LITURGICAL CALENDAR FOR IRELAND 2023

2023 LITURGICAL CALENDAR FOR IRELAND

For the celebration of Mass
and the Liturgy of the Hours
during the liturgical year
2022/2023

VERITAS

The *Liturgical Calendar for Ireland 2023*
is an adaptation for use in the dioceses of Ireland
of the *Universal Norms for the Liturgical Year* and
the *General Roman Calendar*

Published 2022 by
Veritas Publications
7–8 Lower Abbey Street
Dublin 1
for the National Secretariat for Liturgy

Email publications@veritas.ie
Website veritas.ie

Edited by Patrick Jones

Copyright © Irish Episcopal Commission for Liturgy, 2022

ISBN 978 1 80097 037 3

Pastoral and homiletic notes
with ecclesiastical permission according to Canon 830:3
✠ Dermot Farrell
Archbishop of Dublin

1 October 2022

Design and typesetting by Colette Dower, Veritas Publications
Cover image: *St Brigid Feeding the Poor* by Imogen Stuart, used with permission
Printed in the Republic of Ireland by Walsh Colour Print, Kerry

LITURGICAL CALENDAR 2022–2023

In this *Liturgical Calendar for 2022–2023* each day is observed by the celebration of Mass and the Liturgy of the Hours. Often on weekdays this is the combination of the season weekday or weekday in Ordinary Time with the commemoration of a saint.

National Proper

The Mass texts for the National Proper are included in the sequence of the Proper of Saints in the third edition of the *Roman Missal*.

The readings for the solemnity of St Patrick and the feasts of St Brigid, St Columba (Colum Cille) and All the Saints of Ireland are available on www.catholicbishops.ie

Four optional memorials of the General Calendar displaced by higher ranking observances of the National Calendar have been assigned new dates. See *Liturgical Note 24*, p. 24.

General Calendar

Additions to the General Calendar since the publication of the third edition of the *Roman Missal* are included on pp. 180–183. See *Liturgical Note 24*, p. 24.

Ordinary Time

Ordinary Time in 2023 consists of thirty-four weeks. There are seven weeks from 9 January (Monday after the feast of the Baptism of the Lord) until 21 February (Tuesday before Ash Wednesday).

After Pentecost, Ordinary Time resumes from the 8th Week on 29 May (Monday after Pentecost Sunday).

Lectionary

In the *Lectionary*, the Sunday readings are from Cycle A in Ordinary Time, the Year of Matthew, and the weekday readings are Cycle 1.

The Pope's Intentions

The Pope's Prayer Intentions for each month, entrusted to the Worldwide Prayer Network (Apostleship of Prayer), are given on pp. 26–27.

Saints

Some biographical notes may seem uneven or incomplete, very often as a result of page space. Supplementary resources are readily available. The biographical notes for the Irish Calendar are given on pp. 184–192. Many of the notes cite traditional material where historical data is lacking.

Diocesan Observances

Included in the Calendar on the appropriate date are the commemorations of diocesan feasts, including their patrons, the anniversaries of the Dedication of Cathedrals and the episcopal ordination of the Bishops.

CONTENTS

MOVEABLE FEASTS OF THE LITURGICAL YEAR

	2022–2023	2023–2024
First Sunday of Advent	27 November 2022	3 December 2023
The Holy Family	30 December 2022	31 December 2023
The Baptism of the Lord	8 January 2023	7 January 2024
Ash Wednesday	22 February 2023	14 March 2024
Easter Sunday	9 April 2023	31 March 2024
The Ascension of the Lord	21 May 2023	12 May 2024
Pentecost Sunday	28 May 2023	19 May 2024
The Holy Trinity	4 June 2023	26 May 2024
The Body and Blood of Christ	11 June 2023	2 June 2024
The Sacred Heart of Jesus	16 June 2023	7 June 2024
Christ the King	26 November 2023	24 November 2024

HOLYDAYS OF OBLIGATION IN IRELAND
(Sundays and these dates are noted in the Calendar by ✠)

	2022–2023	2023–2024
The Immaculate Conception	Thu, 8 December 2022	Fri, 8 December 2023
The Nativity of the Lord	Sun, 25 December 2022	Mon, 25 December 2023
The Epiphany of the Lord	Fri, 6 January 2023	Sat, 6 January 2024
St Patrick	Fri, 17 March 2023	Sun, 17 March 2024
The Assumption of the BVM	Tue, 15 August 2023	Thu, 15 August 2024
All Saints	Wed, 1 November 2023	Fri, 1 November 2024

Future Dates	Ash Wednesday	Easter Sunday	Pentecost
2024	14 February	31 March	19 May
2025	5 March	20 April	8 June
2026	18 February	5 April	24 May
2027	10 February	28 March	16 May
2028	1 March	16 April	4 June
2029	14 February	1 April	20 May
2030	6 March	21 April	9 June

ABBREVIATIONS

RM Roman Missal (third edition, 2011)
Lect Lectionary (second edition, 1981)
GIRM General Instruction of the Roman Missal
GILH General Instruction of the Liturgy of the Hours
ILect Introduction to the Lectionary
UNLYC Universal Norms for the Liturgical Year and the Calendar

LG Vatican II, *Lumen Gentium*, Dogmatic Constitution on the Church
SC Vatican II, *Sacrosanctum Concilium*, Constitution on the Sacred Liturgy
GetS Vatican II, *Gaudium et Spes,* Pastoral Constitution on the Church in the Modern World

✠ indicates Sundays and holydays of obligation.

LITURGICAL NOTES

LITURGICAL NOTE 1
Table of Liturgical Days
According to their Order of Preference

I

1. The Paschal Triduum of the Passion and Resurrection of the Lord.
2. The Nativity of the Lord, the Epiphany, the Ascension and Pentecost.
   Sundays of Advent, Lent and Easter.
   Ash Wednesday.
   Weekdays of Holy Week from Monday up to and including Thursday.
   Days within the Octave of Easter.
3. Solemnities inscribed in the General Calendar, whether of the Lord, of the Blessed Virgin Mary or of Saints.
   The Commemoration of All the Faithful Departed.
4. Proper Solemnities, namely:
   a) The Solemnity of the principal patron of the place, city or state;
   b) The Solemnity of the dedication and of the anniversary of the dedication of one's own church;
   c) The Solemnity of the Title of one's own church;
   d) The Solemnity either of the Title or of the Founder or of the principal patron of an Order or Congregation.

II

5. Feasts of the Lord inscribed in the General Calendar.
6. Sundays of Christmas Time and the Sundays in Ordinary Time.
7. Feasts of the Blessed Virgin Mary and of the Saints in the General Calendar.
8. Proper Feasts, namely:
   a) The Feast of the principal patron of the diocese;
   b) The Feast of the anniversary of the dedication of the cathedral church;
   c) The Feast of the principal patron of a region or province, or a country, or of a wider territory;
   d) The Feast of the Title, Founder, or principal patron of an Order or Congregation and of a religious province, without prejudice to the prescriptions given under no. 4;
   e) Other Feasts proper to an individual church;
   f) Other Feasts inscribed in the Calendar of each diocese or Order or Congregation.
9. Weekdays of Advent from 17 December up to and including 24 December.
   Days within the Octave of Christmas.
   Weekdays of Lent.

III

10. Obligatory Memorials in the General Calendar.
11. Proper Obligatory Memorials, namely:
    a) The Memorial of a secondary patron of the place, diocese, region or religious province;
    b) Other Obligatory Memorials inscribed in the Calendar of each diocese, or Order or Congregation.
12. Optional Memorials, which, however, may be celebrated, in the special manner described in the *General Instruction of the Roman Missal* and of the Liturgy of the Hours, even on the days listed in no. 9.
    In the same manner, Obligatory Memorials may be celebrated as Optional Memorials if they happen to fall on Lenten weekdays.

13.	Weekdays of Advent up to and including 16 December.
	Weekdays of Christmas Time from 2 January until the Saturday after the Epiphany.
	Weekdays of Easter Time from Monday after the Octave of Easter up to and including the Saturday before Pentecost.
	Weekdays in Ordinary Time.

LITURGICAL NOTE 2
The Liturgical Day

UNLYC, 3–5, 8–16
The Liturgical Day in General
3.	Each and every day is sanctified by the liturgical celebrations of the People of God, especially by the Eucharistic Sacrifice and the Divine Office.
	The liturgical day runs from midnight to midnight. However, the celebration of Sunday and of Solemnities begins already on the evening of the previous day.

Sunday
4.	On the first day of each week, which is known as the Day of the Lord or the Lord's Day, the Church, by an apostolic tradition that draws its origin from the very day of the resurrection of Christ, celebrates the paschal mystery. Hence, Sunday must be considered the primordial feast day.
5.	Because of its special importance, the celebration of Sunday gives way only to Solemnities and Feasts of the Lord; indeed, the Sundays of Advent, Lent and Easter have precedence over all Feasts of the Lord and over all Solemnities. In fact, Solemnities occurring on these Sundays are transferred to the following Monday unless they occur on Palm Sunday or on the Sunday of the Lord's Resurrection.

Solemnities, Feasts and Memorials
8.	In the cycle of the year, as she celebrates the mystery of Christ, the Church also venerates with a particular love the Blessed Mother of God, Mary, and proposes to the devotion of the faithful the Memorials of the Martyrs and other Saints.
9.	The saints who have universal importance are celebrated in an obligatory way throughout the whole Church; other saints are either inscribed in the Calendar, but for optional celebration, or are left to be honoured by a particular church, or nation, or religious family.
10.	Celebrations, according to the importance assigned to them, are hence distinguished one from another and termed: Solemnity, Feast, Memorial.
11.	*Solemnities* are counted among the most important days, whose celebration begins with First Vespers (Evening Prayer I) on the preceding day. Some Solemnities are also endowed with their own Vigil Mass, which is to be used on the evening of the preceding day, if an evening Mass is celebrated.
12.	The celebration of the two greatest Solemnities, Easter and the Nativity, is extended over eight days. Each Octave is governed by its own rules.
13.	*Feasts* are celebrated within the limits of the natural day; accordingly they have no First Vespers (Evening Prayer I), except in the case of Feasts of the Lord that fall on a Sunday in Ordinary Time or in Christmas Time and which replace the Sunday Office.
14.	*Memorials* are either obligatory or optional; their observance is integrated into the celebration of the occurring weekday in accordance with the norms set forth in the *General Instruction of the Roman Missal* and of the Liturgy of the Hours.
	Obligatory Memorials which fall on weekdays of Lent may only be celebrated as Optional Memorials.

If several Optional Memorials are inscribed in the Calendar on the same day, only one may be celebrated, the others being omitted.

15. On Saturdays in Ordinary Time when no Obligatory Memorial occurs, an Optional Memorial of the Blessed Virgin Mary may be celebrated.

16. The days of the week that follow Sunday are called weekdays; however, they are celebrated differently according to the importance of each.

LITURGICAL NOTE 3
The Choice of the Mass and its Parts

GIRM

352. The pastoral effectiveness of a celebration will be greatly increased if the texts of the readings, the prayers and the liturgical chants correspond as aptly as possible to the needs, the preparation and the culture of the participants. This will be achieved by appropriate use of the many possibilities of choice described below.

Hence in arranging the celebration of Mass, the priest should be attentive rather to the common spiritual good of the People of God than to his own inclinations. He should also remember that choices of this kind are to be made in harmony with those who exercise some part in the celebration, including the faithful, as regards the parts that more directly pertain to them.

Since, indeed, many possibilities are provided for choosing the different parts of the Mass, it is necessary for the deacon, the readers, the psalmist, the cantor, the commentator and the choir to know properly before the celebration the texts that concern each and that are to be used, and it is necessary that nothing be in any sense improvised. For harmonious ordering and carrying out of the rites will greatly help in disposing the faithful for participation in the Eucharist.

I. The Choice of Mass

353. On Solemnities, the priest is obliged to follow the Calendar of the church where he is celebrating.

354. On Sundays, on the weekdays during Advent, Christmas Time, Lent and Easter Time, on Feasts and on Obligatory Memorials:
   a) If Mass is celebrated with the people, the priest should follow the Calendar of the church where he is celebrating;
   b) If Mass is celebrated with the participation of one minister only, the priest may choose either the Calendar of the church or his proper Calendar.

355. On Optional Memorials,
   a) On the weekdays of Advent from 17 December to 24 December, on days within the Octave of the Nativity of the Lord, and on the weekdays of Lent, except Ash Wednesday and during Holy Week, the Mass texts for the current liturgical day are used; but the Collect may be taken from a Memorial which happens to be inscribed in the General Calendar for that day, except on Ash Wednesday and during Holy Week. On weekdays of Easter Time, Memorials of Saints may rightly be celebrated in full.
   b) On weekdays of Advent before 17 December, on weekdays of Christmas Time from 2 January, and on weekdays of Easter Time, one of the following may be chosen: either the Mass of the weekday, or the Mass of the Saint or of one of the Saints whose Memorial is observed, or the Mass of any Saint inscribed in the Martyrology for that day.
   c) On weekdays in Ordinary Time, there may be chosen either the Mass of the weekday, or the Mass of an Optional Memorial which happens to occur on that day, or the Mass of any Saint inscribed in the Martyrology for that day, or a Mass for Various Needs or a Votive Mass.

If he celebrates with the people, the priest will take care not to omit too frequently and without sufficient reason the readings assigned each day in the *Lectionary* to the weekdays, for the Church desires that a richer portion at the table of God's Word should be spread before the people (cf. SC, 51).

For the same reason he should choose Masses for the Dead in moderation, for every Mass is offered for both the living and the dead, and there is a commemoration of the dead in the Eucharistic Prayer.

Where, however, the Optional Memorials of the Blessed Virgin Mary or of the Saints are dear to the faithful, the legitimate devotion of the latter should be satisfied.

Moreover, as regards the option of choosing between a Memorial inscribed in the General Calendar and one inserted in a diocesan or religious Calendar, preference should be given, all else being equal and in keeping with tradition, to the Memorial in the particular Calendar.

II. The Choice of Texts for the Mass

356. In choosing texts for the different parts of the Mass, whether for the time of the year or for saints, the norms that follow should be observed.

The Readings

357. Sundays and Solemnities have assigned to them three readings, that is, from a Prophet, an Apostle and a Gospel, by which the Christian people are instructed in the continuity of the work of salvation according to God's wonderful design. These readings should be followed strictly. In Easter Time, according to the tradition of the Church, instead of being from the Old Testament, the reading is taken from the Acts of the Apostles.

For Feasts, two readings are assigned. If, however, according to the norms a Feast is raised to the rank of a Solemnity, a third reading is added, and this is taken from the Common.

For Memorials of Saints, unless proper readings are given, the readings assigned for the weekday are normally used. In certain cases, particularised readings are provided, that is to say, readings which highlight some particular aspect of the spiritual life or activity of the saint. The use of such readings is not to be insisted upon, unless a pastoral reason truly suggests it.

358. In the *Lectionary* for weekdays, readings are provided for each day of every week throughout the entire course of the year; hence, these readings will in general be used on the days to which they are assigned, unless there occurs a Solemnity, a Feast, or Memorial that has its own New Testament readings, that is to say, readings in which mention is made of the saint being celebrated.

Should, however, the continuous reading during the week from time to time be interrupted, on account of some Solemnity or Feast, or some particular celebration, then the priest shall be permitted, bearing in mind the scheme of readings for the entire week, either to combine parts omitted with other readings or to decide which readings are to be given preference over others.

In Masses for special groups, the priest shall be allowed to choose texts more particularly suited to the particular celebration, provided they are taken from the texts of an approved *Lectionary*.

359. In addition, in the *Lectionary* a special selection of texts from Sacred Scripture is given for Ritual Masses into which certain Sacraments or Sacramentals are incorporated, or for Masses that are celebrated for certain needs.

Sets of readings of this kind have been so prescribed so that through a more apt hearing of the Word of God the faithful may be led to a fuller understanding of the mystery in which they are participating, and may be educated to a more ardent love of the Word of God.

Therefore, the texts proclaimed in the celebration are to be chosen keeping in mind both an appropriate pastoral reason and the options allowed in this matter.

360. At times, a longer and shorter form of the same text is given. In choosing between these two forms, a pastoral criterion should be kept in mind. On such an occasion, attention should be paid to the capacity of the faithful to listen with fruit to a reading of greater or lesser length, and to their capacity to hear a more complete text, which is then explained in the homily (GILH, 80).

361. When a possibility is given of choosing between one or other text laid down, or suggested as optional, attention shall be paid to the good of participants, whether, that is to say, it is a matter of using an easier text or one more appropriate for a given gathering, or of repeating or setting aside a text that is assigned as proper to some particular celebration while being optional for another (GILH, 81), just as pastoral advantage may suggest.

Such a situation may arise either when the same text would have to be read again within a few days, as, for example, on a Sunday and on a subsequent weekday, or when it is feared that a certain text might give rise to some difficulties for a particular group of the Christian faithful. However, care should be taken that, when choosing scriptural passages, parts of Sacred Scripture are not permanently excluded.

362. In addition to the options noted above for choosing certain more suitable texts, the Conference of Bishops has the faculty, in particular circumstances, to indicate some adaptations as regards readings, provided that the texts are chosen from a duly approved Lectionary.

The Orations

363. In any Mass the orations proper to that Mass are used, unless otherwise noted.

On Memorials of Saints, the proper Collect is said or, if this is lacking, one from an appropriate Common. As to the Prayer over the Offerings and the Prayer after Communion, unless these are proper, they may be taken either from the Common or from the weekday of the current time of year.

On the weekdays in Ordinary Time, however, besides the orations from the previous Sunday, orations from another Sunday in Ordinary Time may be used, or one of the Prayers for Various Needs provided in the Missal. However, it shall always be permissible to use from these Masses the Collect alone.

In this way a richer collection of texts is provided, by which the prayer life of the faithful is more abundantly nourished.

However, during the more important times of the year, provision has already been made for this by means of the orations proper to these times of the year that exist for each weekday in the Missal.

LITURGICAL NOTE 4
The Eucharistic Prayers of the *Roman Missal*
Eucharistic Prayers I–IV
GIRM

364. The numerous Prefaces with which the Roman Missal is endowed have as their purpose to bring out more fully the motives for thanksgiving within the Eucharistic Prayer and to set out more clearly the different facets of the mystery of salvation.

365. The choice between the Eucharistic Prayers found in the Order of Mass is suitably guided by the following norms:

a) Eucharistic Prayer I, or the Roman Canon, which may always be used, is especially suited for use on days to which a proper text for the *Communicantes (In communion with those whose memory we venerate)* is assigned or in Masses endowed with a proper form of the *Hanc igitur (Therefore, Lord, we pray)* and also in the celebrations of the Apostles and of the Saints mentioned in the Prayer itself; likewise it is especially suited for use on Sundays, unless for pastoral reasons Eucharistic Prayer III is preferred.

b) Eucharistic Prayer II, on account of its particular features, is more appropriately used on weekdays or in special circumstances. Although it is provided with its own Preface, it may also be used with other Prefaces, especially those that sum up the mystery of salvation, for example, the Common Prefaces. When Mass is celebrated for a particular deceased person, the special formula given may be used at the proper point, namely, before the part *Remember also our brothers and sisters.*

c) Eucharistic Prayer III may be said with any Preface. Its use should be preferred on Sundays and festive days. If, however, this Eucharistic Prayer is used in Masses for the Dead, the special formula for a deceased person may be used, to be included at the proper place, namely after the words: *in your compassion, O merciful Father, gather to yourself all your children scattered throughout the earth.*

d) Eucharistic Prayer IV has an invariable Preface and gives a fuller summary of salvation history. It may be used when a Mass has no Preface of its own and on Sundays in Ordinary Time. On account of its structure, no special formula for a deceased person may be inserted into this prayer.

Eucharistic Prayers for Reconciliation I–II

RM, p. 641

The Eucharistic Prayers for Reconciliation may be used in Masses in which the mystery of reconciliation is conveyed to the faithful in a special way, as, for example, in the Masses for Promoting Harmony, For Reconciliation, For the Preservation of Peace and Justice, In Time of War or Civil Disturbance, For the Forgiveness of Sins, For Charity, of the Mystery of the Holy Cross, of the Most Holy Eucharist, of the Most Precious Blood of our Lord Jesus Christ, as well as in Masses during Lent. Although these Eucharistic Prayers have been provided with a proper Preface, they may also be used with other Prefaces that refer to penance and conversion, as, for example, the Prefaces of Lent.

Eucharistic Prayer for Use in Masses for Various Needs (Forms I–IV)

RM, pp. 657–84

I – The Church on the Path of Unity ... is appropriately used with Mass formularies such as, For the Church, For the Pope, For the Bishop, For the Election of a Pope or a Bishop, For a Council or Synod, For Priests, For the Priest Himself, For Ministers of the Church, and For a Spiritual or Pastoral Gathering.

II – God Guides His Church along the Way of Salvation ... is appropriately used with Mass formularies such as, For the Church, For Vocations to Holy Orders, For the Laity, For the Family, For Religious, For Vocations to Religious Life, For Charity, For Relatives and Friends, and For Giving Thanks to God.

III – Jesus, the Way to the Father ... is appropriately used with Mass formularies such as, For the Evangelisation of Peoples, For Persecuted Christians, For the Nation or State, For Those in Public Office, For a Governing Assembly, At the Beginning of the Civil Year, and For the Progress of Peoples.

IV – Jesus, Who Went about Doing Good ... is appropriately used with Mass formularies such as, For Refugees and Exiles, In Time of Famine or For Those Suffering Hunger, For Our Oppressors, For Those Held in Captivity, For Those in Prison, For the Sick, For the Dying, For the Grace of a Happy Death, and In Any Need.

Eucharistic Prayers for Masses with Children I–III are not included in the *Roman Missal* but are published separately in English and Irish (Veritas, 2020) amended for use with the *Roman Missal*, third edition (Prot. 187/19, 13 June 2020). 'The use of these Eucharistic Prayers is strictly limited to Masses celebrated with children and for those children who have not entered the period of preadolescence, or for those Masses in which the majority of the participants are children of that age' (Introduction, 9).

LITURGICAL NOTE 5
Name of St Joseph in Eucharistic Prayers

The name of St Joseph, Spouse of the Blessed Virgin Mary, was added to Eucharistic Prayers II, III, and IV by decree of the Congregation for Divine Worship and the Discipline of the Sacraments (Prot. N. 215/11/L, 1 May 2013, made public 19 June 2013).

The name of St Joseph was added to Eucharistic Prayer I (Roman Canon) in 1962. The additions in the other three Eucharistic Prayers are as follows:

Eucharistic Prayer II

Latin: *ut cum beata Dei Genetrice Virgine Maria, beato Ioseph, eius Sponso, beatis Apostolis*

English: *that with the Blessed Virgin Mary, Mother of God, with blessed Joseph, her Spouse, with the blessed Apostles*

Eucharistic Prayer III

Latin: *cum beatissima Virgine, Dei Genetrice, Maria, cum beato Ioseph, eius Sponsus, cum beatis Apostolis*

English: *with the most Blessed Virgin Mary, Mother of God, with blessed Joseph, her Spouse, with your blessed Apostles and glorious Martyrs*

Eucharistic Prayer IV

Latin: *cum beata Virgine, Dei Genetrice, Maria, cum beato Ioseph, eius Sponso, cum Apostolis*

English: *with the Blessed Virgin Mary, Mother of God, with blessed Joseph, her Spouse, and with your Apostles*

LITURGICAL NOTE 6
Anticipating the Sunday and Holyday Masses
on the Previous Evening

The obligation of assisting at Mass is satisfied wherever Mass is celebrated in a Catholic rite, either on a holyday itself or on the evening of the previous day (*Can.* 1248).

In Ireland this First Mass of a Sunday or holyday must not be celebrated before 6 p.m. No other Saturday Masses are permitted in the evening. Wedding Masses particularly should be held early in the afternoon or in the morning.

The Mass celebrated is that of the Obligation, and the homily and universal prayer or Prayer of the Faithful are not to be omitted. The general principle is to be followed in choosing the Mass texts of giving precedence to the celebration which is of obligation, regardless of the liturgical grade of the two occurring celebrations (*Notitiae*, 20 [1984] 603).

LITURGICAL NOTE 7
Holydays of Obligation

At the October 1996 meeting of the Episcopal Conference, the bishops announced the removal of the obligation on the feasts of the Ascension of the Lord and the Most Holy Body and Blood of Christ (Corpus Christi), and the consequent transfer of these two feasts to the following Sundays in accordance with the universal liturgical law. This decision has been confirmed by the Congregation for Divine Worship (Prot. 1355/96, 9 October 1996).

LITURGICAL NOTE 8
Explanation of Some Rubrics

Funeral Mass. In this liturgical note, the term Funeral Mass means a Mass when the prayer texts and biblical readings are from Masses for the Dead.

No other celebrations, even/except funeral Masses, are permitted today. This rubric respects the order of precedence in the table of liturgical days (*Lit. Note* 1) and in the table of rules concerning Ritual and Votive Masses, Masses for Various Needs and Occasions and Masses for the Dead (see *Lit. Note* 12). The celebration of the day where this rubric appears uses the readings and prayer texts of the day. Other readings and prayer texts, except when Funeral Masses are permitted, are not used. Thus, at a marriage celebrated during the Octave of Easter, the readings and prayers are taken from those of the day.

No Masses for the dead, except funeral Masses, are permitted today. This rubric follows the table of rules for Votive Masses, in this case, the daily Mass for the Dead (see *Lit. Note* 13). Thus, at a funeral on a Feast or Memorial, the texts used may be those for the dead.

No Masses for the dead, except funeral Masses and first anniversaries, are permitted today. This rubric applies to the days after Christmas.

Memorial may be made of St N. This rubric appears in the last week of Advent, during the Octave of Christmas and during Lent indicating that the Mass of the day is celebrated but the Collect may be taken from the memorial (*GIRM*, 355a).

HOURS Proper of the memorial. Some memorials have proper antiphons with psalms of Sunday I at Morning Prayer and psalms of the Commons at Evening Prayer.

MASS of the memorial. The Collect and other prayers that are proper to the memorial or taken from the Commons are used. The readings are of the weekday, except when proper readings are given (or accommodated readings are used. See *Lit. Note* 15).

Preface: Common or of the Saint(s). This note appears on Mass of a memorial and indicates that the Preface may be from the Common Prefaces I–VI (*RM*, pp. 478–89) or Saints I–II, Martyrs I–II, Pastors, Virgins & Religious (*RM*, pp. 466–77) as appropriate.

LITURGICAL NOTE 9
Nuptial Mass

When marriage is celebrated within the Mass, the Mass for the celebration of Marriage, *RM*, pp. 1082–100, is said, and white vestments are used. On Sundays of Advent, Lent and Easter, on holydays of obligation, where the celebration of marriage is permitted, however, the Mass of the day is said, but the nuptial blessing is given, and the special final blessing may be used. On the Sundays of the Christmas season and on Sundays in Ordinary Time, where the celebration of marriage is permitted, in Masses which are not parish Masses, the Ritual Mass may be said without change.

LITURGICAL NOTE 10
Order of Christian Funerals

The *Order of Christian Funerals* (© Irish Conference of Bishops, 1991) has been the approved text in the dioceses of Ireland since Easter 1992. The pastoral notes give a comprehensive guide to the carrying out of the rites by which the Church manifests its care for the dead, and takes into consideration the spiritual and psychological needs of the family and friends of the deceased.

The responsibility for the ministry of consolation rests with the believing community. Each Christian shares in this ministry according to the various gifts and offices in the Church.

Among the priest's responsibilities are: (1) to be at the side of the sick and dying; (2) to impart catechesis on the meaning of Christian death; (3) to comfort the family of the deceased, to sustain them amid the anguish of their grief, and to prepare them for a funeral celebration that has meaning for them; (4) to fit the liturgy for the dead into the total setting of the liturgical life of the parish and his own pastoral ministry.

The *Order of Christian Funerals* makes provision for the minister, in consultation with the family, to choose those rites and texts that are most suitable to the situation; those that most closely apply to the needs of the mourners, the circumstances of death and the customs of the local Christian community.

The celebration of the funeral liturgy is especially entrusted to parish priests. When no priest is available, deacons preside at funeral rites, except for the Mass. When there is no priest or deacon, it is recommended that lay persons carry out the stations at the home and cemetery and all vigils for the dead. The vigil services indeed should usually be entrusted to lay people who have been suitably prepared for this service.

Funeral Rites and Readings (Veritas, 1995) is a helpful aid for all who wish to assist at the funeral rites. The readings in Irish are available in *Léachtaí do Dheasghnátha na Marbh* (An Sagart, 1995).

A brief homily based on the readings should always be given at the funeral liturgy, but never any kind of eulogy.

Masses for the Dead

1. The Funeral Mass has first place among the Masses for the Dead and may be celebrated on any day except solemnities that are days of obligation, Holy Thursday, the Easter Triduum, and the Sundays of Lent and Easter. It may be celebrated during the Octaves of Christmas and Easter. On Holy Thursday, Good Friday and Holy Saturday, a celebration of the Word takes place with the Rite of Final Commendation and Farewell, but Holy Communion may not be distributed.
2. On the occasion of the news of a death, final burial or the first anniversary, Mass for the Dead may be celebrated even on days within the Christmas Octave, on obligatory memorials and on weekdays, except Ash Wednesday and during Holy Week.
3. Daily Masses for the Dead may be celebrated on weekdays in Ordinary Time even when there is an optional memorial or the office of the weekday is used, provided such Masses are actually offered for the dead.
4. Masses for the Dead are in the *Missal, RM*, pp. 1277–318, with Prefaces, *RM*, pp. 490–9. Funeral Masses are *RM*, pp. 1277–86.

LITURGICAL NOTE 11
Saturday Mass of the Blessed Virgin Mary

On Saturdays in Ordinary Time when no obligatory memorial is to be celebrated, an optional memorial of Mary may be observed. This is celebrated as a memorial. Green or white vestments may be worn.

The texts may be chosen from the *Roman Missal* (RM, pp. 954–66, pp. 1252–8) or *the Collection of Masses of the Blessed Virgin Mary* (Veritas, 1987). Irish language texts are available in *An Leabhar Aifrinn* and *Díolaim d'Aifrinn na Maighdine Beannaithe Muire* (An Sagart, 2000).

The ferial readings are to be preferred, but common texts may be selected from the *Lectionary* or the lectionary from the *Collection of Masses of the Blessed Virgin Mary, An Leiceanáir* or *Díolaim d'Aifrinn na Maighdine Beannaithe Muire* (see also *Lit. Note 16*). A homily should be given and general intercessions prepared. This Mass is permitted only in Ordinary Time, and never during the seasons of Advent, Christmas, Lent or Easter.

LITURGICAL NOTE 12
Diocesan Celebrations

a) Proper Celebration of the Principal Patron
The feast of the principal patron of the diocese does not have precedence over any Sunday.

However, for pastoral reasons, the feast of the principal patron of the diocese may be celebrated as a solemnity. As such, it would then have precedence over other feasts in the General Calendar, and over Sundays in Ordinary Time. When it falls on other Sundays or solemnities it should be transferred to the closest day which is not a day listed in Nos. 1–8 in the table of precedence (*Lit. Note* 1).

The *General Instruction of the Roman Missal*, 374, also provides for the situation: When a serious need or pastoral advantage is present, at the direction of the diocesan bishop or with his permission, an appropriate Mass may be celebrated on any day except solemnities, the Sundays of Advent, Lent and the Easter Season, Ash Wednesday, Holy Week. The Octave of Easter and the Commemoration of All the Faithful Departed (see also *Instructio Calendaria Particularia*, II. 9, 24 June [1970]).

b) Celebration of the Anniversary of the Dedication of the Cathedral
In order that the importance and dignity of the local church may stand out with greater clarity, the anniversary of the dedication of its cathedral is to be celebrated, with the rank of a solemnity in the cathedral itself, and with the rank of a feast in the other churches of the diocese, on the date on which the dedication recurs.

It is desirable that the faithful of the entire diocese come together on the day of the celebration to celebrate the Eucharist with the bishop.

If the date is always impeded, the celebration is assigned to the nearest date open (see *Notitiae*, 8:103 [1972]).

The dedication anniversary in the cathedral itself ranks as a solemnity and thus takes precedence over Sundays in Ordinary Time and in the Christmas season. When it falls on other Sundays or solemnities it should be transferred to the closest day which is not a day listed in Nos. 1–8 in the table of precedence (Lit. Note 1).

But the celebration throughout the diocese ranks as a feast, proper to the diocese, and therefore does not have precedence over Sundays in Ordinary Time and in the Christmas season. The bishop may, however, use the power granted him in *GIRM*, 374, noted above.

LITURGICAL NOTE 13
Ritual and Votive Masses, Masses for Various Needs and Occasions, Masses for the Dead: A Table of the Rules

V1 =   Ritual Masses (*GIRM*, 372): Masses at the direction of the local ordinary or with his permission when a serious need or pastoral advantage is present (*GIRM*, 374)

V2 =   Masses at the discretion of the rector of the church or the celebrant when some genuine need or pastoral advantage requires it (*GIRM*, 376)

V3 =   Masses for various needs and votive Masses in accord with the piety of the faithful and chosen by the celebrant (*GIRM*, 373)

D1 =   Funeral Masses (*GIRM*, 380)

D2 =   Masses on learning of a death, on final burial, and first anniversary (*GIRM*, 381)

D3 =   Daily Masses applied for the dead. When D1 and D2 are not permitted, so also are D3 (*GIRM*, 381)

+ =   Permitted

– =   Not permitted

1.	Solemnities that are Holydays of Obligation	V1–		
2.	Sundays of Advent, Lent and Easter	V1– D1–		
3.	Holy Thursday, Paschal Triduum	V1– D1–		
4.	Solemnities other than Holydays of Obligation, All Souls' Day	V1– D1+	D2–	
5.	Ash Wednesday, weekdays of Holy Week	V1– D1+	D2–	
6.	Days within the Easter Octave	V1– D1+	D2–	
7.	Sundays of Christmas and Sundays of Ordinary Time	V1+ D1+	V2– D2–	
8.	Feasts	V1+ D1+	V2– D2–	
9.	Weekdays 17–24 December	V1+ D1+	V2– D2+	D3–
10.	Weekdays within the Octave of Christmas	V1+ D1+	V2– D2+	D3–

11.	Weekdays of Lent	V1+	V2–	
		D1+	D2+	D3–
12.	Obligatory Memorials	V1+	V2–	V3–
		D1+	D2+	D3–
13.	Weekdays of Advent until 16 December	V1+	V2+	V3–
		D1+	D2+	D3–
14.	Weekdays of Christmas from 2 January	V1+	V2+	V3–
		D1+	D2+	D3–
15.	Weekdays of Easter Time	V1+	V2+	V3–
		D1+	D2+	D3–
16.	Weekdays in Ordinary Time	V1+	V2+	V3+
		D1+	D2+	D3+

LITURGICAL NOTE 14
Lectionary Year A – Year of Matthew

In order to do justice to the intention of the *Lectionary*, the five great 'sermons' in Matthew's Gospel will of necessity be the focal points of preaching and instruction. The narrative sections, which are placed between the sermons, are composed in such a way that there is a unity and coherence in the whole work. Discourse and narrative stand side by side, so that the narrative chapters prepare the way for what follows in the discourses. Recognising the way in which the *Lectionary* has reflected the structure of Matthew's Gospel will enable preachers and readers to see the context of the readings from one week to the next.

The division of St Matthew's Gospel through Year A

Unit I   The figure of Jesus the Messiah
          The Baptism of Jesus; the witness of John the Baptist   Sundays 1–2
Unit II   Christ's design for life in God's kingdom
          Narrative: the call of the first disciples
          Discourse: the sermon on the mount   Sundays 3–9
Unit III The spread of God's kingdom
          Narrative: the call of Levi
          Discourse: the mission sermon   Sundays 10–13
Unit IV   The mystery of God's kingdom
          Narrative: the revelation to the simple
          Discourse: the parable sermon   Sundays 14–17
Unit V   God's kingdom on earth – the Church of Christ
          Narrative: the feeding of five thousand; Jesus walks on the waters;
          the Canaanite woman; Peter's confession – the primacy conferred;
          the passion prophesied – discipleship
          Discourse: the community sermon   Sundays 18–24
Unit VI   Authority and invitation – the ministry ends
          Narrative: the parables of the labourers, the two sons,
          he wicked vinedressers, and the marriage feast
          Discourse: the final sermon   Sundays 25–33
Unit VII God's kingdom fulfilled
          Christ the King   Sunday 34

(See *Introduction to the Lectionary*, vol. I, pp. xlviii–xlix.)

LITURGICAL NOTE 15
Certain Readings

In response to a request of the Irish Episcopal Conference, the Congregation for Divine Worship and the Discipline of the Sacraments (Prot. N.2410/93/L) has given permission (23 March 1994) for the inclusion of two alternative readings of scripture in the *Lectionary*:

i *Colossians* 3:12-17 as an alternative reading to *Colossians* 3:12-21. This occurs on the Feast of the Holy Family, Year A and in the Wedding Lectionary.

ii *Ephesians* 5:25-33 as an alternative reading to *Ephesians* 5:21-33. This occurs on the 21st Sunday in Ordinary Time, Year B, on Tuesday of the 30th Week in Ordinary Time, Year 2, and in the Wedding Lectionary.

LITURGICAL NOTE 16
Use of the *Lectionary* on Celebration of Saints

Three readings are assigned for solemnities. Feasts and memorials of saints have only two readings: the first can be chosen from either the Old Testament or from an apostle; the second is from the gospels. Following the Church's traditional practice, however, the first reading during the Easter season is to be taken from an apostle, the second, as far as possible, from the Gospel of St John (*ILect*, 83–4).

Proper readings: when they exist, biblical passages about the saint are given, and these must take the place of the weekday readings even on memorials. These are clearly noted in the *Lectionary* on the day.

Accommodated readings: passages from the Commons are suggested to bring out some particular aspect of a saint's life or apostolate; use of such does not seem binding, except for compelling pastoral reasons. The first concern of a priest celebrating with a congregation is the spiritual benefit of the faithful and he will be careful not to impose his personal preference on them. Above all, he will make sure not to omit too often or needlessly the readings assigned for each day in the weekday *Lectionary*: the Church's desire is to provide the faithful with a richer share of the table of God's word (*ILect*, 83).

LITURGICAL NOTE 17
The Celebration of the Divine Office

Sundays (*GILH*, 204–7)
a) Everything is done as in the Ordinary, in the Psalter and in the Proper, according to the varying seasons.
b) Both First Evening Prayer and Second Evening Prayer are said.
c) At the Office of readings, after the second reading and responsory, the *Te Deum* is said, except in Lent.

Solemnities (*GILH*, 225–30)
a) At First Evening Prayer everything is taken from the Proper or the Common.
b) Night Prayer following First Evening Prayer is the First Night Prayer of Sunday.
c) At the Office of Readings, everything is taken from the Proper or the Common and the *Te Deum* is said.
d) At Morning Prayer everything is taken from the Proper or the Common, using the psalms of Sunday Week 1.
e) At the Day Hour: (1) the hymn is taken from the Ordinary; (2) the antiphons, short reading, versicle and response and the prayer are taken from the Proper or the Common; (3) the psalms: if particular psalms are given they are said. If no particular psalms are given for a solemnity which occurs on a Sunday, the psalms are those of Sunday Week 1. In all other cases, the psalms are the complementary psalms.

f) At Second Evening Prayer everything is taken from the Proper or the Common.

g) Night Prayer following Second Evening Prayer is the Second Night Prayer of Sunday.

Feasts (*GILH*, 231–3)

a) First Evening Prayer is said only on Feasts of the Lord which fall on a Sunday.

b) At the Office of Readings, everything is taken from the Proper or the Common and the *Te Deum* is said.

c) At Morning Prayer everything is taken from the Proper or the Common, using the psalms of Sunday Week 1.

d) At the Day Hour: (1) the hymn is taken from the Ordinary; (2) the short reading, versicle and response and the prayer are taken from the Proper or the Common; (3) the antiphons (unless there are proper ones) and psalms are taken from the current day of the week.

e) At Second Evening Prayer everything is taken from the Proper or the Common.

f) Night Prayer is that of the particular day of the week.

Memorials (*GILH*, 220, 234–6)

a) At Morning Prayer, Evening Prayer and the Office of Readings: (1) the psalms and their antiphons are those of the weekday. (If there are proper antiphons for Morning Prayer, they are used with the psalms of Sunday Week 1; if there are proper antiphons for Evening Prayer, they are used with the psalms from the Common); (2) hymns, short readings with their versicle and response, the *Benedictus* and *Magnificat* antiphons and intercessions – if there are proper texts, these are used, otherwise they may be from the Common or the particular weekday; (3) the prayer is that of the memorial.

b) At the Office of Readings, the biblical reading is from the present season, the second reading is of the saint or in the absence of a proper reading for the saint, the reading is taken from the weekday.

c) The Day Hour and Night Prayer is that of the weekday.

Weekdays

a) Everything is taken from the Ordinary, from the Psalter and from the Proper, according to the season.

b) The prayer at the Office of Readings is taken from the Proper, at other Hours in Ordinary Time from the Psalter, and in the seasons from the Proper.

LITURGICAL NOTE 18
On the Reception of Holy Communion

Can. 917 One who has received the blessed Eucharist may receive it again on the same day only within a eucharistic celebration in which that person participates, without prejudice to the provision of *Can.* 921.2.

Can. 921.1. Christ's faithful who are in danger of death, from whatever cause, are to be strengthened by Holy Communion as Viaticum.

Can. 921.2. Even if they have already received Holy Communion that same day, it is nevertheless strongly suggested that in danger of death they should communicate again.

Can. 921.3. While the danger of death persists, it is recommended that Holy Communion be administered a number of times, but on separate days.

Holy Communion under Both Kinds

'Holy Communion has a fuller form as a sign when it is distributed under both kinds. For in this form the sign of the Eucharistic banquet is more clearly evident and clear expression is given to the divine will by which the new and eternal

Covenant is ratified in the Blood of the Lord, as also the relationship between the Eucharistic banquet and the eschatological banquet in the Father's kingdom.

'Sacred pastors should take care to ensure that the faithful who participate in the rite or are present at it are as fully aware as possible of the Catholic teaching on the form of Holy Communion as set forth by the Ecumenical Council of Trent. Above all, they should instruct the Christian faithful that the Catholic faith teaches that Christ, whole and entire, and the true Sacrament, is received even under only one species, and consequently that as far as the effects are concerned, those who receive under only one species are not deprived of any of the grace that is necessary for salvation.

'They are to teach, furthermore, that the Church, in her stewardship of the Sacraments, has the power to set forth or alter whatever provisions, apart from the substance of the Sacraments, that she judges to be most conducive to the veneration of the Sacraments and the wellbeing of the recipients, in view of changing conditions, times and places. At the same time, the faithful should be encouraged to seek to participate more eagerly in this sacred rite, by which the sign of the Eucharistic banquet is made more fully evident' (*GIRM*, 281–2).

In response to a request of the Irish Episcopal Conference, the Congregation for Divine Worship and the Discipline of the Sacraments (Prot. N/CD 653/91) has given permission (26 October 1991) for Holy Communion to be distributed under both kinds to the faithful at Masses on Sundays and holydays of obligation and on weekdays, if, in the judgement of the ordinary, Communion can be given in an orderly and reverent way. Each local bishop in Ireland can implement this permission in accordance with the norms that apply.

These norms are recalled in the letter of permission.

1. Adequate catechetical instruction must be given to the faithful concerning the doctrine of the Church on the form of Holy Communion.
2. The decision to receive or not to receive from the chalice is left to the individual communicant.
3. The directives already given in the various instructions are to be observed:
   (a) The consecrated wine must be consumed after the distribution (except in the case of someone who is ill and cannot receive solid food). Only the necessary amount of wine should be consecrated;
   (b) The proper ministers are to be provided;
   (c) The form and material of the sacred vessels must follow the norms. Rules for the purification are to be observed.

Reverent and careful celebration and reception of Holy Communion under both kinds is to be observed.

The letter of permission states that Communion should not be distributed under both kinds in the following situations:

(a) At Masses celebrated in the open with a great number of communicants;
(b) At other Masses where the number of communicants is so great as to make it difficult for Communion under both kinds to be given in an orderly and reverent way;
(c) At Masses where the assembled congregation is of such a diverse nature that it is difficult to ascertain whether those present have been sufficiently instructed about receiving Communion under both kinds;
(d) When circumstances do not permit the assurance that due reverence towards the consecrated wine can be maintained during and after the celebration (see *Inaestimabile donum*, 13–14).

LITURGICAL NOTE 19
Days of Prayer

World Day of Peace	Sunday, 1 January 2023
Week of Prayer for Christian Unity	begins Wednesday, 18 January 2023
Sunday of the Word of God	Sunday, 22 January 2023
World Day for Consecrated Life	Thursday, 2 February 2023
International Day of Prayer and Awareness against Human Trafficking	
	Wednesday, 8 February 2023
World Day of the Sick	Saturday, 11 February 2023
Worldwide Day of Prayer for Survivors and Victims of Sexual Abuse	
	Friday, 24 February 2023
Day of Prayer for Vocations	Sunday, 30 April, 2023
World Communications Day	Sunday, 21 May 2023
Day of Prayer for the Church in China	Wednesday, 24 May 2023
World Day of Prayer for Priests	Friday, 16 June 2023
World Day of Grandparents and the Elderly	Sunday, 23 July 2023
World Day of Prayer for the Care of Creation	Friday, 1 September 2023
World Day of Migrants and Refugees	Sunday, 24 September 2023
Mission Sunday	Sunday, 22 October 2023
World Day of the Poor	Sunday, 19 November 2023

Additional Days for Ireland:

Catholic Schools Week	begins Sunday, 22 January 2023
Day of Prayer for Temperance	Sunday, 19 February 2023
Day of Prayer for Emigrants	Friday, 17 March 2023
Day for Life	Sunday, 1 October 2023
Children's Day of Mission Prayer	Friday, 6 October 2023
Prisoners' Sunday	Sunday, 5 November 2023

LITURGICAL NOTE 20
Exposition of the Holy Eucharist

Exposition of the Holy Eucharist, either in the ciborium or in the monstrance, is intended to acknowledge Christ's marvellous presence in the sacrament. Exposition invites us to the spiritual union with him that culminates in sacramental communion. Thus it fosters very well the worship which is due to Christ in spirit and in truth.

Full texts and rubrics for this exposition are to be found in *Exposition and Benediction of the Blessed Sacrament/Taispeáint agus Beannacht na Naomh-Shacraiminte*, published by the Irish Institute of Pastoral Liturgy (now National Centre for Liturgy, Maynooth), 1982.

LITURGICAL NOTE 21
Friday Penance
Statement from the Irish Bishops on Canons 1249–53
November 1983

Following the example of Christ
The new Code of Canon Law reminds us that all of Christ's faithful are obliged to do penance. The obligation arises in imitation of Christ himself and in response to his call. During his life on earth, not least at the beginning of his public ministry, our Lord undertook voluntary penance. He invited his followers to do the same. The penance he invited would be a participation in his own suffering, an expression of inner conversion and a form of reparation for sin. It would be a personal sacrifice made out of love for God and our neighbour. It follows that if we are to be true, as Christians, to the spirit of Christ, we must practise some form of penance.

Special penitential days

So that all may be united with Christ and with one another in a common practice of penance, the Church sets aside certain penitential days. On those days the faithful are to devote themselves in a special way to prayer, self-denial and works of charity. Such days are not designed to confine or isolate penance but to intensify it in the life of the Christian throughout the year.

Lent: a time of fast and abstinence

Lent is the traditional season of renewal and penance in the Church. The new Code reaffirms this. It also prescribes that Ash Wednesday and Good Friday are to be observed as days of fast and abstinence. Fasting means that the amount of food we eat is considerably reduced. Abstinence means that we give up a particular kind of food or drink or form of amusement.

The subjects of penitential observance

Those over eighteen are bound by the law of fasting until the beginning of their sixtieth year, while all over fourteen are bound by the law of abstinence. Priests and parents are urged to foster the spirit and practice of penance among those too young to be the subjects of either law.

Friday: a special penitential day

Because Friday recalls the crucifixion of our Lord, it too is set aside as a special penitential day. The Church does not prescribe, however, that fish must be eaten on Fridays. It never did. Abstinence always meant the giving up of meat rather than the eating of fish as a substitute. What the Church does require, according to the new Code, is that its members abstain from meat or some other food or that they perform some alternative work of penance laid down by the Bishops' Conference.

The style of Friday abstinence

In accordance with the mind of the universal Church, the Irish bishops remind their people of the obligation of Friday penance, and instruct them that it may be fulfilled in one or more of the following ways:

(i) By abstaining from meat or some other food;
(ii) By abstaining from alcoholic drink, smoking or some form of amusement;
(iii) By making the special effort involved in family prayer, taking part in the Mass, visiting the Blessed Sacrament or praying the Stations of the Cross;
(iv) By fasting from all food for a longer period than usual and perhaps by giving what is saved in this way to the needy at home and abroad;
(v) By going out of our way to help somebody who is poor, sick, old or lonely.

Friday penance is a serious obligation

While the form of penance is an option and doesn't have to take the same form every Friday, the obligation to do penance is not. There is a serious obligation to observe Friday as a penitential day. We are confident that the Irish people as a whole will take this obligation to heart. We recommend that each person should choose some form of penance for Fridays, in memory, as was Friday abstinence, of the passion and death of our Lord.

LITURGICAL NOTE 22
National Liturgical Agencies

A national liturgical commission and diocesan commissions are established for the renewal of liturgy in *Sacrosanctum Concilium* 44–45.

In changes to the structures of the Episcopal Conference in March 2010, the Irish Episcopal Commission for Liturgy and the Irish Commission for Liturgy became the Council for Liturgy. Its chairperson is Most Rev. Francis Duffy.

There are three advisory committees: Sacred Art and Architecture (chairperson: Mr Brian Quinn; secretary: Rev. Neil X. O'Donoghue); Church Music (chairperson:

Rev. J Columba McCann OSB; secretary: Sr Moira Bergin RSM); Liotúirge i nGaeilge (cathaoirleach: An Dr Marie Whelton; rúnaí: An Dr Micheál Ó Cearúil).

The Irish Episcopal Conference's Secretary for Liturgy is Fr Neil X. O'Donoghue, Columba Centre, Maynooth, Co. Kildare.

The National Centre for Liturgy, as an institute of pastoral liturgy (*Sacrosanctum Concilium,* 44), within the Pontifical University, St Patrick's College, Maynooth, offers programmes of liturgical formation. Through the Pontifical University and its Faculty of Theology it offers the Diploma and Higher Diploma in Pastoral Liturgy and the M.Th degree specialising in liturgy. It also works with the Department of Music, Maynooth University, on a part-time Diploma in Arts (Church Music) course.

LITURGICAL NOTE 23
Copyright

In order to reprint copyright material for liturgies, permission should be obtained beforehand from the publisher/agent/composer, as appropriate.

Most of the texts in our liturgical books are owned by the International Commission on English in the Liturgy (ICEL), a joint commission of Catholic Bishops' Conferences. ICEL's address is 1100 Connecticut Avenue, NW, Suite 710, Washington, D.C. 20036-4101, USA. Tel. 001 202 347 0800. Fax 001 202 347 1839. Website www.icelweb.org. For copyright permission email permission@eliturgy.org .

The copyright of some rites in Ireland, such as the Marriage Rite, and of liturgical texts in Irish is held by the Irish Episcopal Conference. The contact address is the National Secretariat for Liturgy, St Patrick's College, Maynooth, Co. Kildare.

The copyright of scripture texts is held by the publishers of the various versions. The publisher of *An Bíobla Naofa* (Bíobla Má Nuad) is An Sagart, Daingean, Trá Lí, Co. Chiarraí.

The copyright of music (words and music) is held by the composers and/or publishers/agents. An annual reprint licence and once-off publication permission, covering much of the music used in worship (GIA, OCP, Taizé, McCrimmon, Weston Priory, Grail and Revised Grail Psalms, WLP, Iona Community, Veritas Publications, etc.) including the former Calamus licence, are available from One License, at https://www.onelicense.net.

LITURGICAL NOTE 24
Additions to the Calendar

Four optional memorials of the General Calendar displaced by higher ranking observances of the National Calendar as approved in 1998 have been assigned new dates: St Ephrem, deacon and doctor of the Church – 10 June, St Peter Claver, priest – 10 September, St Martin de Porres, religious – 5 November and St Clement I, pope and martyr – 25 November (Prot. N. 354/16, 11 July 2016).

The higher ranking celebrations of the proper calendar for Ireland are unchanged: St Columba (Colum Cille), feast – 9 June; and three obligatory memorials, St Ciaran – 9 September, St Malachy – 3 November and St Columban – 23 November.

The memorial of Blessed Virgin Mary, Mother of the Church (Monday after Pentecost Sunday) was added by decree of the Congregation for Divine Worship and Discipline of the Sacraments (11 February 2018).

The optional memorials of St John XXIII (11 October) and St John Paul II (22 October) were added by decree of the Congregation for Divine Worship and Discipline of the Sacraments (29 May 2014), St Paul VI (29 May) by decree (25 January 2019), Our Lady of Loreto (10 December) by decree (7 October 2019), St Faustina Kowalska (5 October) by decree (18 May 2020). The memorial of St Mary Magdalene (22 July) was raised to the rank of feast (decree 3 June 2016). The memorial of Ss Martha, Mary and Lazarus replaces the memorial of St Martha (29 July) (decree 2 February 2021).

LITURGICAL NOTE 25
Liturgical Websites

General Links
catholicbishops.ie
For information and news on the Church in Ireland, bishops and on the agencies and commissions of the Irish Bishops' Conference.

catholicireland.net
Gives information on Mass times in parishes in Ireland. It provides news, features and liturgical material.

maynoothcollege.ie
This is the site of St Patrick's College, Maynooth and gives information on courses offered, including the liturgy programmes of the National Centre for Liturgy.

maynoothuniversity.ie
Gives access to the Department of Music at Maynooth University where a Diploma in Arts (Church Music) is available. This part-time course is conducted in association with the National Centre for Liturgy.

icmamusic.ie
The site of the Irish Church Music Association with links to other sites on liturgical music.

cumannnasagart.ie
The website of Cumann na Sagart provides texts for liturgy through the medium of Irish.

vatican.va
The website of the Holy See, including the Congregation for Divine Worship and the Discipline of the Sacraments.

Liturgy Resources
virc.at
Readings for Sunday Mass in several western and eastern European languages.

osb.org/liturgy
This is a comprehensive site for liturgical history, documentation and prayer texts.

catholic-resources.org
A website with a variety of materials on bible and liturgy.

liturgyoffice.org.uk
The website of the Liturgy Office of the Conference of Bishops of England and Wales.

Prayer Site
sacredspace.ie
This site offers Sacred Space, a daily reflection.

Irish publishers of books on liturgy, etc.
Columba Press – *columba.ie*
Dominican Publications – *dominicanpublications.com*
The Furrow – *thefurrow.ie*
Messenger Publications – *messenger.ie*
Redemptorist Communications – *redcoms.org*
Veritas Publications – *veritas.ie*

NOVEMBER 2022
For children who suffer
We pray for children who are suffering, especially those who are homeless, orphans, and victims of war; may they be guaranteed access to education and the opportunity to experience family affection.

DECEMBER 2022
For volunteer not-for-profit organisations
We pray that volunteer non-profit organisations committed to human development find people dedicated to the common good and ceaselessly seek out new paths to international cooperation.

JANUARY 2023
For educators
We pray that educators may be credible witnesses, teaching fraternity rather than competition and helping the youngest and most vulnerable above all.

FEBRUARY 2023
For parishes
We pray that parishes, placing communion at the centre, may increasingly become communities of faith, fraternity and welcome towards those most in need.

MARCH 2023
For victims of abuse
We pray for those who have suffered harm from members of the Church; may they find within the Church herself a concrete response to their pain and suffering.

APRIL 2023
For a culture of peace and non-violence
We pray for the spread of peace and non-violence, by decreasing the use of weapons by States and citizens.

MAY 2023
For church movements and groups
We pray that Church movements and groups may rediscover their mission of evangelisation each day, placing their own charisms at the service of needs in the world.

JUNE 2023
For the abolition of torture
We pray that the international community may commit in a concrete way to ensuring the abolition of torture and guarantee support to victims and their families.

JULY 2023
For a Eucharistic life
We pray that Catholics may place the celebration of the Eucharist at the heart of their lives, transforming human relationships in a very deep way and opening to the encounter with God and all their brothers and sisters.

AUGUST 2023
For World Youth Day
We pray the World Youth Day in Lisbon will help young people to live and witness the Gospel in their own lives.

SEPTEMBER 2023
For people living on the margins
We pray for those persons living on the margins of society, in inhumane life conditions; may they not be overlooked by institutions and never considered of lesser importance.

OCTOBER 2023
For the Synod
We pray for the Church, that she may adopt listening and dialogue as a lifestyle at every level, and allow herself to be guided by the Holy Spirit towards the peripheries of the world.

NOVEMBER 2023
For the Pope
We pray for the Holy Father; as he fulfils his mission, may he continue to accompany the flock entrusted to him, with the help of the Holy Spirit.

DECEMBER 2023
For persons with disabilities
We pray that people living with disabilities may be at the centre of attention in society, and that institutions may offer inclusive programmes which value their active participation.

ADVENT-CHRISTMAS-EPIPHANY

Advent has a twofold character, for it is a time of preparation for the Solemnities of Christmas, in which the First Coming of the Son of God to humanity is remembered, and likewise a time when, by remembrance of this, minds and hearts are led to look forward to Christ's Second Coming at the end of time. For these two reasons, Advent is a period of devout and expectant delight.

Advent begins with First Vespers (Evening Prayer I) of the Sunday that falls on or closest to 30 November and it ends before First Vespers (Evening Prayer I) of Christmas.

The Sundays of this time of year are named the First, Second, Third and Fourth Sundays of Advent.

The weekdays from 17 December up to and including 24 December are ordered in a more direct way to prepare for the Nativity of the Lord.

After the annual celebration of the paschal mystery, the Church has no more ancient custom than celebrating the Memorial of the Nativity of the Lord and of his first manifestations, and this takes place in Christmas Time.

Christmas Time runs from First Vespers (Evening Prayer I) of the Nativity of the Lord up to and including the Sunday after Epiphany or after 6 January.

The Vigil Mass of the Nativity is used on the evening of 24 December, either before or after First Vespers (Evening Prayer I).

On the day of the Nativity of the Lord, following ancient Roman tradition, Mass may be celebrated three times, that is, in the night, at dawn and during the day.

The Nativity of the Lord has its own Octave, arranged thus:
  a) Sunday within the Octave or, if there is no Sunday, 30 December, is the Feast of the Holy Family of Jesus, Mary and Joseph;
  b) 26 December is the Feast of St Stephen, the First Martyr;
  c) 27 December is the Feast of St John, Apostle and Evangelist;
  d) 28 December is the Feast of the Holy Innocents;
  e) 29, 30 and 31 December are days within the Octave;
  f) 1 January, the Octave Day of the Nativity of the Lord, is the Solemnity of Mary, the Holy Mother of God, and also the commemoration of the conferral of the Most Holy Name of Jesus.

The Sunday falling between 2 and 5 January is the Second Sunday after the Nativity.

The Epiphany of the Lord is celebrated on 6 January, unless, where it is not observed as a Holyday of Obligation, it has been assigned to the Sunday occurring between 2 and 8 January.

The Sunday falling after 6 January is the Feast of the Baptism of the Lord.

UNLYC, 32–42

Advent is a time of waiting, conversion and of hope:
* waiting–memory of the first, humble coming of the Lord in our mortal flesh; waiting–supplication for his final, glorious coming as Lord of History and Universal Judge;
* conversion, to which the liturgy at this time often refers quoting the prophets, especially John the Baptist, 'Repent for the kingdom of heaven is at hand' (*Mt* 3:2);
* joyful hope that the salvation already accomplished by Christ (cf. *Rm* 8:24-25) and the reality of grace in the world will mature and reach their fullness, thereby granting us what is promised by faith, and 'we shall become like him for we shall see him as he really is' (*Jn* 3:2).

Popular piety is particularly sensitive to Advent, especially when seen as the memory of the preparation for the coming of the Messiah. The Christian people are deeply conscious of the long period of expectation that preceded the birth of our Saviour. The faithful know that God sustained Israel's hope in the coming of the Messiah by the prophets.

Various expressions of popular piety connected with Advent have emerged throughout the centuries. These have sustained the faith of the people, and from one generation to the next, they have conserved many valuable aspects of the liturgical season of Advent.

The Advent Wreath

Placing four candles on green fronds has become a symbol of Advent in many Christian homes, especially in Germanic countries and in North America.

The Advent wreath, with the progressive lighting of its four candles, Sunday after Sunday, until the Solemnity of Christmas, is a recollection of the various stages of salvation history prior to Christ's coming and a symbol of the prophetic light gradually illuminating the long night prior to the rising of the Sun of justice (cf. *Mal* 3:20; *Lk* 1:78).

The Blessed Virgin Mary and Advent

The liturgy frequently celebrates the Blessed Virgin Mary in an exemplary way during the season of Advent. It recalls the women of the Old Testament who prefigured and prophesied her mission; it exalts her faith and the humility with which she promptly and totally submitted to God's plan of salvation; it highlights her presence in the events of grace preceding the birth of the Saviour. Popular piety also devotes particular attention to the Blessed Virgin Mary during Advent, as is evident from the many pious exercises practised at this time – especially the novena of the Immaculate Conception and of Christmas. The novena of the Immaculate Conception, wherever it is celebrated, should highlight the prophetical texts which begin with Genesis 3:15, and end in Gabriel's salutation of the one who is 'full of grace' (*Lk* 1:31-33).

However, the significance of Advent, 'that time which is particularly apt for the cult of the Mother of God' (*Marialis Cultus*, 4), is such that it cannot be represented merely as a 'Marian month'.

In the Calendars of the Oriental Churches, the period of preparation for the celebration of the manifestation (Advent) of divine salvation (Theophany) in the mysteries of Christmas-Epiphany of the Only Son of God, is markedly Marian in character. Attention is concentrated on preparation for the Lord's coming in the *Deipara*. For the Orientals, all Marian mysteries are Christological mysteries since they refer to the mystery of our salvation in Christ. The Byzantine Rite prepares for Christmas with a whole series of Marian feasts and rituals.

The Feast of the Immaculate Conception, which is profoundly influential among the faithful, is an occasion for many displays of popular piety and especially for the novena of the Immaculate Conception. There can be no doubt that the feast of the pure and sinless Conception of the Virgin Mary, which is a fundamental preparation for the Lord's coming into the world, harmonises perfectly with many of the salient themes of Advent. This feast also makes reference to the long messianic waiting for the Saviour's birth and recalls events and prophecies from the Old Testament, which are also used in the Liturgy of advent.

Directory on Popular Piety and the Liturgy, 96–8, 100, 102

The Mass Lectionary in Advent
Sunday Readings

Each gospel reading has a distinctive theme: first Sunday – the Lord's coming at the end of time; second and third – John the Baptist; and fourth – the events preparatory to the Lord's birth. The Old Testament readings, usually from Isaiah, are messianic prophecies. The readings from an apostle are exhortations and proclamations in keeping with the themes of Advent.

Weekday Readings

There are two series of readings: the first continues until 16 December; the second is according to date from 17 December.

On the first days of Advent, the Gospel passage is chosen in relation to the selected passage from Isaiah.

On Thursday of the second week, the Gospel passages are about St John the Baptist, and the first reading is either a continuation of Isaiah or a text chosen in view of the Gospel.

From 17 December, Gospel passages are chosen about the events that immediately prepared for the birth of Christ. The first readings are from different books of the Old Testament in view of the Gospel readings and include the most important messianic prophecies. See Liturgical Note 8 in regard to commemorations of saints.

NOVEMBER 2022

READINGS Sunday Cycle A — Psalter Week 1

26 Saturday
Violet — FIRST EVENING PRAYER of the **First Sunday of Advent**

Volume I of the Divine Office is used from this evening.

---

27 Sunday — **FIRST SUNDAY OF ADVENT**
Violet ✠ — HOURS Proper. Te Deum. Psalter Week 1
MASS Proper. No Gloria. Creed. Preface: Advent I
READINGS — **Is 2:1-5. Ps 121:1-2, 4-5, 6-9, R/ cf. v 1. Rm 13:11-14. Mt 24:37-44.** *Lect* I:3

The liturgy of the day directs our minds to the Last Day, to the Second Coming of Christ, to the Day of Judgement. We look at this not as individuals, but as a great gathering of all peoples. The suddenness of the coming of the Lord may make us fear, but we should look forward in joy – rejoice when we hear them say 'Let us go to God's house'. St Paul tells us how to live in the meantime: be fully awake and cast off the works of darkness.
No other celebrations, not even funeral Masses, are permitted today (see Lit. Note 8)
St Fergal, bishop and missionary is not celebrated this year.

---

28 Monday — **1st Week of Advent**
Violet — HOURS Psalter Week 1. MASS Proper. Preface: Advent I
READINGS — **Is 4:2-6. Ps 121:1-2, 4-5, 6-9, R/ cf. v 1. Mt 8:5-11.** *Lect* I:11

On these first days of Advent the gospel passage is chosen in consideration of the selected texts from Isaiah. For this reason the Church, especially during Advent and Lent, and above all at the Easter Vigil, re-reads and re-lives the great events of salvation history in the 'today' of her liturgy.

---

29 Tuesday — **1st Week of Advent**
Violet — HOURS Psalter Week 1. MASS Proper. Preface: Advent I
READINGS — **Is 11:1-10. Ps 71:1-2, 7-8, 12-13, 17, R/ cf. v 7. Lk 10:21-24.** *Lect* I:13

The prophet speaks of the one on whom the Spirit rests. Integrity and faithfulness shall characterise him. And in those days there shall be peace. Jesus, filled with the joy of the Holy Spirit, gives thanks to the Father for revealing the fulfilment of the prophecies.
Kildare and Leighlin — **Dedication of the Cathedral** (see *Lit. Note* 12)

30 Wednesday ST ANDREW, APOSTLE   Feast
Red   HOURS Proper. Te Deum. Psalter Week 1 at Day Hour
                       MASS Proper. Gloria. Preface: Apostles I-II
READINGS   **Rm 10:9-18. Ps 18:2-5, R/ v 5. Mt 4:18-22.** *Lect*
                       II:1279

St Andrew from Bethsaida was a disciple of John the Baptist when he was called by Jesus. He in turn brought his brother Peter to Jesus. He is said to have suffered martyrdom by crucifixion on this date, but the tradition of an X-shaped cross is much later. Patron of Scotland, Russia and fishermen.
No Masses for the dead, except funeral Masses, are permitted today (Lit. Note 8)

DECEMBER 2022

1 Thursday   **1st Week of Advent**
Violet   HOURS Psalter Week 1. MASS Proper. Preface: Advent I
READINGS   **Is 26:1-6. Ps 117:1, 8-9, 19-21, 25-27, R/ v 26. Mt 7:21, 24-27.** *Lect* I:18

It is the upright nation, the faithful people, which will enter the kingdom. To be part of that people each one must hear the word of God and do God's will.

---

2 Friday   **1st Week of Advent**
Violet   HOURS Psalter Week 1. MASS Proper. Preface: Advent I
READINGS   **Is 29:17-24. Ps 26:1, 4, 13-14, R/ v 1. Mt 9:27-31.** *Lect* I:20

One of the signs of the Day of the Lord is that the eyes of the blind will see. Jesus cures two blind men because of their faith in him. In Christ, the true light, we can truly see, have visions, discern with wisdom.

---

3 Saturday   **1st Week of Advent**
                     St Francis Xavier, priest   Memorial
White   HOURS of the memorial. Psalter Week 1
                      MASS of the memorial. Preface: Advent I or of the Saint
READINGS   **Is 30:19-21, 23-26. Ps 146:1-6, R/ Is 30:18. Mt 9:35–10:1, 6-8.** *Lect* I:22

God's ears are not deaf to the cries of the needy. Jesus, as a shepherd, feels compassion for those who have lost the way.
St Francis Xavier, 1506–52, one of the first seven Jesuits, was sent to India by St Ignatius. He converted many in Goa and later in Japan. He died as he attempted to enter China. A patron of the missions.

DECEMBER 2022

4 Sunday — SECOND SUNDAY OF ADVENT

Violet ✠
HOURS Proper. Te Deum. Psalter Week 2
MASS Proper. No Gloria. Creed. Preface: Advent I
READINGS **Is 11:1-10. Ps 71:1-2, 7-8, 12-13, 17, R/ cf. v 7. Rm 15:4-9. Mt 3:1-12.** *Lect* I:24

John the Baptist is a prophetic voice for all ages: his message speaks to us today, for conversion is always part of the Christian way of living. Conversion to each other is called for by St Paul, so that we can be tolerant of each other, united in mind and heart.
No other celebrations, not even funeral Masses, are permitted today (see Lit. Note 8)
St John Damascene, priest and doctor of the Church is not celebrated this year.

---

5 Monday — 2nd Week of Advent

Violet
HOURS Psalter Week 2. MASS Proper. Preface: Advent I
READINGS **Is 35:1-10. Ps 84:9-14, R/ Is 35:4. Lk 5:17-26.** *Lect* I:33

The marvellous vision of God's saving love is expressed in some of the most poetic language of the prophet. This vision is realised in the life and works of Jesus Christ.

---

6 Tuesday — 2nd Week of Advent

Violet
HOURS Psalter Week 2. MASS Proper. Preface: Advent I
White
Optional memorial of **St Nicholas, bishop**
Galway   St Nicholas, bishop   Feast
City of Galway St Nicholas, bishop   Solemnity
READINGS **Is 40:1-11. Ps 95:1-3, 10-13, R/ cf. Is 40:9-10. Mt 18:12-14.** *Lect* I:35

Isaiah's words of comfort breathe the very spirit of Advent. The nation's slavery is ended and God will lead his people in a new Exodus. The road must be prepared for God to travel on.
St Nicholas is a fourth-century Bishop of Myra in modern-day Turkey of whom little is known. He is patron of Russia, of sailors, of pawnbrokers and of children.

The O Antiphons

A feature of the Liturgy of the Hours in Advent is the singing of the Magnificat antiphon on the seven evenings before the Vigil of Christmas. They were popular especially during the Middle Ages in the Monastic Office. Intoning the antiphon was the special privilege of office holders in the community, the chant had a special distinction, and the great bell of the monastery was tolled throughout. The ritual and the meanings created the atmosphere of expectation for the Christmas feast. These antiphons are still in the Liturgy of the Hours today. They are also used in the daily *Lectionary* as the versicle for the Gospel Acclamation. An Advent Prayer Service can be built around the singing of the antiphons, using appropriate readings and prayers.

7 Wednesday 2nd Week of Advent
St Ambrose, bishop and doctor of the Church
Memorial

White   HOURS of the memorial. Psalter Week 2
               MASS of the memorial. Preface: Advent I or of the Saint
READINGS   **Is 40:25-31. Ps 102:1-4, 8, 10, R/ v 1. Mt 11:28-30.**
               Lect I:38

The people are not to grow weary and tired, thinking that the Lord has deserted them. Those who hope in him will renew their strength, they will sprout wings like eagles. Jesus promises rest to the weary and overburdened.

St Ambrose, 339-397, became governor of the Roman province whose seat was in Milan. In 374, the laity insisted on his becoming bishop though he was still not baptised. He defended orthodoxy in brilliant preaching and through his writing. Patron of Milan, bee-keepers, and domestic animals.

White   FIRST EVENING PRAYER of the **Immaculate Conception**

---

8 Thursday THE IMMACULATE CONCEPTION OF THE BLESSED VIRGIN MARY
Solemnity

White ✠   HOURS Proper. Te Deum. Complementary Psalms at Day Hour
               MASS Proper. Gloria. Creed. Preface: Proper
READINGS   **Gn 3:9-15, 20. Ps 97:1-4, R/ v 1. Eph 1:3-6, 11-12.**
               Lk 1:26-38. *Lect* I:1009 or II:1289

The Immaculate Conception of the Blessed Virgin Mary. We celebrate Mary who, from the first instant of her existence in the womb of her mother Anne, was 'by a singular grace and privilege of almighty God, and in view of the merits of Jesus Christ, Saviour of the human race, preserved free from all stain of original sin'.

               EVENING PRAYER of the Solemnity
No Masses for the dead, except funeral Masses, are permitted today (see Lit. Note 8)

---

9 Friday 2nd Week of Advent
Violet   HOURS Psalter Week 2. MASS Proper. Preface: Advent I
White   Optional memorial of **St Juan Diego Cuauhtlatoatzin**
READINGS   **Is 48:17-19. Ps 1:1-4, 6, R/ cf. Jn 8:12. Mt 11:16-19.**
               Lect I:42

The people of Jesus' own time have acted in a self-willed way, never consistent nor satisfied, and have refused the offer of salvation. Neither the ascetical John, nor Jesus with his free and easy way at table with sinners, can bring them to faith.

St Juan Diego Cuauhtlatoatzin, 1474–1548, saw the vision of Our Lady of Guadalupe in December 1531.

---

10 Saturday **2nd Week of Advent**
Violet HOURS Psalter Week 2. MASS Proper. Preface: Advent I
White Optional memorial of **Blessed Virgin Mary of Loreto**
(see Collect, p. 181)
READINGS **Eccles (Sir) 48:1-4, 9-11. Ps 79:2-3, 15-16, 18-19, R/ v 4. Mt 17:10-13.** Lect I:44

Going before Jesus in the spirit and power of Elijah, John bears witness to Christ in his preaching, by his baptism of conversion, and through his martyrdom.

Our Lady of Loreto. This celebration helps all people, especially families, youth and religious to imitate the virtues of that perfect disciple of the gospel, the Virgin Mother, who, in conceiving the Head of the Church also accepted us as her own. **Is 7:10-14, 8:10** (Lect II:1428)**. Ps Lk 1:46-53, R/ 54-55** (II:1423)**. Lk 1:26-38** (II:1443)**.**

Our Lady of Loreto (10 December)

Loreto is a hill town near the Adriatic Sea port of Ancona, on the east coast of Italy. A decree from the Congregation for Divine Worship published at the end of October 2019 adds the optional memorial of Our Lady of Loreto to our Calendar, to be observed on 10 December. It stated, 'This celebration will help all people, especially families, youth and religious to imitate the virtues of that perfect disciple of the gospel, the Virgin Mother, who, in conceiving the Head of the Church also accepted us as her own.' Pilgrims go to Loreto to pray at the Holy House where Mary was born and was visited by the Angel Gabriel at the Annunciation and where the Holy Family later lived. 'This shrine,' the decree adds, 'recalls the mystery of the Incarnation, leading all those who visit it to consider "the fullness of time," when God sent his Son, born of a woman, as well as to meditate on the words of the Angel announcing the Good News and on the words of the Virgin in response to the divine call.'

According to tradition, the small house was carried by angels from Nazareth to Loreto on the night of 9–10 December, 1294, after three years in Tersatto in present-day Croatia.

Loreto is Italy's most popular Marian shrine city. The decree says, 'Before the image of the Mother of the Redeemed and of the Church, saints and blessed have responded to their vocation, the sick have invoked consolation in suffering, the people of God have begun to praise and plead with Mary using the Litany of Loreto, which is known throughout the world.'

THE PROCLAMATION OF CHRISTMAS

The first entry in the *Martyrologium Romanum* (Roman Martyrology) for 25 December is a proclamation of 'the Nativity of Our Lord Jesus Christ according to the flesh'. It may be used before or at the beginning of Midnight Mass. Its inclusion after Evening Prayer or at the Office of Readings is also appropriate.

The twenty-fifth day of December.
After the passage of countless centuries from the creation of the world, when in the beginning God created heaven and earth and formed man in his own image; and very many centuries from the time when after the flood the Almighty had set his bow in the clouds,
a sign of the covenant and of peace;
in the twenty-first century from the migration of Abraham, our father in faith, from Ur of the Chaldees;
in the thirteenth century from the departure of the people of Israel from Egypt under the leadership of Moses;
in about the one-thousandth year from the anointing of David as king according to the prophecy of Daniel;
in the 194th Olympiad;
in the 752nd year from the foundation of the City of Rome;
in the 42nd year of the rule of Caesar Octavian Augustus;
while the whole world was at peace, Jesus Christ, eternal God and Son of the Eternal Father, desiring to consecrate the world by his most gracious coming, having been conceived of the Holy Spirit, and when nine months had passed after his conception, is born as man in Bethlehem of Judah from the Virgin Mary:
the Nativity of Our Lord Jesus Christ according to the flesh.

ANNOUNCEMENT OF EASTER

The season of Christmas ends with the celebration of the Baptism of the Lord. As the season draws to an end, the solemnity of the Epiphany offers an opportunity to proclaim the centrality of Christ's paschal mystery: dying he destroyed our death and rising he restored our life. The Easter Triduum of the passion, death and resurrection of Christ is the culmination of the entire liturgical year. The proclamation of the date of Easter may be announced on the solemnity of the Epiphany after the homily or after the Prayer after Communion. The Announcement with music is to be found in *RM*, pp. 1351–2.

Know, dear brothers and sisters that, as we have rejoiced at the Nativity of our Lord Jesus Christ, so by leave of God's mercy we announce to you also the joy of his resurrection, who is our Saviour.

On the twenty-second day of February will fall Ash Wednesday, and the beginning of the fast of the most sacred Lenten season.
On the ninth day of April you will celebrate with joy Easter Day, the Paschal feast of our Lord Jesus Christ.
On the twenty-first day of May will be the Ascension of our Lord Jesus Christ.
On the twenty-eighth day of May, the feast of Pentecost.
On the eleventh day of June, the feast of the Most Holy Body and Blood of Christ.
On the third day of December, the First Sunday of the Advent of our Lord Jesus Christ,
to whom is honour and glory for ever and ever.
Amen.

DECEMBER 2022

11 Sunday — THIRD SUNDAY OF ADVENT
(Gaudete Sunday)

Violet or Rose ✠ HOURS Proper. Te Deum. Psalter Week 3
MASS Proper. No Gloria. Creed. Preface: Advent I

READINGS **Is 35:1-6, 10. Ps 145:6-10, R/ cf. Is 35:4. Jas 5:7-10. Mt 11:2-11.** *Lect* I:46

The joy of the kingdom is anticipated. The signs of the kingdom already come are given to the messengers of John the Baptist, and they are familiar with the prophecy of Isaiah. Patient waiting for the fulfilment is our Christian duty. There should be no complaining, no giving up or losing heart. Joy, prayer and thanksgiving should characterise the Christian community.

No other celebrations, not even funeral Masses, are permitted today (see Lit. Note 8)
St Damasus I, pope is not celebrated this year.

---

12 Monday — 3rd Week of Advent

Violet   HOURS Psalter Week 3. MASS Proper. Preface: Advent I
White   Optional memorial of **Our Lady of Guadalupe**
White   Optional memorial of **St Finnian, bishop**
Meath   **St Finnian, bishop**
READINGS   **Num 24:2-7, 15-17. Ps 24:4-9, R/ v 4. Mt 21:23-27.** *Lect* I:53

On the issue of the authority of John's baptism the leaders refuse to take a public stand, either for or against it. As a result they are shown up as not being able to act with authority. Jesus shows his superiority by refusing to submit his teaching authority to their judgement.

Our Lady of Guadalupe is patron of the Americas. This memorial recalls the apparitions in December 1531 to Juan Diego Cuauhtlatoatzin on Tepeyac hill, near Mexico city.

St Finnian, see *The Irish Calendar*, p. 192.

---

13 Tuesday — 3rd Week of Advent
St Lucy, virgin and martyr   Memorial

Red   HOURS of the memorial. Psalter Week 3
MASS of the memorial. Preface: Advent I or of the Saint
READINGS   **Zeph 3:1-2, 9-13. Ps 33:2-3, 6-7, 16, 18-19, 23, R/ v 7. Mt 21:28-32.** *Lect* I:56

The poor and marginalised are given hope through the coming of Christ. There is no place for the proud and overbearing in the kingdom of God.

St Lucy, desiring to remain consecrated to Christ alone, was martyred in 304 in Sicily during the persecution of Diocletian.

---

14 Wednesday 3rd Week of Advent
St John of the Cross, priest and doctor of the Church
Memorial

White   HOURS of the memorial. Psalter Week 3.

MASS of the memorial. Preface: Advent I or of the Saint

READINGS   **Is 45:6-8, 18, 21-26. Ps 84:9-14, R/ cf. Is 45:8. Lk 7:19-23.** *Lect* I:58

John the Baptist encourages his disciples to find the true Messiah. Our prayer is the ancient *Rorate Coeli*: send victory like a dew.

St John of the Cross, 1542-1591, a Carmelite who, despite opposition and imprisonment, worked for spreading the reform of the Carmelites. He was a man of prayer, an outstanding poet, a spiritual writer, declared doctor of the Church.

---

15 Thursday   3rd Week of Advent
Violet   HOURS Psalter Week 3. MASS Proper. Preface: Advent I

READINGS   **Is 54:1-10. Ps 29:2, 4-6, 11-13, R/ v 2. Lk 7:24-30.** *Lect* I:61

There is a tension between living fully this present life and at the same time waiting for the happiness that is to come. May we have the courage and strength that the promise and hope of heaven will guide our way on earth.

---

16 Friday   3rd Week of Advent
Violet   HOURS Psalter Week 3. MASS Proper. Preface: Advent I

READINGS   **Is 56:1-3, 6-8. Ps 66:2-3, 5, 7-8, R/ v 4. Jn 5:33-36.** *Lect* I:63

John was as a lamp lighting the way, but Jesus is the true light that enlightens all peoples. The promise of salvation is given to all who serve and love the Lord.

17–24 December Preparation for Christmas

For the Liturgy of the Hours the texts are proper for each day (see Divine Office, I, pp. 117 ff.). Mass texts are proper also according to the date. Votive Masses and daily Masses for the dead are not permitted. See Liturgical Note 8 in regard to commemorations of saints.

17 Saturday   3rd Week of Advent
Violet   HOURS Psalter Week 3. MASS Proper. Preface: Advent II

READINGS   **Gn 49:2, 8-10. Ps 71:1-4, 7-8, 17, R/ cf. v 7. Mt 1:1-17.** *Lect* I:76

'When the Church celebrates the liturgy of Advent each year, she makes present this ancient expectancy of the Messiah, for by sharing in the long preparation for the Saviour's first coming, the faithful renew their ardent desire for his second coming' (CCC, 524). 'Wisdom of the Most High, teach us the way of truth.'

DECEMBER 2022

18 Sunday FOURTH SUNDAY OF ADVENT
Violet ✠ HOURS Proper. Te Deum. Psalter Week 4
MASS Proper. No Gloria. Creed. Preface: Advent II
READINGS **Is 7:10-14. Ps 23:1-6, R/ cf. vv 7, 10. Rm 1:1-7. Mt 1:18-24.** *Lect* I:68

Our attention is now directed fully to the coming of Christ in the Christmas mystery. The Preface calls us to wonder at this great happening, to prepare for Christmas in prayer and praise. The psalm tells us to purify our hearts as preparation. Prayer and reconciliation should be features of these days.
No other celebrations, not even funeral Masses, are permitted today (see Lit. Note 8)
St Flannan, bishop is not celebrated this year.

---

19 Monday 4th Week of Advent
Violet HOURS Psalter Week 4. MASS Proper. Preface: Advent II
READINGS **Jg 13:2-7, 24-25. Ps 70:3-6, 16-17, R/ cf. v 8. Lk 1:5-25.** *Lect* I:81

Samson and John are specially chosen messengers whose births are announced by an angel. Each of us is a messenger to tell the praise of God's glory every day. 'Root of Jesse, do not delay to come and save us.'

---

20 Tuesday 4th Week of Advent
Violet HOURS Psalter Week 4. MASS Proper. Preface: Advent II
Memorial may be made of **St Fachanan, bishop** (see *Lit. Note 8*)
Kilfenora **St Fachanan, bishop**   Feast
READINGS **Is 7:10-14. Ps 23:1-6, R/ v 7, 10. Lk 1:26-38.** *Lect* I:83

'The faithful who carry the spirit of Advent from the liturgy into their own lives perceive the inexpressible love in the Virgin Mary's welcoming of her Son. Thus the Advent liturgy leads them to keep Mary before their own eyes as a model and to prepare the way for the coming Saviour, with wonder and praise (*Marialis Cultus*). 'Key of David, come to liberate those who are captive in darkness.'
St Fachanan, see *The Irish Calendar*, p. 192.

---

21 Wednesday 4th Week of Advent
Violet HOURS Psalter Week 4. MASS Proper. Preface: Advent II
Memorial may be made of **St Peter Canisius, priest and doctor of the Church** (see *Lit. Note 8*)
READINGS **Song 2:8-14 or Zeph 3:14-18. Ps 32:2-3, 11-12, 20-21, R/ vv 1, 3. Lk 1:39-45.** *Lect* I:85

Elizabeth is honoured by a visit from the mother of her Lord, and the child leaps for joy. Our Advent joy arises from Christ's coming among us. 'Emmanuel, our king and our law-giver, come and save us, Lord our God.'
St Peter Canisius, 1521–97, was born in Holland. He intended to become a lawyer but joined the Jesuits. Through courtesy and learning he promoted the Catholic revival after the Council of Trent. His greatest work was a catechism of 211 questions and answers, published in 1555.

---

22 Thursday   **4th Week of Advent**
Violet   HOURS Psalter Week 4. MASS Proper. Preface: Advent II
READINGS   **1 Sm 1:24-28. Ps 1 Sm 2:1, 4-8, R/ v 1. Lk 1:46-56.**
                  Lect I:88

'The Almighty has done great things for me': both Hannah and Mary can sing this song to the Lord. So can all who have heard the good news of great joy. 'Root of Jesse, set up as a sign to the peoples, delay no more.'

_____

23 Friday   **4th Week of Advent**
Violet   HOURS Psalter Week 4. MASS Proper. Preface: Advent II
                  Memorial may be made of **St John of Kanty, priest** (see
                  Lit. Note 8)
READINGS   **Mal 3:1-4, 23-24. Ps 24:4-5, 8-9, 10, 14, R/ Lk
                  21:28. Lk 1:57-66.** *Lect* I:90

The birth of John the Baptist is a cause of joy for relations and neighbours. 'King of the peoples and cornerstone of the Church, come and save those whom you made from the dust of the earth.'
St John of Kanty, 1390-1473, taught theology and scripture in the university of Kraków, Poland. He is remembered for his austerity of life and generosity.

_____

24 Saturday   **4th Week of Advent**
Violet   HOURS Psalter Week 4. MASS Proper. Preface: Advent II
READINGS   **2 Sm 7:1-5, 8-12, 14, 16. Ps 88:2-5, 27, 29, R/ cf. v
                  2. Lk 1:67-79.** *Lect* I:92

Zechariah prophesies that the Rising Sun comes to give light to all in darkness and the shadow of death. The tender mercy of our God will bring the rising Sun to shine upon us, to guide our feet into the way of peace. 'Morning Star, sun of justice, come and enlighten those who live in darkness.'

_____

CHRISTMAS TIME

After the annual celebration of the paschal mystery, the Church has no more ancient custom than celebrating the memorial of the Nativity of the Lord and of his first manifestations, and this takes place in Christmas Time.

Christmas Time runs from First Vespers (Evening Prayer I) of the Nativity of the Lord up to and including the Sunday after Epiphany or after 6 January.

The Vigil Mass of the Nativity is used on the evening of 24 December, either before or after First Vespers (Evening Prayer I).

On the day of the Nativity of the Lord, following ancient Roman tradition, Mass may be celebrated three times, that is, in the night, at dawn and during the day.

UNLYC, 32–34

SEASON OF CHRISTMAS

THE NATIVITY OF OUR LORD JESUS CHRIST

24 Saturday **Christmas Eve**   Solemnity with Octave
White ✠   EVENING MASS of the Vigil Proper. Gloria. Creed. Preface:
                Nativity I–III. In the Roman Canon, proper form
READINGS   **Is 62:1-5. Ps 88:4-5, 16-17, 27, 29, R/ cf. v 2. Acts
                13:16-17, 22-25. Mt 1:1-25** (shorter form 1:18-25). *Lect
                I:99*

The Virgin will conceive and give birth to a son and they shall call him Emmanuel.
At all Masses this evening and tomorrow in the Creed all kneel at the words: and
by the Holy Spirit was incarnate.
                FIRST EVENING PRAYER of the Nativity
OFFICE OF READINGS should appropriately be celebrated before the Midnight
Mass as a solemn Vigil.

---

25 Sunday   **THE NATIVITY OF OUR LORD JESUS CHRIST** Solemnity
White ✠   HOURS Proper. Te Deum.
                MASS, at Midnight, Dawn and Day, Proper. Gloria. Creed.
                Preface: Nativity I–III. In the Roman Canon, proper form
READINGS
**Midnight Mass Is 9:1-7. Ps 95:1-3, 11-13, R/ Lk 2:11. Ti 2:11-14. Lk
2:1-14.** *Lect I:104*
I bring you news of great joy. This night a child is born for us, a son given to us.
Dawn Mass   **Is 62:11-12. Ps 96:1, 6, 11-12. Ti 3:4-7. Lk 2:15-20.**
                Lect I:107
The shepherds found Mary and Joseph and the baby, and glorified God.
**Mass during the Day Is 52:7-10. Ps 97:1-6, R/ v 3. Heb 1:1-6. Jn
1:1-18** (shorter form 1:1-5, 9-14). *Lect I:109*
The Word was made flesh, he lived among us, and we saw his glory.
In the Creed all kneel at the words: and by the Holy Spirit was incarnate.
On Christmas Day all priests may celebrate three Masses, provided that they are
celebrated at their proper time.
                EVENING PRAYER of the Nativity.
*No Masses for the dead, not even funeral Masses, are permitted today (see Lit.
Note 8)*

Since their feasts fall on the three days after Christmas, St Stephen, St John the
Apostle and Evangelist, and the Holy Innocents were given the name of *Comites
Christi*, Companions of Christ, in the Middle Ages. They were seen as a cortege or
court of honour accompanying the Christ-child. It was also said that three forms
of martyrdom are represented: voluntary and executed (Stephen), voluntary but
not executed (John), and executed but not voluntary (Holy Innocents).

---

26 Monday   ST STEPHEN, FIRST MARTYR   Feast
Red   HOURS Proper. Te Deum. Psalter Week 1 at Day Hour
                MASS Proper. Gloria. Preface: Nativity I–III. In the Roman
                Canon, proper form
READINGS   **Acts 6:8-10, 7:54-59. Ps 30:3-4, 6, 8, 16-17, R/ v 6.
Mt 10:17-22.** Lect I:125

St Stephen, the first Christian martyr, was one of those in charge of the poor
and needy. He is outstanding for his forgiveness of his enemies. Patron of
deacons, stonemasons and bricklayers.
*No Masses for the dead, except the funeral Mass and Mass on the occasion of the
first anniversary are permitted today (see Lit. Note 8)*

---

27 Tuesday   ST JOHN, APOSTLE AND EVANGELIST   Feast
White   HOURS Proper. Te Deum. Psalter Week 1 at Day Hour
                MASS Proper. Gloria. Preface: Nativity I–III. In the Roman
                Canon, proper form
READINGS   **1 Jn 1:1-4. Ps 96:1-2, 5-6, 11-12, R/ v 12. Jn 20:2-8.**
Lect I:127

St John, brother of James, son of Zebedee, the disciple whom Jesus loved, is
traditionally said to have died in Ephesus. He is considered to be the author of the
Fourth Gospel, the Book of Revelation and three Letters. The Letters especially
teach us the law of love; John is said in his old age to have preached only one
message: love one another.
*No Masses for the dead, except the funeral Mass and Mass on the occasion of the
first anniversary are permitted today (see Lit. Note 8)*

---

28 Wednesday THE HOLY INNOCENTS, MARTYRS   Feast
Red   HOURS Proper. Te Deum. Psalter Week 1 at Day Hour
                MASS Proper. Gloria. Preface: Nativity I–III. In the Roman
                Canon, proper form
READINGS   **1 Jn 1:5-2:2. Ps 123:2-5, 7-8, R/ v 7. Mt 2:13-18.** Lect
I:129

'The flight into Egypt and the massacre of the **Holy Innocents** make manifest the
opposition of darkness to the light: 'He came to his own home, and his own people
received him not.' Christ's whole life was lived under the sign of persecution. His
own share it with him. Jesus' departure from Egypt recalls the exodus and presents
him as the definitive liberator of God's people.' (CCC, 530)
*No Masses for the dead, except the funeral Mass and Mass on the occasion of the
first anniversary are permitted today (see Lit. Note 8)*

29 Thursday   **5th Day in the Octave of Christmas**
White   HOURS Proper. Te Deum. Psalter Week 1 at Day Hour.
    MASS Proper. Gloria. Preface: Nativity I–III. In the Roman Canon, proper form
    Memorial may be made of **St Thomas Becket, bishop and martyr** *(see Lit. Note 8)*
READINGS   **1 Jn 2:3-11. Ps 95:1-3, 5-6, R/ v 11. Lk 2:22-35.** *Lect* I:131
Christmas has its origins in a feast of light to celebrate the victory of the Sun of Justice, a light shining in the darkness.
St Thomas Becket, 1118–1170, as Archbishop of Canterbury, came in conflict with King Henry II over Church rights. He was killed in his cathedral on this date.
No Masses for the dead, except the funeral Mass and Mass on the occasion of the first anniversary are permitted today (see Lit. Note 8)

---

30 Friday   THE HOLY FAMILY OF JESUS, MARY AND JOSEPH   Feast
White   HOURS Proper. Te Deum. Psalter Week 1 at Day Hour.
    MASS Proper. Gloria. Creed. Preface: Nativity I–III. In the Roman Canon, proper form
READINGS   **Eccles (Sir) 3:2-6, 12-14 or Col 3:12-21** (shorter form 3:12-17)**. Ps 127:1-5, R/ cf. v 1. Mt 2:13-15, 19-23.** *Lect* I:114
    Col 3:12-17 *(first two paragraphs of Lectionary reading) is recommended as alternative reading.* See Lit. Note 15.
The Holy Family is seen as the model for the human family, the religious community, and the Church itself. The celebration of the Incarnation has brought us to see God's closeness. In the Holy Family we see the ordinariness of the life of Jesus, the simple acceptance by Mary and Joseph of the marvels of God. In the daily life of family and community we can touch the divine, we can come close to God. But we have to learn to live centred on God, with respect and love for each other.
No Masses for the dead, except the funeral Mass and Mass on the occasion of the first anniversary are permitted today (see Lit. Note 8)

---

31 Saturday   **7th Day in the Octave of Christmas**
White   HOURS Proper. Te Deum. Psalter Week 1 at Day Hour.
    MASS Proper. Gloria. Preface: Nativity I–III. In the Roman Canon, proper form
    Memorial may be made of **St Sylvester, pope** *(see Lit. Note 8)*
READINGS   **1 Jn 2:18-21. Ps 95:1-2, 11-13, R/ v 11. Jn 1:1-18.** *Lect* I:136
'This end of the civil year affords an opportunity for the faithful to reflect on "the mystery of time", which passes quickly and inexorably. Such should give rise to a dual feeling: of penance and sorrow for the lost occasions of grace; and of thanks to God for the graces and blessings He has given during the past year. These sentiments have given rise to two pious exercises: prolonged exposition of the Blessed Sacrament, and the singing of the *Te Deum* as an act of community praise and thanksgiving to God for the graces received from Him as the year draws to a close' (*Directory on Popular Piety and the Liturgy*, 126).
St Sylvester died in 335 after being pope for twenty-one years. Being elected in the year after the Edict of Milan he was free to build many churches in Rome.
    FIRST EVENING PRAYER of **Mary, Mother of God**
No Masses for the dead, except the funeral Mass and Mass on the occasion of the first anniversary are permitted today (see Lit. Note 8)

1 Sunday	**MARY, THE HOLY MOTHER OF GOD** Solemnity
	World Day of Peace Octave of Christmas
White ✠	HOURS Proper. Te Deum. Complementary Psalms at Day Hour.
	MASS Proper. Gloria. Creed. Preface of BVM I. In the Roman Canon, proper form
	EVENING PRAYER of the Solemnity
READINGS	**Num 6:22-27. Ps 66:2-3, 5, 6, 8, R/ v 2. Gal 4:4-7. Lk 2:16-21.** Lect I:139

Mary, Mother of God. At the message of the angel, the Virgin Mary received the Word of God in her heart and in her body, and gave Life to the world. Hence she is acknowledged and honoured as being truly the Mother of God and Mother of the Redeemer (*Lumen Gentium*, 52).

No Masses for the dead, not even funeral Masses, are permitted today (see Lit. Note 8)

A Prayer for our Earth

All powerful God,
you are present in the universe
and in the smallest of your creatures.
You embrace with your tenderness all that exists.
Pour out upon us the power of your love,
that we may protect life and beauty.
Fill us with your peace, that we may live
as brothers and sisters, harming no one.
O God of the poor,
help us to rescue the abandoned
and forgotten of this earth,
so precious in your eyes.
Bring healing to our lives,
that we may protect the world and not prey on it,
that we may sow beauty,
not pollution and destruction.
Touch the hearts
of those who look only for gain
at the expense of the poor and the earth.
Teach us to discover the worth of each thing,
to be filled with awe and contemplation,
to recognize that we are profoundly united
with every creature
as we journey towards your infinite light.
We thank you for being with us each day.
Encourage us, we pray, in our struggle,
for justice, love and peace.
(*Laudato Si'*)

JANUARY 2023

2 Monday   **Before Epiphany**
                  Ss Basil the Great and Gregory Nazianzen, bishops,
                  doctors of the Church   Memorial
White   HOURS of the memorial. Psalter Week 2
                  MASS of the memorial. Preface: Nativity I–III or of the Saints
READINGS   **1 Jn 2:22-28. Ps 97:1-4, R/ v 3. Jn 1:19-28.** *Lect* I:146
'To become "children of God" we must be "born from above" or "born of God".'
The mystery of Christmas is fulfilled in us when Christ is formed in us.
St Basil, 330–79, Bishop of Caesarea, lived an ascetic life establishing norms for
monastic life. He was a theologian of distinction. **St Gregory**, 329–89, a friend
of Basil, was Bishop of Sasima and later of Constantinople. He retired to live a
monastic life.

---

3 Tuesday   **Before Epiphany**
White   HOURS Psalter Week 2. MASS Proper. Preface: Nativity I–III
White   Optional memorial of **The Holy Name of Jesus**
White   Optional memorial of **St Munchin (Mainchin), bishop**
Limerick   **St Munchin (Mainchin), bishop**   Feast
READINGS   **1 Jn 2:29-3:6. Ps 97:1, 3-6, R/ v 3. Jn 1:29-34.**
                  Lect I:148
'The whole life of Jesus Christ will make manifest "how God anointed Jesus of
Nazareth with the Holy Spirit and with power"' (CCC, 486).
The Holy Name of Jesus: Phil 2:1-11. Ps 8:4-9. Lk 2:21-24.
St Munchin (Mainchin) see *The Irish Calendar*, p. 184.

---

4 Wednesday   **Before Epiphany**
White   HOURS Psalter Week 2. MASS Proper. Preface: Nativity I–III
READINGS   **1 Jn 3:7-10. Ps 97:1, 7-9, R/ v 3. Jn 1:35-42.**
                  Lect I:150
The Christmas message is that we have found the Messiah. Jesus Christ, the
Incarnate Word, has appeared to undo the work of the devil.

---

5 Thursday   **Before Epiphany**
White   HOURS Psalter Week 2. MASS Proper. Preface: Nativity I–III
Dublin   Optional memorial of **St Charles of St Andrew, priest**
READINGS   **1 Jn 3:11-21. Ps 99, R/ v 1. Jn 1:43-51.** *Lect* I:152
'The Epiphany shows that "the full number of the nations" now takes its "place in
the family of the patriarchs" and acquires *Israelitica dignitas* (is made "worthy of
the heritage of Israel")' (CCC, 528).
                  FIRST EVENING PRAYER of the **Epiphany**
St Charles of St Andrew see *The Irish Calendar*, p. 184.

---

6 Friday **THE EPIPHANY OF THE LORD** Solemnity
White ✠ HOURS Proper. Te Deum.
MASS Proper. Gloria. Creed. Preface: Epiphany. In the Roman
Canon, proper form
READINGS **Is 60:1-6. Ps 71:1-2, 7-8, 10-13, R/ cf. v 11. Eph 3:2-3, 5-6. Mt 2:1-12.** Lect I:161

'The Epiphany is the manifestation of Jesus as Messiah of Israel, Son of God and Saviour of the world. The great feast of Epiphany celebrates the adoration of Jesus by the wise men (magi) from the East, together with his baptism in the Jordan and the wedding feast at Cana in Galilee. In the magi, representatives of the neighbouring pagan religions, the gospel sees the first-fruits of the nations, who welcome the good news of salvation through the Incarnation' (CCC, 528).

EVENING PRAYER of the Epiphany

Three wonders mark this day we celebrate:
today the star led the Magi to the manger;
today water was changed into wine at the marriage feast;
today Christ desired to be baptised by John in the river Jordan to bring us salvation, alleluia.
(Magnificat antiphon of Evening Prayer)

No other celebrations, not even funeral Masses, are permitted today (see Lit. Note 8) After the gospel and homily or after the Prayer after Communion, the announcement of the moveable feasts may be made. See Announcement of Easter, p. 35 and RM, pp. 1351–2

Dublin Today is the anniversary of the episcopal ordination of Most Rev. Diarmuid Martin, 6 January 1999.

---

7 Saturday **After Epiphany**
White HOURS Psalter Week 2. MASS Proper. Preface: Epiphany or Nativity I–III
White Optional memorial of **St Raymond of Penafort, priest**
READINGS **1 Jn 3:22-4:6. Ps 2:7-8, 10-11, R/ v 8. Mt 4:12-17, 23-25.** Lect I:164

Jesus, God made man, works signs and wonders among his people. We lose the message of Christmas if we see only a baby in a crib and do not wonder at the great mystery unfolded for us.

St Raymond of Penafort, 1175–1275, was a very brilliant lawyer when, at the age of forty-seven, he became a Dominican. Later he became Master General of the Dominicans and Archbishop of Tarragona.

FIRST EVENING PRAYER of the **Baptism of the Lord**

8 Sunday   **THE BAPTISM OF THE LORD**   Feast
White ✠   HOURS Proper. Te Deum. Psalter Week 3 at Day Hour
              MASS Proper. Gloria. Creed. Preface: Proper
READINGS   **Is 42:1-4, 6-7. Ps 28:1-4, 9-10, R/ v 11. Acts 10:34-38. Mt 3:13-17.** *Lect* I:179 or I:639

The Baptism of the Lord. Jesus is anointed with the Spirit and his power. He is proclaimed Messiah. He now goes about doing good, working the signs that make him known as the Servant of God. He is the one who brings good news to the poor and tells of salvation. Through our baptism each one of us is ordered to the life of Christ – Priest, Prophet and King – and the Father looks on us with favour.

              EVENING PRAYER of the Feast
No other celebrations, except funeral Masses, are permitted today (see Lit. Note 8)

ORDINARY TIME

Ordinary Time begins on Monday after the feast of the Baptism of the Lord

READINGS Sunday Cycle A/Weekday Cycle 1   Psalter Week 1

9 Monday   **1st Week in Ordinary Time**
Green   HOURS Psalter Week 1. MASS of choice
READINGS   **Heb 1:1-6. Ps 96:1-2, 6-7, 9, R/ cf. v 7. Mk 1:14-20.** *Lect* II:3

The Letter to the Hebrews is to be understood as a homily, rather than a letter. Just as for the people of his time so for us today the message of forgiveness, the call to courage and to hope, the challenge to risk are relevant. For God has spoken in his Son to us today.

---

10 Tuesday   **1st Week in Ordinary Time**
Green   HOURS Psalter Week 1. MASS of choice
READINGS   **Heb 2:5-12. Ps 8:2, 5-9, R/ v 7. Mk 1:21-28.** *Lect* II:5
The humanity of Jesus is strongly stressed: he is immersed in our human existence. Like us he suffered and was tempted.

---

11 Wednesday 1st Week in Ordinary Time
Green   HOURS Psalter Week 1. MASS of choice
READINGS   **Heb 2:14-18. Ps 104:1-4, 6-9, R/ v 8. Mk 1:29-39.** *Lect* II:7

Jesus is the pioneer of our salvation, the one who leads us forward into a new land. The new High Priest, chosen from the people, has entered the presence of God, offered sacrifice for sin, and removed the burden of guilt. He continues his merciful intercession; for through his own experience he understands our temptations.

12 Thursday   **1st Week in Ordinary Time**
Green   HOURS Psalter Week 1. MASS of choice
READINGS   **Heb 3:7-14. Ps 94:6-11, R/ v 8. Mk 1:40-45.** Lect II:9
Let us not be foolish and reject the word spoken to us today, and in turn lose our
own entrance into God's presence, into the Promised Land.

---

13 Friday   **1st Week in Ordinary Time**
Green   HOURS Psalter Week 1. MASS of choice
White   Optional memorial of **St Hilary, bishop and doctor of
              the Church**
READINGS   **Heb 4:1-5, 11. Ps 77:3-4, 6-8, R/ cf. v 7. Mk 2:1-12.**
              Lect II:11
The temptation to give up, to disregard the word of God, to take his gifts lightly –
these are dangers for Christians at all times.
St Hilary, c. 315–c. 367, was elected (c. 353) bishop of Potiers and distinguished
himself by his stand against Arianism. In exile (356–59) by order of Emperor
Constantius, he used his time to write. His major works include De Trinitate, a study
of the Trinity.

---

14 Saturday   **1st Week in Ordinary Time**
Green   HOURS Psalter Week 1. MASS of choice
White/Green   Saturday Mass of the **Blessed Virgin Mary**
READINGS   **Heb 4:12-16. Ps 18:8-10, 15, R/ cf. Jn 6:63. Mk
                2:13-17.** Lect II:13
We stand before God's judgement with Jesus who feels for our weaknesses.

WEEK OF PRAYER FOR CHRISTIAN UNITY
18–25 January 2023

The theme for 2023 is Do good; seek justice, from Isaiah 1:17 – 'Learn to do good;
seek justice, rescue the oppressed, defend the orphan, plead for the widow'.

Isaiah challenged God's people in his day to learn to do good together; to seek
justice together, to rescue the oppressed together, to defend the orphan and plead
for the widow together. The prophet's challenge applies equally to us today. How
can we live our unity as Christians so as to confront the evils and injustices of our
time? How can we engage in dialogue, increase awareness, understanding and
insight about one another's lived experiences? These prayers and encounters of the
heart have the power to transform us – individually and collectively. Let us be open
to God's presence in all our encounters with each other as we seek to be
transformed, to dismantle the systems of oppression, and to heal the sins of racism.
Together, let us engage in the struggle for justice in our society. We all belong to
Christ.

The theme and resources are prepared by a group of Christians in USA convened
by the Minnesota Council of Churches and published by the Pontifical Council for
Promoting Christian Unity and Commission on Faith and Order of the World
Council of Churches.

JANUARY 2023

15 Sunday — SECOND SUNDAY IN ORDINARY TIME

Green ✠

HOURS Proper. Te Deum. Psalter Week 2

MASS Proper. Gloria. Creed. Preface: Sundays I–VIII

READINGS **Is 49:3, 5-6. Ps 39:2, 4, 7-10, R/ vv 8, 9. 1 Cor 1:1-3. Jn 1:29-34.** Lect I:641

Jesus is chosen by the Spirit to be Lamb and Servant; Paul is chosen to be an apostle. Each of us in baptism is chosen. We are chosen to live a life of holiness, to share in God's life, a life for us of praise and worship, of witness and apostolicity.

No Masses for the dead, except funeral Masses, are permitted today (see Lit. Note 8)

St Ita, virgin is not celebrated this year, except

Limerick **St Ita, virgin** This year as Solemnity

St Ita see *The Irish Calendar*, p. 184.

---

16 Monday — 2nd Week in Ordinary Time

Green

HOURS Psalter Week 2. MASS of choice

White Optional memorial of **St Fursa, abbot and missionary**

READINGS **Heb 5:1-10. Ps 109:1-4, R/ v 4. Mk 2:18-22.** Lect II:15

Jesus grew in suffering and learned to obey God's will. He is the bridegroom who is always with us.

St Fursa see *The Irish Calendar*, p. 184.

---

17 Tuesday — 2nd Week in Ordinary Time

St Anthony, abbot Memorial

White HOURS of the memorial. Psalter Week 2

MASS of the memorial. Preface: Common or of the Saints

READINGS **Heb 6:10-20. Ps 110:1-2, 4-5, 9, 10, R/ v 5. Mk 2:23-28.** Lect II:17

'The celebration of Sunday observes the moral commandment inscribed by nature in the human heart to render to God an outward, visible, public and regular worship "as a sign of his universal beneficence to all"' (CCC, 2176).

St Anthony, died 356, 'Father of monasticism,' lived a life of solitude but also attracted many others to form communities of hermits.

From 18–25 January, the Week of Prayer for Christian Unity is held. The texts for the Masses for Christian Unity are given in the Missal, pp. 1176–81. These can be used on days which allow a choice throughout the Week of Prayer. The Eucharistic Prayer for Various Needs, form I (The Church on the Path of Unity), may be used each day. During the Week of Prayer for Christian Unity readings may be taken from Lect III:508–28.

18 Wednesday 2nd Week in Ordinary Time
Week of Prayer for Christian Unity begins today
Green   HOURS Psalter Week 2. MASS of choice
READINGS   **Heb 7:1-3, 15-17. Ps 109:1-4, R/ v 4. Mk 3:1-6.** *Lect* II:19

'Sunday worship fulfils the moral command of the Old Covenant, taking up its rhythm and spirit in the weekly celebration of the Creator and Redeemer of his people' (CCC, 2176).

---

19 Thursday   2nd Week in Ordinary Time
Green   HOURS Psalter Week 2. MASS of choice
READINGS   **Heb 7:25-8:6. Ps 39:7-10, 17, R/ cf. vv 8, 9. Mk 3:7-12.** *Lect* II:21

'Christ always gives his Church the gift of unity, but the Church must always pray and work to maintain, reinforce, and perfect the unity that Christ wills for her' (CCC, 820).

---

20 Friday   2nd Week in Ordinary Time
Green   HOURS Psalter Week 2. MASS of choice
Red   Optional memorial of **St Fabian, pope and martyr**
Red   Optional memorial of **St Sebastian, martyr**
READINGS   **Heb 8:6-13. Ps 84:8, 10-14, R/ v 11. Mk 3:13-19.** *Lect* II:23

Jesus founded the better covenant, as prophesied by Jeremiah: 'I will put my laws into their minds and write them on their hearts.' The preaching of the apostles is to enable all to know God's love, the least no less than the greatest.

St Fabian had been Pope for fourteen years when martyred under Decius in the year 250.

St Sebastian may have been a soldier and was martyred in the persecution of Diocletian. He sustained many others in their trials.

Ferns Today is the anniversary of the episcopal ordination of Most Rev. Brendan Comiskey, SSCC, 20 January 1980.

---

21 Saturday   2nd Week in Ordinary Time
St Agnes, virgin and martyr   Memorial
Red   HOURS Proper of the memorial. Psalter Week 2 at Day Hour
              MASS of the memorial. Preface: Common or of the Saint
READINGS   **Heb 9:2-3, 11-14. Ps 46:2-3, 6-9, R/ v 6. Mk 3:20-21.** *Lect* II:25

'Relations between Christians call for every possible form of practical co-operation at all levels: pastoral, cultural and social, as well as that of witnessing to the gospel message … Unity of action leads to the full unity of faith' (*Ut Unum Sint*, 40).

St Agnes, wealthy and beautiful, was martyred for her virginity in the last persecutions in Rome, in the early fourth century. Patron of betrothed couples, gardeners and young girls.

JANUARY 2023

22 Sunday	**THIRD SUNDAY IN ORDINARY TIME**
	Sunday of the Word of God.
	Catholic Schools Week begins today
Green ✠	HOURS Proper. Te Deum. Psalter Week 3
	MASS Proper. Gloria. Creed. Preface: Sundays I–VIII
READINGS	**Is 8:23-9:3. Ps 26:1, 4, 13-14, R/ v 1. 1 Cor 1:10-13,**
	17. Mt 4:12-23 (shorter form 4:12-17)**.** *Lect* I:644

The semi-continuous reading of St Matthew's Gospel on each Sunday begins today with the calling of the first disciples. The prophecy of Isaiah is fulfilled: the people that lived in darkness have seen a great light. The scriptures are fulfilled in the person and work of Jesus who begins his preaching with the message: repent, for the kingdom of heaven is close at hand.

No Masses for the dead, except funeral Masses, are permitted today (see Lit. Note 8)
St Vincent, deacon and martyr is not celebrated this year.

SUNDAY OF THE WORD OF GOD
Third Sunday in Ordinary Time – 22 January 2023

Saint Luke tells us that, just before his Ascension, the Risen Lord appeared to the apostles, and broke bread with them. 'He then opened their minds to understand the Scriptures' (24:45). This is how Pope Francis begins his apostolic letter, *Aperuit illis*, issued 30 September 2019, the feast of St Jerome, instituting the Sunday of the Word of God. 'The relationship between the Risen Lord, the community of believers and sacred Scripture is essential to our identity as Christians. Without the Lord who opens our minds to them, it is impossible to understand the scriptures in depth. Yet the contrary is equally true: without the scriptures, the events of the mission of Jesus and of his Church in this world would remain incomprehensible. Hence, Saint Jerome could rightly claim: "Ignorance of the scriptures is ignorance of Christ."'

At the end of the Year of Mercy Pope Francis had proposed setting aside 'a Sunday given entirely to the word of God, so as to appreciate the inexhaustible riches contained in that constant dialogue between the Lord and his people.' He declares the Third Sunday in Ordinary Time (this year: 22 January 2023) to be devoted to the celebration, study and dissemination of the word of God. He notes this as a fitting time 'to strengthen our bonds with the Jewish people and to pray for Christian unity.' As well as highlighting the proclamation of the word of the Lord and emphasising it in the homily he suggests a celebration of the commissioning of readers, renewed efforts to provide them with 'training needed to be genuine proclaimers of the word' and the giving of the Bible or one of its books to the entire assembly 'as a way of showing the importance of learning how to read, appreciate and pray daily with sacred scripture, especially through the practice of *lectio divina*.'

The need for a serious and vital liturgical formation

How do we recover the capacity to live completely the liturgical action? This was the objective of the Council's reform. The challenge is extremely demanding because modern people – not in all cultures to the same degree – have lost the capacity to engage with symbolic action, which is an essential trait of the liturgical act.

With post-modernity people feel themselves even more lost, without references of any sort, lacking in values because they have become indifferent, completely orphaned, living a fragmentation in which a horizon of meaning seems impossible. And so, it is even more weighed down by the burdensome inheritance that the previous epoch left us, consisting in individualism and subjectivism (which evokes once again the Pelagian and gnostic problems). It consists also in an abstract spiritualism which contradicts human nature itself, for a human person is an incarnate spirit and therefore as such capable of symbolic action and of symbolic understanding.

It is with this reality of the modern world that the Church, united in Council, wanted to enter into contact, reaffirming her awareness of being the sacrament of Christ, the *Light of the nations* (*Lumen Gentium*), putting herself in a devout listening to the *Word of God* (*Dei Verbum*), and recognising as her own *the joys and the hopes* (*Gaudium et Spes*) of the people of our times. The great Constitutions of the Council cannot be separated one from the other, and it is not an accident that this single huge effort at reflection by the Ecumenical Council – which is the highest expression of synodality in the Church and whose richness I, together with all of you, am called to be the custodian – began with reflection on the liturgy. (*Sacrosanctum Concilium*)

Pope Francis, *Desiderio Desideravi*, 27–29

* * *

From all that we have said about the nature of the liturgy it becomes clear that knowledge of the mystery of Christ, the decisive question for our lives, does not consist in a mental assimilation of some idea but in real existential engagement with his person. In this sense, liturgy is not about 'knowledge,' and its scope is not primarily pedagogical, even though it does have great pedagogical value. (cf. SC, 33) Rather, liturgy is about praise, about rendering thanks for the Passover of the Son whose power reaches our lives. The celebration concerns the reality of our being docile to the action of the Spirit who operates through it until Christ be formed in us. (cf. Gal 4:19) The full extent of our formation is our conformation to Christ. I repeat: it does not have to do with an abstract mental process, but with becoming him. This is the purpose for which the Spirit is given, whose action is always and only to confect the Body of Christ. It is that way with the eucharistic bread, and with every one of the baptised called to become always more and more that which was received as a gift in baptism, namely, being a member of the Body of Christ. Leo the Great writes, 'Our participation in the Body and Blood of Christ has no other end than to make us become that which we eat.'

Pope Francis, *Desiderio Desideravi*, 41

23 Monday   **3rd Week in Ordinary Time**
Green   HOURS Psalter Week 3. MASS of choice
READINGS   **Heb 9:15, 24-28. Ps 97:1-6, R/ v 1. Mk 3:22-30.** *Lect*
                II:27

We now live in the new covenant times when Jesus has conquered sin. But we await the final consummation when he returns in glory to claim us for himself.

---

24 Tuesday   **3rd Week in Ordinary Time**
                 St Francis de Sales, bishop and doctor of the Church
                                                              Memorial
White   HOURS of the memorial. Psalter Week 3
                 MASS of the memorial. Preface: Common or of the Saints
READINGS   **Heb 10:1-10. Ps 39:2, 4, 7-8, 10, 11, R/ cf. vv 8, 9.**
                 Mk 3:31-35. *Lect* II:29

In the story of God's relationship with his people there is an often repeated warning about sacrifices which are purely external. In Christ we have the supreme expression of conformity to God's will in a sacrificial life.

St Francis de Sales, 1567–1622, bishop of Geneva, founder of the Visitation Sisters. He worked with gentleness and love to rebuild the Catholic faith after the Reformation. Patron saint of writers, editors and journalists.

---

25 Wednesday THE CONVERSION OF ST PAUL, APOSTLE   Feast
White   HOURS Proper. Te Deum. Psalter Week 3 at Day Hour
                 MASS Proper. Gloria. Preface: Apostles I-II
READINGS   **Acts 22:3-16 or Acts 9:1-22. Ps 116:1-2, R/ Mk**
                 16:15. Mk 16:15-18. *Lect* II: 928

St Paul preached the power of God at work in the lives of each one of us. His own conversion shows that power in his life. Out of a persecutor God made a preacher and teacher of the peoples. Paul never ceased to express thanks and wonder for this grace. But he still prayed for perseverance.

No Masses for the dead, except funeral Masses, are permitted today (see Lit. Note 8)

---

26 Thursday **3rd Week in Ordinary Time**
White   **Ss Timothy and Titus, bishops**   Memorial
                 HOURS of the memorial. Psalter Week 3
                 MASS of the memorial. Preface: Common or of the Saints
READINGS   **2 Tm 1:1-8 or Ti 1:1-5. Ps 95:1-3, 7-8, 10, R/ v 3. Lk**
                 10:1-9. *Lect* II:931

Ss Timothy and Titus were close to St Paul as followers and later in their work with him. Tradition makes Timothy the first bishop of Ephesus. And from Paul's advice to him to take some wine for his stomach's sake, he has been invoked as a patron in cases of stomach complaint. Titus was sent to organise the Church in Crete.

---

27 Friday   **3rd Week in Ordinary Time**
Green   HOURS Psalter Week 3. MASS of choice
White   Optional memorial of **St Angela Merici, virgin and religious**
READINGS   **Heb 10:32-39. Ps 36:3-6, 23-24, 39-40, R/ v 39. Mk 4:26-34.** Lect II:35

We recall our first fervour in the faith and recognise that God's grace is with us always to the end. The faith in us should grow like the mustard seed.

St Angela Merici, 1474–1540, founder of the Ursulines, devoted herself to Christian education based on love, kindness with firmness, and concern for the individual.

Galway Today is the anniversary of the episcopal ordination of Most Rev. Brendan Kelly, 27 January 2008.

Cloyne Today is the anniversary of the episcopal ordination of Most Rev.William Crean, 27 January 2013.

---

28 Saturday   **3rd Week in Ordinary Time**
   St Thomas Aquinas, priest and doctor of the Church
   Memorial
White   HOURS of the memorial. Psalter Week 3.
   MASS of memorial. Preface: Common or of the Saint
READINGS   **Heb 11:1-2, 8-19. Ps Lk 1:69-75, R/ cf. v 68. Mk 4:35-41.** Lect II:37

It was for faith that our ancestors were commended and that faith is praised in Abraham. Jesus expects faith in his disciples.

St Thomas Aquinas was born in Italy in 1224. He died in 1274. Thomas taught that Christian revelation and human knowledge are aspects of a single truth and cannot be in conflict with one another. One of the greatest theologians, he is patron of schools, universities, students and booksellers.

JANUARY 2023

29 Sunday   FOURTH SUNDAY IN ORDINARY TIME

Green ✠   HOURS Proper. Te Deum. Psalter Week 4

MASS Proper. Gloria. Creed. Preface: Sundays I–VIII

READINGS   **Zeph 2:3, 3:12-13. Ps 145:7-10, R/ Mt 5:3. 1 Cor 1:26-31. Mt 5:1-12.** *Lect* I:647

The Beatitudes are in the life of Jesus himself and, in turn, they tell his followers what make for true happiness. Blessed are they who are poor in spirit, gentle, hungry and thirsty for justice, merciful, pure in heart, peacemaking, suffering for Christ.

No Masses for the dead, except funeral Masses, are permitted today (see Lit. Note 8)

Meath Today is the anniversary of the episcopal ordination of Most Rev. Michael Smith, 29 January 1984.

---

30 Monday   4th Week in Ordinary Time

Green   HOURS Psalter Week 4. MASS of choice

White   Optional memorial of **St Aidan, bishop**

Ferns   **St Aidan, bishop**   Feast

Dublin   Optional memorial of **Bl. Margaret Ball and Francis Taylor, martyrs**

Meath   Optional memorial of **Bl. Margaret Ball and Francis Taylor, martyrs**

READINGS   **Heb 11:32-40. Ps 30:20-24, R/ v 25. Mk 5:1-20.** *Lect* II:40

These witnesses of faith who endured so much did not receive the promises. We are indeed blessed in that we have been chosen.

St Aidan see *The Irish Calendar*, p. 184.

Bl Margaret Ball and Francis Taylor see *The Irish Calendar*, p. 184.

---

31 Tuesday   4th Week in Ordinary Time

               St John Bosco, priest   Memorial

White   HOURS of the memorial. Psalter Week 4.

MASS of memorial. Preface: Common or of the Saint

READINGS   **Heb 12:1-4. Ps 21:26-28, 30-32, R/ cf. v 27. Mk 5:21-43.** *Lect* II:42

'Jesus hears the prayer of faith, expressed in words by Jairus or in silence by the woman who touches his clothes. The urgent request of the blind men has been renewed in the traditional prayer to Jesus known as the Jesus Prayer: "Lord Jesus Christ, Son of God, have mercy on me, a sinner!"' (CCC, 2616).

St John Bosco, 1815–88, born in Piedmont, founded the Salesians to educate boys for life. He also became involved in publishing catechetical material for youth. He is a patron saint of youth and of Catholic publishers.

---

1 Wednesday ST BRIGID, ABBESS, SECONDARY PATRON OF IRELAND Feast
White HOURS Proper (Divine Office, II, p. 192*)
Te Deum. Psalter Week 4 at Day Hour
MASS Proper. Gloria. Preface: Proper
READINGS **Job 31:16-20, 24-25, 31-32 or Eph 3:14-21. Ps 106:35-38, 41-42, R/ v 1. Lk 6:32-38.** National Proper
EVENING PRAYER of St Brigid

No Masses for the dead, except funeral Masses, are permitted today (see Lit. Note 8)
St Brigid see *The Irish Calendar*, p. 185.

---

2 Thursday THE PRESENTATION OF THE LORD Feast
White *World Day for Consecrated Life*
HOURS Proper. Te Deum. Psalter Week 4 at Day Hour.
MASS Proper. Gloria. Preface: Proper: Presentation
Blessing of Candles and Procession, *RM*, pp. 704–8
READINGS **Mal 3:1-4 or Heb 2:14-18. Ps 23:7-10, R/ v 10. Lk 2:22-40** (shorter form 2:22-32)**.** Lect I:967 or II:940

The Presentation of the Lord. This feast is a remembrance of the Lord and Mary, mother of the Lord. With candles in their hands, the people go out to meet the Lord and to acclaim him like Simeon, who recognised Christ as 'a light to reveal God to the nations'.

No Masses for the dead, except funeral Masses, are permitted today (see Lit. Note 8)
Kilmore Today is the anniversary of the episcopal ordination of Most Rev. Leo O'Reilly, 2 February 1997.

Who celebrates?

The entire Body of Christ, animated by the Holy Spirit, celebrates the liturgy. The celebrating assembly is the community of the baptised. Liturgy is not a matter of private prayer, but a public act of worship by the faithful gathered together by the power of the Spirit under the authority of the bishop, their teacher and shepherd. 'Mother Church earnestly desires that all the faithful should be led to that full, conscious and active participation in liturgical celebrations which is demanded by the very nature of the liturgy, and to which the Christian people … have a right and an obligation by reason of their Baptism' (CCC, no. 1141). The faithful are called to come to the liturgy consciously prepared to make their thoughts agree with what they say and hear and to cooperate with divine grace.

Within the assembly, the ordained have a unique function of service. 'These servants are chosen and consecrated by the sacrament of Holy Orders, by which the Holy Spirit enables them to act in the person of Christ the head, for the service of all the members of the Church' (CCC, no. 1142). Thus, for example, priests preside at the Eucharist, in which the elements of bread and wine are changed into the Body and Blood of Christ. Priests act in the person of Christ, the Head of the Church, and in the name of the Church when presenting to God the prayers and self-offering of the people and when offering the Eucharistic sacrifice, above all as they proclaim the Eucharistic Prayer.

Irish Catholic Catechism for Adults,
Irish Episcopal Conference, Veritas, 2014, p. 190

3 Friday   **4th Week in Ordinary Time**
Green   HOURS Psalter Week 4. MASS of choice
Red   Optional memorial of **St Blaise, bishop and martyr**
White   Optional memorial of **St Ansgar, bishop**
READINGS   **Heb 13:1-8. Ps 26:1, 3, 5, 8-9, R/ v 1. Mk 6:14-29.**
Lect II:49

The law of love covers all situations and it remembers strangers and prisoners.
The marriage state is to be honoured and authority in the Church respected.

St Ansgar, a Frenchman, who became Archbishop of Hamburg in the ninth century, and preached the gospel in Denmark and Sweden. Apostle of Scandinavia. Patron of Denmark.

St Blaise, died 315. Bishop of Sebaste, martyred in Armenia. Tradition states that he was a physician before becoming a bishop. Since the eighth century he has been venerated as patron of those who suffer from disease of the throat.

The blessing of St Blaise is a sign of our faith in God's protection and love for us and for the sick. Using two crossed and unlighted candles, blessed on the memorial of St Blaise or on the feast of the Presentation of the Lord, the minister touches the throat of each person, saying, 'Through the intercession of St Blaise, bishop and martyr, may God deliver you from all ailments of the throat and from every other evil [or from every disease of the throat and from every other illness]. In the name of the Father, and of the Son, and of the Holy Spirit. Amen.'

---

4 Saturday   **4th Week in Ordinary Time**
Green   HOURS Psalter Week 4. MASS of choice
White/Green   Saturday Mass of the **Blessed Virgin Mary**
READINGS   **Heb 13:15-17, 20-21. Ps 22, R/ v 1. Mk 6:30-34.** *Lect* I:51

Jesus took pity on the crowd for they were like sheep without a shepherd. May the Good Shepherd make us always ready to do God's will in every kind of good action.

We could say that there are different 'models' of presiding. Here is a possible list of approaches, which even though opposed to each other, characterise a way of presiding that is certainly inadequate: rigid austerity or an exasperating creativity, a spiritualising mysticism or a practical functionalism, a rushed briskness or an overemphasised slowness, a sloppy carelessness or an excessive finickiness, a superabundant friendliness or priestly impassibility. Granted the wide range of these examples, I think that the inadequacy of these models of presiding have a common root: a heightened personalism of the celebrating style which at times expresses a poorly concealed mania to be the centre of attention. Often this becomes more evident when our celebrations are transmitted over the air or online, something not always opportune and that needs further reflection. Be sure you understand me: these are not the most widespread behaviours, but still, not infrequently assemblies suffer from being thus abused.

Pope Francis, *Desiderio Desideravi*, 54

FEBRUARY 2023

5 Sunday   **FIFTH SUNDAY IN ORDINARY TIME**
Green ✠   HOURS Proper. Te Deum. Psalter Week 1
             MASS Proper. Gloria. Creed. Preface: Sundays I–VIII
READINGS   **Is 58:7-10. Ps 111:4-9, R/ v 4. 1 Cor 2:1-5. Mt 5:13-16.** *Lect* I: 650

Christians who have the Beatitudes as their rule of life become the salt of the earth and the light of the world. We should recognise the dignity that is ours as we share in the work of Christ. Like him we are to lead all people to praise the wonderful deeds of God. The Spirit-filled community can bring about a new world. Christian love will make light rise in the darkness of our world.

No Masses for the dead, except funeral Masses, are permitted today (see Lit. Note 8)
St Agatha, virgin and martyr is not celebrated this year.

---

6 Monday   **5th Week in Ordinary Time**
             Ss Paul Miki and Companions, martyrs   Memorial
Red   HOURS of the memorial. Psalter Week 4.
             MASS of the memorial. Preface: Common or of the Saint
READINGS   **Gn 1:1-19. Ps 103:1-2, 5-6, 10, 12, 24, 35, R/ v 31. Mk 6:53-56.** *Lect* II:54

The blessing of water at baptism recalls the Spirit of God over the primitive waters from which came life. We are reborn by water and the Spirit to the new life of Christ.

Ss Paul Miki and Companions martyred at Nagasaki, Japan, in 1597. The six Franciscans, seventeenth Franciscan Tertiaries, and three Jesuits died suspended on crosses.

---

7 Tuesday   **5th Week in Ordinary Time**
Green   HOURS Psalter Week 1. MASS of choice
White   Optional memorial of **St Mel, bishop**
Ardagh and
Clonmacnois   **St Mel, bishop**   Feast
READINGS   **Gn 1:20-2:4. Ps 8:4-9, R/ v 2. Mk 7:1-13.** *Lect* II:56

We are the crown of God's creation, yet we fail to carry out the work of conserving the earth that God gave to our stewardship. Our responsibility towards conservation of the earth's resources and beauty is a God-given trust.

St Mel see *The Irish Calendar*, p. 185.

---

8 Wednesday   5th Week in Ordinary Time
International Day of Prayer and Awareness against Human Trafficking
Green   HOURS Psalter Week 1. MASS of choice
White   Optional memorial of **St Jerome Emiliani**
White   Optional memorial of **St Josephine Bakhita, virgin**
READINGS   **Gn 2:4-9, 15-17. Ps 103:1-2, 27-30, R/ v 1. Mk 7:14-23.** *Lect* II:59

The readings contrast the innocence of human beings in the Garden and the evil that lurks in the hearts of fallen humanity.

St Jerome Emiliani, d. 1537, after a military career he founded the Clerks Regular of Somaschi for the care of orphans and the poor. Patron saint of orphans.

St Josephine Bakhita, 1868–1947, a native of Sudan, brought as a slave to Italy where she became a Christian and later entered the Institute of Canossian Daughters of Charity in Venice.

Today is *International Day of Prayer and Awareness against Human Trafficking*, first observed in 2015 and on the memorial of St Josephine Bakhita. Each year, around 2.5 million people are victims of trafficking and slavery. For those engaged in trafficking it has become one of the most lucrative illegal activities in the world.
Through the Day of Prayer we reflect on the experience of those who have suffered but also we are called to reach out to victims and survivors.

---

9 Thursday   5th Week in Ordinary Time
Green   HOURS Psalter Week 1. MASS of choice
READINGS   **Gn 2:18-25. Ps 127:1-5, R/ v 1. Mk 7:24-30.** *Lect* II:61

Woman is created as the equal of the man. Her qualities are to complement his. The growth and development of God's creation is now a joint enterprise of man and woman.

---

10 Friday   5th Week in Ordinary Time
                St Scholastica, virgin   Memorial
White   HOURS of the memorial. Psalter Week 1
                 MASS of the memorial. Preface: Common or of the Saint
READINGS   **Gn 3:1-8,. Ps 31:1-2, 5-7, R/ v 1. Mk 7:31-37.** *Lect* II:63

Sin enters human life, the great roots being pride and selfishness. Comparing ourselves with others, desiring more and more, lead to dissatisfaction with what we have. In the end all can be lost through overpowering greed.

St Scholastica, died c. 543, sister of St Benedict. She spent her life as a consecrated virgin. Patron of convulsive children.

Clogher Today is the anniversary of the episcopal ordination of Most Rev. Larry Duffy, 10 February 2019

---

11 Saturday   **5th Week in Ordinary Time**
World Day of the Sick

Green   HOURS Psalter Week 1. MASS of choice
White   Optional memorial of **Our Lady of Lourdes**
White   Optional memorial of **St Gobnait, virgin**
READINGS   **Gn 3:9-24. Ps 89:2-6, 12-13, R/ v 1. Mk 8:1-10.** *Lect* II:65

Our human form comes from the soil and the earth is the stage on which we live our lives. Child-bearing and work are blessings and yet they can be accompanied by pain and sorrow. We believe and trust in God, who is generous and gives us more than is wanted.

Our Lady of Lourdes: Is 66:10-14. Ps Jud 13:18-19, R/ 15:19. Jn 2:1-11. *Lect* II:955

On this day in 1858, Our Lady first appeared to the fourteen-year-old Bernadette Soubirous. Later Bernadette was to learn that the mysterious lady was the Blessed Virgin and to hear from her lips, 'I am the Immaculate Conception'. In 1992 Pope John Paul II instituted the World Day of the Sick to be held on the commemoration of Our Lady of Lourdes.

St Gobnait see *The Irish Calendar*, p. 185.

THE UNIVERSAL PRAYER

In the Universal Prayer or Prayer of the Faithful, the people respond in some sense to the Word of God which they have received in faith and, exercising the office of their baptismal priesthood, offer prayers to God for the salvation of all. It is desirable that there usually be such a form of prayer in Masses celebrated with the people, so that petitions may be offered for holy Church, for those who govern with authority over us, for those weighed down by various needs, for all humanity, and for the salvation of the whole world (SC, 53).

The series of intentions is usually to be:
a) for the needs of the Church;
b) for public authorities and the salvation of the whole world;
c) for those burdened by any kind of difficulty;
d) for the local community.

Nevertheless, in any particular celebration, such as a Confirmation, a Marriage, or at a Funeral, the series of intentions may be concerned more closely with the particular occasion.

It is for the priest celebrant to regulate this prayer from the chair. He himself begins it with a brief introduction, by which he calls upon the faithful to pray, and likewise he concludes it with an oration. The intentions announced should be sober, be composed with a wise liberty and in few words, and they should be expressive of the prayer of the entire community.

They are announced from the ambo or from another suitable place, by the deacon or by a cantor, a reader, or one of the lay faithful (*Inter Oecumenici*, 56).

The people, for their part, stand and give expression to their prayer either by an invocation said in common after each intention or by praying in silence.

GIRM, 69–71

FEBRUARY 2023

12 Sunday   SIXTH SUNDAY IN ORDINARY TIME
Green ✠   HOURS Proper. Te Deum. Psalter Week 2
           MASS Proper. Gloria. Creed. Preface: Sundays I–VIII
READINGS   **Eccles (Sir) 15:15-20. Ps 118:1-2, 4-5, 17-18, 33-34, R/ v 1. 1 Cor 2:6-10. Mt 5:17-37** (shorter form 5:20-22, 27-28, 33-34, 37). *Lect* I:652

Human beings have been given the freedom to obey God's laws or not. Christ calls us to choose love as the fulfilling of the law. His followers do not measure out the minimum legal requirements but choose the fullness of life. 'You have heard that it was said … but I say to you.'
No Masses for the dead, except funeral Masses, are permitted today (see Lit. Note 8)

---

13 Monday   6th Week in Ordinary Time
Green   HOURS Psalter Week 2. MASS of choice
READINGS   **Gn 4:1-15, 25. Ps 49:1, 8, 16-17, 20-21, R/ v 14. Mk 8:11-13.** *Lect* II:68

Envy and jealousy lead to murder in the story of Cain and Abel. Self-control is the gift of the Spirit given to all who are redeemed in Christ.

---

14 Tuesday   SS CYRIL, MONK, AND METHODIUS, BISHOP, PATRONS OF EUROPE   Feast
White   HOURS Proper. Te Deum. Psalter Week 2 at Day Hour.
           MASS Proper. Gloria. Preface: Saints I–II
READINGS   **Acts 13:46-49. Ps 116, R/ v Mk 16:15. Lk 10:1-9.** *Lect* II:957

St Cyril, 826-69, and **St Methodius**, 815-85, were brothers from Thessalonica in Greece. They preached the gospel in Moravia using their own translation of the scriptures and the liturgy in the local language. These translations into Slavonic were in an alphabet, now called Cyrillic, which they devised. They are honoured as apostles of the Slavic peoples and in 1980 Pope John Paul II declared them Patrons of Europe.
No Masses for the dead, except funeral Masses, are permitted today (see Lit. Note 8)

---

15 Wednesday 6th Week in Ordinary Time
Green   HOURS Psalter Week 2. MASS of choice
READINGS   **Gn 8:6-13, 20-22. Ps 115:12-15, 18-19, R/ v 17. Mk 8:22-26.** *Lect* II:72

Noah offers a sacrifice of thanksgiving at the end of the Flood. God promises that nature will keep its course for ever. How can we repay the Lord for his daily acts of goodness to us?

---

16 Thursday   **6th Week in Ordinary Time**
Green   HOURS Psalter Week 2. MASS of choice
READINGS   **Gn 9:1-13. Ps 101:16-21, 29, 22-23, R/ v 20. Mk 8:27-33.** Lect II:74

The rainbow is the sign given of the renewed covenant that God makes with humankind. The final covenant is to be made through the death and resurrection of Jesus, the Christ.

---

17 Friday   **6th Week in Ordinary Time**
Green   HOURS Psalter Week 2. MASS of choice
White   Optional memorial of **Seven Holy Founders of the Servite Order**
White   Optional memorial of **St Fintan, abbot**
READINGS   **Gn 11:1-9. Ps 32:10-15, R/ v 12. Mk 8:34-9:1.** Lect II:76

The Tower of Babel symbolises the pride of the human race trying to be as God. Jesus warns of the folly of trying to gain the whole world at the expense of the real life.
Servite Founders. In the early thirteenth century seven young merchants of Florence decided to help one another live more perfect Christian lives. As the result of a vision, they became known as the 'Servants of Mary' and followed the Rule of Saint Augustine.
St Fintan see *The Irish Calendar*, p. 185.

---

18 Saturday   **6th Week in Ordinary Time**
Green   HOURS Psalter Week 2. MASS of choice
White/Green   Saturday Mass of the **Blessed Virgin Mary**
READINGS   **Heb 11:1-7. Ps 144:2-5, 10-11, R/ cf. v 1. Mk 9:2-13.** Lect II:78

The faith of the patriarchs is praised. Jesus brings Peter, James, and John to the mountaintop to help deepen their faith to face the trials to come.

Lent and Christian Initiation

7. The whole rite of Christian initiation has a markedly paschal character, since it is therein that the sacramental participation in the death and Resurrection of Christ takes place for the first time. Therefore, Lent should have its full character as a time of purification and enlightenment, especially through the scrutinies and by the presentations; naturally the paschal Vigil should be regarded as the proper time to celebrate the sacraments of initiation.

8. Communities that do not have any catechumens should not, however, fail to pray for those who in the forthcoming paschal Vigil will receive the sacraments of Christian initiation. Pastors should draw the attention of the faithful to those moments of significant importance in their spiritual life, which are nourished by their baptismal profession of faith, and which they will be invited to renew in the Easter Vigil – 'the fullness of the Lenten observance'.

9. In Lent, there should be catechesis for those adults who, although baptised when infants, were not brought up in the faith and, consequently, have not been confirmed nor have they received the Eucharist. During this period, penitential services should be arranged to help prepare them for the sacrament of reconciliation.

10. The Lenten season is also an appropriate time for the celebration of penitential rites on the model of the scrutinies for unbaptised children who are at an age to be catechised and also for children already baptised, before being admitted to the sacrament of penance.

The bishop should have particular care to foster the catechumenate of both adults and children and, according to circumstances, to preside at the prescribed rites, with the devout participation of the local community.

Celebrations During the Lenten Season

11. The Sundays of Lent take precedence over all feasts and all solemnities. Solemnities occurring on these Sundays are observed on the preceding Saturday. The weekdays of Lent have precedence over obligatory memorials.

12. The catechesis on the paschal mystery and the sacraments should be given a special place in the Sunday homilies. The text of the *Lectionary* should be carefully explained, particularly the passages of the Gospel that illustrate the diverse aspects of Baptism and the other sacraments and the mercy of God.

13. Pastors should frequently and as fully as possible explain the word of God in homilies on weekdays, in celebrations of the word of God, in penitential celebrations, in various reunions, in visiting families, or on the occasion of blessing families. The faithful should try and attend weekday Mass and where this is not possible they should at least be encouraged to read the lessons, either with their family or in private.

14. 'The Lenten season should retain something of its penitential character' (*Paenitemini*, II,1). 'As regards catechesis, it is important to impress on the minds of the faithful not only the social consequences of sin but also that aspect of the virtue of penance, which involves the detestation of sin as an offence against God' (*Cer. Bishops*, 251).

The virtue and practice of penance form a necessary part of the preparation for Easter. From that inner conversion of heart should spring the practice of penance, both for the individual Christian and the whole community; which while being adapted to the conditions of the present time should nevertheless witness to the evangelical spirit of penance and also be to the advantage of others.

The role of the Church in penitential practices is not to be neglected and encouragement is to be given to pray for sinners. This intention should be included in the prayer of the faithful.

15. 'The faithful are to be encouraged to participate in an ever more intense and fruitful way in the Lenten liturgy and in penitential celebrations. They are to be clearly reminded that both according to the law and tradition, they should approach the sacrament of penance during this season, so that with purified heart they may participate in the paschal mysteries. It is appropriate that during Lent the

sacrament of penance be celebrated according to the rite for the reconciliation of several penitents with individual confession and absolution, as given in the Roman Ritual' (*Cer. Bishops*, 251).

Pastors should devote themselves to the ministry of reconciliation and provide sufficient time for the faithful to avail themselves of this sacrament.

16. 'All Lenten observances should be of such a nature that they also witness to the life of the local Church and foster it. The Roman tradition of the 'stational' churches can be recommended as a model for gathering the faithful in one place. In this way, the faithful can assemble in larger numbers, especially under the leadership of the bishop of the diocese, or at the tombs of the saints, or in the principle churches of the city or sanctuaries, or some place of pilgrimage which has a special significance for the diocese' (*Cer. Bishops*, 260).

17. 'In Lent, the altar should not be decorated with flowers, and musical instruments may be played only to give necessary support to the singing' (*Cer. Bishops*, 252). This is in order that the penitential character of the season be preserved.

18. Likewise, from the beginning of Lent until the Paschal Vigil, 'Alleluia' is to be omitted in all celebrations, even on solemnities and feasts.

19. The chants to be sung in celebrations, especially of the Eucharist, and also at devotional exercises should be in harmony with the spirit of the season and the liturgical texts.

20. Devotional exercises that harmonise with the Lenten season are to be encouraged, for example, 'The Stations of the Cross.' They should help foster the liturgical spirit with which the faithful can prepare themselves for the celebration of Christ's paschal mystery.

21. 'On the Wednesday before the first Sunday of Lent, the faithful receive the ashes, thus entering into the time established for the purification of their souls. This sign of penance, a traditionally biblical one, has been preserved among the Church's customs until the present day. It signifies the human condition of the sinner, who seeks to express his guilt before the Lord in an exterior manner, and by so doing express his interior conversion, led on by the confident hope that the Lord will be merciful. This same sign marks the beginning of the way of conversion, which is developed through the celebration of the sacraments of penance during the days before Easter' (*Cer. Bishops*, 252).

The blessing and imposition of ashes should take place either in the Mass or outside of the Mass. In the latter case, it is to be part of a liturgy of the word and conclude with the prayer of the faithful.

22. Ash Wednesday is to be observed as a day of penance in the whole Church, one of both abstinence and fasting.

23. The first Sunday of Lent marks the beginning of the annual Lenten observance. In the Mass of this Sunday, there should be some distinctive elements that underline this important moment (e.g., the entrance procession with litanies of the saints). During the Mass of the first Sunday in Lent, the bishop should celebrate the rite of election in the cathedral or in some other church, as seems appropriate.

24. The Gospel pericopes of the Samaritan woman, of the man blind from birth, and the resurrection of Lazarus are assigned to the III, IV and V Sundays of Lent of year A. Of particular significance in relation to Christian initiation, they can also be read in years B and C, especially in places where there are catechumens.

On the fourth Sunday of Lent, *Laetare*, and in solemnities and feasts, musical instruments may be played and the altar decorated with flowers. Rose coloured vestments may be worn on this Sunday.

26. The practice of covering the crosses and images in the church may be observed, if the episcopal conference should so decide. The crosses are to be covered until the end of the celebration of the Lord's Passion on Good Friday. Images are to remain covered until the beginning of the Easter Vigil.

Congregation for Divine Worship, *Paschale solemnitatis*
Letter on the Preparation and Celebration of the Easter Feasts

FEBRUARY 2023

19 Sunday   SEVENTH SUNDAY IN ORDINARY TIME
Day of Prayer for Temperance

Green ✠   HOURS Proper. Te Deum. Psalter Week 3

               MASS Proper. Gloria. Creed. Preface: Sundays I–VIII

READINGS   **Lev 19:1-2, 17-18. Ps 102:1-4, 8, 10, 12-13, R/ v 8. 1 Cor 3:16-23. Mt 5:38-48.** *Lect* I: 656

Christ's call becomes most challenging – to be perfect as God is perfect. To be perfect as God means to be full of compassion, slow to anger, rich in mercy.

No Masses for the dead, except funeral Masses, are permitted today (see Lit. Note 8)

Armagh Today is the anniversary of the episcopal ordination of His Eminence Cardinal Seán Brady, 19 February 1995.

---

20 Monday   7th Week in Ordinary Time
Green   HOURS Psalter Week 3. MASS of choice

READINGS   **Eccles (Sir) 1:1-10. Ps 92:1-2, 5 R/ v 1. Mk 9:14-29.** *Lect* II:81

The wisdom which Ben Sira commends comes from God. It is the source of happiness, and the young should form their character from it. This wisdom is closely associated with the Law of Moses, especially in carrying out religious duties, notably the liturgy.

---

21 Tuesday   7th Week in Ordinary Time
Green   HOURS Psalter Week 3. MASS of choice

White   Optional memorial of **St Peter Damian, bishop and doctor of the Church**

READINGS   **Eccles (Sir) 2:1-11. Ps 36:3-4, 18-19, 27-28, 39-40 R/ v 5. Mk 9:30-37.** *Lect* II:83

Fear of the Lord is the key to endurance. In time of trial we must stand firm, there must be no giving way to apostasy. Jesus himself is our example, being delivered into the hands of men who put him to death.

St Peter Damian, 1007–72, gave up teaching to become a hermit. Later he was Cardinal Bishop of Ostia. He was an outstanding reformer of Church life and discipline.

---

22 Wednesday ASH WEDNESDAY   Day of Fast and Abstinence
Violet   HOURS Psalter Week 4
                          Psalms of Friday Week 3 may be used at Morning Prayer
                          MASS Proper. Preface: Lent III or IV
READINGS   **Jl 2:12-18. Ps 50:3-6, 12-14, 17, R/ v 3. 2 Cor 5:20-6:2. Mt 6:1-6, 16-18.** *Lect* I:191

In the readings today there is a great consciousness of our sinfulness, as we pray 'Have mercy on us, O Lord, for we have sinned'. There is also a sense that the time to repent and turn back is now. The gospel tells us how to approach that renewal of our lives. It puts before us the remedy in prayer, fasting and almsgiving. These three strands of Lenten observance are as ancient as Christianity itself. There is no substitute for them. 'Fasting is the soul of prayer, mercy is the lifeblood of fasting. If we have not all three together, we have nothing,' says St Peter Chrysologus.

No Masses for the dead, except funeral Masses, are permitted today (see Lit. Note 8)

The Chair of St Peter, apostle is not celebrated this year.

---

23 Thursday   **After Ash Wednesday**
Violet   HOURS Psalter Week 4
                    MASS Proper. Preface: Lent I–IV
                    Memorial may be made of **St Polycarp, bishop and martyr** (see *Lit. Note 8*)
READINGS   **Deut 30:15-20. Ps 1:1-4, 6, R/ Ps 39:5. Lk 9:22-25.** *Lect* I:194

Today we are called to make a choice, a choice between life and death. 'Let us cast off the works of darkness and put on the armour of light, that having sailed across the great sea of the Fast, we may reach, on the third day, the resurrection of our Lord Jesus Christ, the Saviour of our souls' (Byzantine vespers).

St Polycarp was bishop of Smyrna or Izmir in modern Turkey. Born around the year 69, he was a disciple of St John the Apostle. He was martyred in 155.

---

24 Friday **After Ash Wednesday**
Worldwide Day of Prayer for Survivors and Victims of Sexual Abuse

Violet HOURS Psalter Week 4
MASS Proper. Preface: Lent I–IV

READINGS **Is 58:1-9. Ps 50:3-6, 18-19, R/ v 19. Mt 9:14-15.** *Lect* I:196

Christian fasting began as a voluntary practice, as a support to prayer, as penance for sin, as a way to save something for the poor, and as a way to prepare for a feast. It was a suitable practice to prepare for the celebration of Easter. The need for fasting is still there.

---

25 Saturday **After Ash Wednesday**
Violet HOURS Psalter Week 4.
MASS Proper. Preface: Lent I–IV

READINGS **Is 58:9-14. Ps 85:1-6, R/ v 11. Lk 5:27-32.** Lect I:198

Isaiah calls out for greater service of God and fellow human beings. Lent gives us the opportunity to jettison much that is unnecessary and unhelpful in our way of life. The following of Christ implies a leaving behind of much that causes unhappiness in our own lives and in the lives of others.

Lord, we are sorry
for what some of us did to your children:
treated them so cruelly,
especially in their hour of need.
We have left them with a lifelong suffering.
This was not your plan for them or us.
Please help us to help them.
Guide us, Lord, Amen.

Prayer inscribed on the healing stone unveiled at the
50th International Eucharistic Congress in 2012 in Dublin,
which now has a permanent home at Lough Derg

FEBRUARY 2023

26 Sunday   **FIRST SUNDAY OF LENT**
Violet ✠   HOURS Psalter Week 1
                MASS Proper. No Gloria. Creed. Preface: Proper (The Temptation
                of the Lord)
READINGS   **Gn 2:7-9, 3:1-7. Ps 50:3-6, 12-14, 17. R/ cf. v 3. Rm**
                5:12-19 (shorter form 5:12, 17-19)**. Mt 4:1-11.** *Lect* I:201

The Church has in mind the catechumens throughout the world who set out today
on their great preparation for the Easter Vigil when they will become Christians.
The faithful, who are already baptised, are the concern of the Church too. They
must be awakened once more to the meaning of being in Christ. The faithful join
with the catechumens in the struggle against the powers of darkness, confident
that where sin abounded, grace abounds still more.

                The Rite of Election of Catechumens is celebrated today
No other celebrations, not even funeral Masses, are permitted today (see Lit. Note 8)

---

27 Monday   **1st Week of Lent**
Violet   HOURS Psalter Week 1. MASS Proper. Preface: Lent I–IV
                Memorial may be made of **St Gregory of Narek, abbot**
                and doctor of the Church (see *Lit. Note* 8)
READINGS   **Lev 19:1-2, 11-18. Ps 18:8-10, 15, R/ Jn 6:64. Mt**
                25:31-46. *Lect* I:210

The gospel reminds us that Jesus came to preach good news to the poor. At the
beginning of Lent we again get a reminder that good works are essential to our
proper observance of the season, along with prayer and fasting.

St Gregory of Narek, c. 950–1003, was a monk of the Armenian Church, a
mystic and poet. His best known writing is *Lamentations*, also called simply *Narek*,
a collection of 95 prayers, each with the title 'Conversation with God from the
depth of the heart'. Pope Francis declared Gregory a doctor of the Church in
2015.

---

28 Tuesday   **1st Week of Lent**
Violet   HOURS Psalter Week 1. MASS Proper. Preface: Lent I–IV
READINGS   **Is 55:10-11. Ps 33:4-7, 16-19, R/ v 18. Mt 6:7-15.**
                Lect I:212

The model for our prayer is the Lord's Prayer. It is a summary of the whole gospel,
the most perfect of all prayers. Being taught and given to us by our Lord it is
indeed the word of God that goes out and succeeds in what it was sent to do. It is
the foundation of the daily prayer of all Christians.

---

1 Wednesday 1st Week of Lent
Violet   HOURS Psalter Week 1. MASS Proper. Preface: Lent I–IV

                    Memorial may be made of **St David, bishop** (see *Lit. Note* 8)

READINGS   **Jon 3:1-10. Ps 50:3-4, 12-13, 18-19, R/ v 19. Lk 11:29-32.** *Lect* I:214

In Lent our eyes are fixed on the Cross of Christ from which comes our salvation, and the grace to accept it.

St David see *The Irish Calendar*, p. 185.

---

2 Thursday 1st Week of Lent
Violet   HOURS Psalter Week 1. MASS Proper. Preface: Lent I–IV

READINGS   **Est 4:17. Ps 137:1-3, 7-8, R/ v 3. Mt 7:7-12.** *Lect* I:216

Queen Esther knew the practical things to be done and did them, but she did not rely on them. Her prayer shows that her confidence was in God: 'I have no one but you, Lord.' We can show a practical lack of faith. Sometimes we are hesitant to ask in prayer, maybe because it is only our last resort.

---

3 Friday 1st Week of Lent
Violet   HOURS Psalter Week 1. MASS Proper. Preface: Lent I–IV

READINGS   **Ez 18:21-28. Ps 129, R/ v 3. Mt 5:20-26.** *Lect* I:218

As we prepare to celebrate the Eucharist, St Cyprian reminds us: 'To God the better offering is peace, community concord and a people made one in the unity of the Father, Son and Holy Spirit.'

---

4 Saturday 1st Week of Lent
Violet   HOURS Psalter Week 1. MASS Proper. Preface: Lent I–IV

                    Memorial may be made of **St Casimir** (see *Lit. Note* 8)

READINGS   **Deut 26:16-19. Ps 118:1-2, 4-5, 7-8, R/ v 1. Mt 5:43-48.** *Lect* I:221

The Lord Jesus, the divine Teacher and Model of all perfection, preached holiness of life to each and every one of his disciples of every condition. He himself stands as the author and consummator of this holiness of life (*Lumen Gentium*, 40).

St Casimir, 1458–84, strove to promote peace and the unity of western Europe. Though a young prince, he chose a life of prayer and penance. Patron saint of Poland.

CONFESSIO OF PATRICK

1. I am Patrick, a sinner, the most rustic and least of all the faithful, the most contemptible in the eyes of a great many people. My father was Calpornius, a deacon and the son of the presbyter Potitus. He came from the village of Bannaventaberniae where he had a country residence nearby. It was there that I was taken captive. I was almost sixteen at the time and I did not know the true God. I was taken into captivity to Ireland with many thousands of people. We deserved this fate because we had turned away from God; we neither kept his commandments nor obeyed our priests who used to warn us about our salvation. The Lord's fury bore down on us and he scattered us among many heathen peoples, even to the ends of the earth. This is where I now am, in all my insignificance, among strangers.

2. The Lord there made me aware of my unbelief that I might at last advert to my sins and turn whole-heartedly to the Lord my God. He showed concern for my weakness, and pity for my youth and ignorance; he watched over me before I got to know him and before I was wise or distinguished good from evil. In fact he protected me and comforted me as a father would his son.

3. I cannot be silent then, nor indeed should I, about the great benefits and grace that the Lord saw fit to confer on me in the land of my captivity. This is the way we repay God for correcting us and taking notice of us; we honour and praise his wonders before every nation under heaven.

4. There is no other God, there never was and there never will be, than God the Father unbegotten and without beginning, from whom is all beginning, holding all things as we have learned; and his son Jesus Christ whom we declare to have been always with the Father and to have been begotten spiritually by the Father in a way that baffles description, before the beginning of the world, before all beginning; and through him are made all things, visible and invisible. He was made man, defeated death and was received into heaven by the Father, who has given him all power over all names in heaven, on earth, and under the earth; and every tongue should acknowledge to him that Jesus Christ is the Lord God. We believe in him and we look for his coming soon as judge of the living and of the dead, who will treat every man according to his deeds. He has poured out the Holy Spirit on us in abundance, the gift and guarantee of eternal life, who makes those who believe and obey sons of God and joint heirs with Christ. We acknowledge and adore him as one God in the Trinity of the holy name.

5. He himself has said through the prophet: *Call upon me in the day of your trouble; and I will deliver you, and you shall glorify me. He also says: It is honourable to reveal and confess the works of God.*

6. Although I am imperfect in many ways I want my brothers and relatives to know what kind of man I am, so that they may perceive the aspiration of my life.

7. I know well the statement of the Lord which he makes in the psalm: *You will destroy those who speak falsely.* He says again: *A lying mouth destroys the soul.* The same Lord says in the Gospel: *On the day of judgement men will render account for every careless word they utter.*

8. I ought therefore to dread with fear and trembling the sentence of that day when no one will be able to escape or hide, but when all of us will have to give an account of even our smallest sins before the court of the Lord Christ.

taken from *Patrick in his Own Words*,
Bishop Joseph Duffy, Veritas Publications, 2019

MARCH 2023

5 Sunday   SECOND SUNDAY OF LENT
Violet ✠   HOURS Psalter Week 2
                MASS Proper. No Gloria. Creed. Preface: Proper (The
                Transfiguration of the Lord)
READINGS   **Gn 12:1-4. Ps 32:4-5, 18-20, 22, R/ v 22. 2 Tm 1:8-
                10. Mt 17:1-9.** *Lect* I:223

Through his Cross, Christ entered into his glory. We are already at this point in Lent at the heart of the paschal mystery. The catechumens, having been shown the struggle needed, are pointed towards their own exodus. The disciples on the mountaintop, seeing Jesus transfigured, are encouraged for the days when they meet the Cross. We are all called to holiness. If we respond as did Abraham and Jesus, then we will come to a glorious transfiguration.

No other celebrations, not even funeral Masses, are permitted today (see Lit. Note 8)
St Kieran, bishop is not celebrated this year.

---

6 Monday   2nd Week of Lent
Violet   HOURS Psalter Week 2. MASS Proper. Preface: Lent I–IV
Ossory   **St Kieran, bishop**   Feast transferred
READINGS   **Dn 9:4-10. Ps 78:8-9, 11, 13, R/ Ps 102:10. Lk 6:36-
                38.** *Lect* I:231

Daniel sees the goodness and generous love of God and contrasts the wickedness and betrayal of the people. He recognises the community aspect of that sin that has brought punishment on all the people high and low. And only God can heal them, for to him alone mercy and pardon belong.

St Kieran see *The Irish Calendar*, p. 185.

---

7 Tuesday   2nd Week of Lent
Violet   HOURS Psalter Week 2. MASS Proper. Preface: Lent I–IV
                Memorial may be made of **Ss Perpetua and Felicity,
                martyrs** (see *Lit. Note 8*)
READINGS   **Is 1:10, 16-20. Ps 49:8-9, 16-17, 21, 23, R/ v 23. Mt
                23:1-12.** *Lect* I:232

Lent meaning 'springtime' calls to mind new beginnings. Spring cleaning destroys the dirt and grime of dark winter. The harrowing by penance and prayer prepares the Christian for the implanting of the seed that will bring an abundant harvest.

St Perpetua, a young upper-class married woman, and **St Felicity**, a slave girl, were martyred in Carthage, 203.

---

8 Wednesday   2nd Week of Lent
Violet   HOURS Psalter Week 2. MASS Proper. Preface: Lent I–IV
                  Memorial may be made of **St John of God, religious** (see *Lit. Note* 8)
                  Memorial may be made of **St Senan, bishop** (see *Lit. Note* 8)
READINGS   **Jer 18:18-20. Ps 30:5-6, 14-16, R/ v 17. Mt 20:17-28.** *Lect* I:234

'Save me in your love, O Lord.' This prayer to be saved reminds us that salvation comes from God alone. The mother of the two apostles was looking for security for her sons. Jesus had to tell her that her understanding of such safety was wrong. He required abandonment to God's will as the best security.
St John of God, 1495–1550, devoted his life to the care of the poor and the sick. He is patron saint of nurses, the sick, heart patients, printers and booksellers.
St Senan see *The Irish Calendar*, p. 185.

---

9 Thursday   2nd Week of Lent
Violet   HOURS Psalter Week 2. MASS Proper. Preface: Lent I–IV
                  Memorial may be made of **St Frances of Rome, religious** (see *Lit. Note* 8)
READINGS   **Jer 17:5-10. Ps 1:1-4, 6, R/ Ps 39:5. Lk 16:19-31.** *Lect* I:236

The gospel story of the poor man Lazarus is about the choice that each one has to make of life or death. It is a responsible choice because we have Moses and the prophets, and Jesus himself, to show us the alternatives.
St Frances of Rome, d. 1440, lived a happily married life and founded a society of women with the Rule of St Benedict and became a member of it after her husband's death.
Cashel and Emly Today is the anniversary of the episcopal ordination of Most Rev. Dermot Clifford, 9 March 1986

---

10 Friday   2nd Week of Lent
Violet   HOURS Psalter Week 2. MASS Proper. Preface: Lent I–IV
READINGS   **Gn 37:3-4, 12-13, 17-28. Ps 104:16-21, R/ v 5. Mt 21:33-43, 45-46.** *Lect* I:239

Joseph is sold into slavery for twenty pieces of silver. The servants in the vineyard kill the heir. Jesus, the Son of God, is also sold and sentenced to death. But the stone rejected becomes the cornerstone.

---

11 Saturday   2nd Week of Lent
Violet   HOURS Psalter Week 2. MASS Proper. Preface: Lent I–IV
                  Memorial may be made of **St Aengus, bishop and abbot** (see *Lit. Note* 8)
READINGS   **Mic 7:14-15, 18-20. Ps 102:1-4, 9-12, R/ v 8. Lk 15:1-3, 11-32.** *Lect* I:241

In the story of the father welcoming back his son, Jesus shows us in a very human way that we can be like that.
St Aengus see *The Irish Calendar*, p. 185.
Dublin Today is the anniversary of the episcopal ordination of Most Rev. Dermot Farrell, 11 March 2018.

MARCH 2023

12 Sunday **THIRD SUNDAY OF LENT**
Violet ✠
HOURS Psalter Week 3
MASS Proper. No Gloria. Creed. Preface: Proper (The Samaritan Woman)
READINGS **Ex 17:3-7. Ps 94:1-2, 6-9, R/ v 8. Rm 5:1-2, 5-8. Jn 4:5-42** (shorter form 4:5-15, 19-26, 39-42)**.** Lect I:245

The catechumens and the baptised Christians are together on this Lenten pilgrimage. Christ offers the water of life to all who thirst. Today there occurs the first scrutiny or exorcism for the catechumens. By it they are being prepared to accept the Spirit. Through that Spirit the gift of love is poured into our hearts, a gift bought for us by the blood of Christ. The prayer that they grow in wisdom and love echoes the readings, and must still be the prayer of all Christians.

The First Scrutiny is celebrated today

No other celebrations, not even funeral Masses, are permitted today (see Lit. Note 8)

The readings **Ex 17:1-7. Ps 94:1-2, 6-9, R/ v 8. Jn 4:5-42.** Lect I:258 may be used instead of the Lenten readings any day this week.

---

13 Monday **3rd Week of Lent**
Violet
HOURS Psalter Week 3. MASS Proper. Preface: Lent I–IV
READINGS **2 Kg 5:1-15. Pss 41:2-3; 42:3-4, R/ Ps 41:3. Lk 4:24-30.** Lect I:262

Naaman, the Syrian, learned to obey God's will, and went and washed in the Jordan. He was cleansed. Jesus reminds us that salvation is a gift of God. These are reminders to us the baptised and to those preparing for baptism.

Today is the anniversary of the election in 2013 of **Pope Francis** as Supreme Pastor of the Church. An intention for the Holy Father should be included in the Prayer of the Faithful at all Masses.

---

14 Tuesday **3rd Week of Lent**
Violet
HOURS Psalter Week 3. MASS Proper. Preface: Lent I–IV
READINGS **Dn 3:25, 34-43. Ps 24:4-9, R/ v 6. Mt 18:21-35.** Lect I:264

It is in the memory of past favours that Azariah has the confidence to pray to God. His prayer is suitable for all times. God is faithful to his covenant, and Jesus Christ intercedes for us always.

---

15 Wednesday **3rd Week of Lent**
Violet
HOURS Psalter Week 3. MASS Proper. Preface: Lent I–IV
READINGS **Deut 4:1, 5-9. Ps 147:12-13, 15-16, 19-20, R/ v 12. Mt 5:17-19.** Lect I:267

The Law is a great treasure to be safely guarded and to be handed on as a sacred trust. In the new Jerusalem, the Church, the laws of Christ are not to be seen as burdens or out of date. They are the evidence of the love of Christ for us.

---

16 Thursday   3rd Week of Lent
Violet   HOURS Psalter Week 3. MASS Proper. Preface: Lent I–IV
READINGS   **Jer 7:23-28. Ps 94:1-2, 6-9, R/ v 8. Lk 11:14-23.** *Lect* I:268

Hardness of heart is the characteristic of those who have refused to listen to God. Listening to the lies of Satan led human beings to disobey God in the beginning. Satan still acts in our world out of hatred of God and his kingdom in Jesus Christ.
White   FIRST EVENING PRAYER of **St Patrick**

---

17 Friday   ST PATRICK, bishop, principal patron of Ireland
Solemnity

                         Day of Prayer for Emigrants
White ✠   HOURS Proper (Divine Office, II, p. 209*)
                         Te Deum. Complementary Psalms at Day Hour
                         MASS Proper. Gloria, Creed. Preface: Proper
READINGS   **Eccles (Sir) 39:6-10. Ps 115:12-19, R/ v 12. 2 Tm 4:1-8. Mt 13:24-32.** National Proper
                         EVENING PRAYER of St Patrick

No other celebrations, not even funeral Masses, are permitted today (see Lit. Note 8)
St Patrick see *The Irish Calendar*, p. 186.
Cloyne Today is the anniversary of the episcopal ordination of Most Rev. John Magee, 17 March 1987.

---

18 Saturday   3rd Week of Lent
Violet   HOURS Psalter Week 3. MASS Proper. Preface: Lent I–IV
                         Memorial may be made of **St Cyril of Jerusalem, bishop and doctor of the Church** (see *Lit. Note 8*)
READINGS   **Hos 5:15-6:6. Ps 50:3-4, 18-21, R/ cf. Hos 6:6. Lk 18:9-14.** *Lect* I:273

'Only when we humbly acknowledge that "we do not know how to pray as we ought" are we ready to receive freely the gift of prayer. "Man is a beggar before God"' (CCC, 2559).
St Cyril of Jerusalem, 315–86, Bishop of Jerusalem. He excelled as a catechist and administrator, and suffered exile in his fight against Arianism.

THE SCRUTINIES

Catechumens, now the elect, asking for the three sacraments of initiation at the Easter Vigil, take part in the Scrutinies, celebrated on the third, fourth and fifth Sundays of Lent. The scrutinies are meant to uncover, then heal all that is weak, defective, or sinful in the hearts of the elect; to bring out, then strengthen all that is upright, strong and good. For the scrutinies are celebrated in order to deliver the elect from the power of sin and Satan, to protect them against temptation, and to give them strength in Christ, who is the way, the truth and the life. These rites, therefore, should complete the conversion of the elect and deepen their resolve to hold fast to Christ and to carry out their decision to love God above all.
Rite of Christian Initiation of Adults, 128

MARCH 2023

19 Sunday   **FOURTH SUNDAY OF LENT**
                 (Laetare Sunday)
Violet or Rose ✠   HOURS Psalter Week 4
                 MASS Proper. No Gloria. Creed. Preface: Proper (The Man
                 Born Blind)
READINGS   **1 Sm 16:1, 6-7, 10-13. Ps 22, R/ v 1. Eph 5:8-14. Jn**
                 9:1-41 (shorter form 9:6-9, 13-17, 34-38)**.** Lect I:276
The experience of the man born blind helps our understanding of baptism. 'You
went, you washed, you came to the altar, you began to see what you had not seen
before. In short, your eyes were opened in the fountain of the Lord and by the
preaching of the Lord's Passion. You seemed previously to be blind of heart: now
you began to see the light.' So spoke St Ambrose to the recently baptised,
recalling that experience to them.
                 The Second Scrutiny is celebrated today
No other celebrations, not even funeral Masses, are permitted today (see Lit. Note 8)
The readings **Mic 7:7-9. Ps 26:1, 7-9, 13-14, R/ v 1. Jn 9:1-41.** Lect I:287
may be used instead of the Lenten readings any day this week.
Today is the anniversary of the inauguration of the Petrine ministry of **Pope
Francis**, Bishop of Rome in 2013. An intention for the Holy Father should be
included in the Prayer of the Faithful at all Masses.
                 EVENING PRAYER of **Fourth Sunday of Lent**
The Solemnity of **St Joseph, Spouse of the Blessed Virgin Mary** is transferred
to Monday, 20 March

---

20 Monday   **ST JOSEPH, SPOUSE OF THE BLESSED VIRGIN MARY**
                                               Solemnity
White   HOURS Proper. Te Deum. Complementary Psalms at Day Hour
                 MASS Proper. Gloria. Creed. Preface: Proper
READINGS   **2 Sm 7:4-5, 12-14, 16. Ps 88:2-5, 27, 29, R/ v 37.**
                 Rm 4:13, 16-18, 22. Mt 1:16, 18-21, 24 or Lk 2:41-
                 51. Lect I:970 or II:980
'The virtues of **St Joseph** have been the object of ecclesial reflection down through
the centuries, especially the more recent centuries. Among those virtues the following
stand out: faith, with which he fully accepted God's salvific plan; prompt and silent
obedience to the will of God; love for and fulfilment of the law, true piety, fortitude in
time of trial; chaste love for the Blessed Virgin Mary, a dutiful exercise of his paternal
authority, and fruitful reticence' (*Directory on Popular Piety and the Liturgy*, 219).
No Masses for the dead, except funeral Masses, are permitted today (see Lit. Note 8)
                 EVENING PRAYER of the Solemnity

---

21 Tuesday   **4th Week of Lent**
Violet   HOURS Psalter Week 4. MASS Proper. Preface: Lent I–IV
                 Memorial may be made of **St Enda, abbot** (see Lit. Note 8)
READINGS   **Ez 47:1-9, 12. Ps 45:2-3, 5-6, 8-9, R/ v 8. Jn 5:1-3, 5-**
                 16. Lect I:292
The water of baptism gives great joy to the Church. By this water we are healed
and saved. By baptism all sins are forgiven, original sin and all personal sins, as
well as punishments for sin. Nothing remains that would impede the baptised
from entry into the kingdom of God.
St Enda see *The Irish Calendar*, p. 186.

22 Wednesday 4th Week of Lent

Violet   HOURS Psalter Week 4. MASS Proper. Preface: Lent I–IV

READINGS   **Is 49:8-15. Ps 144:8-9, 13-14, 17-18, R/ v 8. Jn 5:17-30.** *Lect* I:294

Pride and joy in belonging to the Church should be part of our inheritance. Today the readings in so many metaphors express the fullness of life in the Church, of the life of God's chosen people. 'Baptism is the sacrament by which its recipients are incorporated into the Church and are built up together in the Spirit into a house where God lives, into a holy nation and a royal priesthood' (Rite of Baptism).

23 Thursday   4th Week of Lent

Violet   HOURS Psalter Week 4. MASS Proper. Preface: Lent I–IV

Memorial may be made of **St Turibius of Mongrovejo, bishop** (see *Lit. Note* 8)

READINGS   **Ex 32:7-14. Ps 105:19-23, R/ v 4. Jn 5:31-47.** *Lect* I:297

Jesus puts before his listeners the remembrance of Moses pleading for his people. The repeated failure of God's people to live up to the covenant serves as a warning for all generations. We also must call on God to give us the grace to turn back again. **St Turibius of Mongrovejo**, 1538–1606, was a layman when he was appointed archbishop of Lima, Peru by King Philip II. He combated all the abuses of the conquerors in Peru and built up the Church there.

24 Friday   4th Week of Lent

Violet   HOURS Psalter Week 4. MASS Proper. Preface: Lent I–IV

Memorial may be made of **St Macartan, bishop** (see *Lit. Note* 8)

Clogher   **St Macartan, bishop**   Feast

READINGS   **Wis 2:1, 12-22. Ps 33:16, 18, 19-21, 23, R/ v 19. Jn 7:1-2, 10, 25-30.** *Lect* I:300

A word of warning today. To take on the Christian way of life is to risk enmity and death. The opposition to Christianity has been violent and bloodstained in many periods of history. Today, the opposition may be by other means – slander and ribaldry, ridicule and negative publicity.

St Macartan see *The Irish Calendar*, p. 186.

White   FIRST EVENING PRAYER of the **Annunciation**

25 Saturday   THE ANNUNCIATION OF THE LORD   Solemnity

White   HOURS Proper. Te Deum. Complementary Psalms at Day Hour

MASS Proper. Gloria. Creed. Preface: Proper

In the Profession of Faith, all genuflect at the words: and was incarnate.

READINGS   **Is 7:10-14, 8:10. Ps 39:7-11, R/ vv 8, 9. Heb 10:4-10. Lk 1:26-38.** *Lect* II:985

The Annunciation of the Lord. 'Giving her consent to God's word, Mary becomes the mother of Jesus. Espousing the divine will for salvation wholeheartedly, without a single sin to restrain her, she gave herself entirely to the person and to the work of her Son; she did so in order to serve the mystery of redemption with him and dependent on him, by God's grace' (CCC, 494).

No Masses for the Dead, except funeral Masses, are permitted today (see Lit. Note 8)

Violet   FIRST EVENING PRAYER of **Fifth Sunday of Lent**

MARCH 2023

26 Sunday   **FIFTH SUNDAY OF LENT**
Violet ✠   HOURS Psalter Week 1
                    MASS Proper. No Gloria. Creed. Preface: Proper (Lazarus)
READINGS   **Ez 37:12-14. Ps 129, R/ v 7. Rm 8:8-11. Jn 11:1-45**
                    (shorter form 11:3-7, 17, 20-27, 33-45). Lect I:305

Lazarus' resurrection is a figure and type of Jesus' resurrection, and of our
resurrection, first to divine life in baptism and to our definitive resurrection at the
end of time. The gospel is a call to a deeper faith in the Spirit living in us, giving life
to our mortal bodies. The catechumens are presented with the Creed in the third
week of Lent and the Lord's Prayer in the coming week after the third scrutiny.
Growth in faith means a deeper love for these two expressions of our way of life.
               The Third Scrutiny is celebrated today
No other celebrations, not even funeral Masses, are permitted today (see Lit. Note 8)
The readings **2 Kg 4:18-21, 32-37. Ps 16:1, 6-8, 15, R/ v 15. Jn 11:1-
45.** Lect I:316 may be used instead of the Lenten readings any day this week.

---

27 Monday   **5th Week of Lent**
Violet   HOURS Psalter Week 1
                    MASS Proper. Preface: Passion I
READINGS   **Dn 13:1-9, 15-17, 19-30, 33-62** (shorter form 13:41-62).
                    Ps 22, R/ v 4. Jn 8:1-11. Lect I:319

Both women in today's readings suffered in their experience of condemnation,
whether guilty or innocent. They were led to the tribunals of judgement and felt
defenceless. Their liberation is an act of God's mercy and provision of help.

---

28 Tuesday   **5th Week of Lent**
Violet   HOURS Psalter Week 1
                    MASS Proper. Preface: Passion I
READINGS   **Num 21:4-9. Ps 101:2-3, 16-21, R/ v 2. Jn 8:21-30.**
                    Lect I:326

Christ lifted up on the Cross is the image which identifies his followers everywhere.
Christians have knelt before the Cross in all times of need and distress. It has
been held before the eyes of those facing death. It has led missionary journeys so
that those who looked upon it might have new life.

DATES OF PASSOVER AND EASTER

At the Council of Nicaea in 325, the date for Easter was fixed as the Sunday after
the full moon after the spring equinox. Sunday, 9 April 2023 is the feast of Easter.
Eastern Christians calculate the date of Easter according to the Julian Calendar, the
Calendar in general use before the Gregorian reform of 1582. One of the reforms
was the removal of ten days from the Calendar and this discrepancy, now thirteen
days, between the Julian and Gregorian Calendars results often in a difference in
the date for Easter in East and West as they follow the two Calendars. This happens
in 2023 when the date of Easter for Eastern Christians is Sunday, 16 April.

The feast of Passover is a seven day feast, beginning at sundown on the
evening of 5 April 2023 (14 Nisan 5783).

29 Wednesday 5th Week of Lent
Violet   HOURS Psalter Week 1
               MASS Proper. Preface: Passion I
READINGS   **Dn 3:14-20, 24-25, 28. Ps Dn 3:52-56, R/ v 52. Jn 8:31-42.** *Lect* I:328

The three young men refused to obey an unjust law – a higher moral law was at stake. God rewarded their faithfulness to the truth and their courage in making a stand for conscience's sake.

---

30 Thursday   5th Week of Lent
Violet   HOURS Psalter Week 1
               MASS Proper. Preface: Passion I
READINGS   **Gn 17:3-9. Ps 104:4-9, R/ v 8. Jn 8:51-59.** *Lect* I:331

The God of Abraham and Jesus is beyond and outside time. He is before the Father now to remember for us the past goodness of God so that now in our present time it may continue. In the Eucharist when we remember his passion, death and resurrection we are in a position to join with him and through him to make intercession for the whole world.

---

31 Friday   5th Week of Lent
Violet   HOURS Psalter Week 1
               MASS Proper. Preface: Passion I
READINGS   **Jer 20:10-13. Ps 17:2-7, R/ cf. v 7. Jn 10:31-42.** *Lect* I:333

To God we must turn in time of trial. It is God who will be the final judge of the rightness of the cause. Both Jesus and Jeremiah faced a lack of belief but were supported by the knowledge that the Lord was on their side.

APRIL 2023

1 Saturday   5th Week of Lent
Violet   HOURS Psalter Week 1
               MASS Proper. Preface: Passion I
               Memorial may be made of **St Ceallach (Celsus), bishop** (see *Lit. Note* 8)
READINGS   **Ez 37:21-28. Ps Jer 31:10-13, R/ v 10. Jn 11:45-56.** *Lect* I:336

In order to gather together scattered humanity, God called Abraham, a wandering Aramean shepherd, to be the father of a multitude of nations. To the people descended from him would be entrusted the promise that one day God would gather all his children into the unity of the Church.
St Ceallach (Celsus) see *The Irish Calendar*, p. 186.

APRIL 2023

HOLY WEEK

2 Sunday	**PALM SUNDAY OF THE LORD'S PASSION**
Red ✠	HOURS Psalter Week 2
	MASS Proper. No Gloria. Creed. Preface: Proper
READINGS	Procession **Mt 21:1-11.** Lect I:343
	Mass **Is 50:4-7. Ps 21:8-9, 17-20, 23-24, R/ v 2. Phil 2:6-11. Mt 26:14-27:66** (shorter form 27:11-54)**.** Lect I:346

No other celebrations, not even funeral Masses, are permitted today (see Lit. Note 8)
St Francis of Paola, hermit is not celebrated this year.

Palm Sunday of the Lord's Passion

Holy Week begins on this Sunday, which joins the foretelling of Christ's regal triumph and the proclamation of the passion. The connection between both aspects of the paschal mystery should be shown and explained in the celebration and catechesis of this day. The commemoration of the entrance of the Lord into Jerusalem is celebrated with a solemn procession which may take place only once, before the Mass which has the largest attendance, even if this should be the evening of Saturday or Sunday. In this procession the faithful carry palm or other branches. The priest and the ministers, also carrying branches, precede the people. The palms or branches are blessed so that they can be carried in the procession. The palms should be taken home, where they will serve as a reminder of the victory of Christ which they celebrated in the procession. Pastors should make every effort to ensure that this procession in honour of Christ the King be so prepared and celebrated that it is of great spiritual significance in the life of the faithful.

The Proclamation of the Passion

The passion narrative occupies a special place. It should be sung or read in the traditional way, that is, by three persons who take the part of Christ, the narrator, and the people. The passion is proclaimed by deacons or priests, or by lay readers; in the latter case the part of Christ should be reserved to the priest. The proclamation of the passion should be without candles and incense, the greeting and the sign of the cross on the book are omitted. For the spiritual good of the faithful the passion should be proclaimed in its entirety, and the readings which precede it should not be omitted. After the passion has been proclaimed, a homily is to be given.

Holy Week

During Holy Week, the Church celebrates the mysteries of salvation accomplished by Christ in the last days of his life on earth, beginning with his messianic entrance into Jerusalem. The Lenten season lasts until the Thursday of this week. The Easter Triduum begins with the evening Mass of the Lord's Supper. The days of Holy Week, from Monday to Thursday inclusive, have precedence over all other celebrations. It is not fitting that baptism and confirmation be celebrated on these days.

End of Lent

It is fitting that the Lenten season should be concluded, both for the individual Christian as well as for the whole Christian community, with a penitential celebration, so that they may be helped to prepare to celebrate more fully the paschal mystery. These celebrations, however, should take place before the Easter Triduum, and should not immediately precede the evening Mass of the Lord's Supper.

3 Monday   **Monday in Holy Week**
Violet   HOURS Psalter Week 2
                  MASS Proper. Preface: Passion II
READINGS   **Is 42:1-7. Ps 26:1-3, 13-14, R/ v 1. Jn 12:1-11.** *Lect* I:374

Our attention is now focused on the great mystery of Christ, dying and rising. The sense of impending doom hovers over the actions of Jesus. Like a lamb led to the slaughter, Christ does not cry out or shout aloud. Mary's anointing becomes one of preparation of the body for burial after death. All things are being readied for the final hour. The chrism is prepared for blessing by the bishop this week: it will be used to sign new Christians with the Cross, to seal them for Christ. This sweet-smelling oil will remind them that they are, as St Paul says, to be the 'aroma of Christ' spreading a fragrance wherever they go (2 Cor 2:14-15).

No other celebrations, except funeral Masses, are permitted today (see Lit. Note 8)

---

4 Tuesday   **Tuesday in Holy Week**
Violet   HOURS Psalter Week 2
                  MASS Proper. Preface: Passion II
READINGS   **Is 49:1-6. Ps 70:1-6, 15, 17, R/ v 15. Jn 13:21-33, 36-38.** *Lect* I:376

The words of Isaiah speak beautifully of our vocation in Christ. Chosen before birth, given great gifts of body and mind, called to be servant of the Most High, and destined to be a light of the nations so that Christ's salvation may be brought to the ends of the earth. Such is our destiny. And yet, we can fail. We can reject this calling, give way to weakness. Both Judas and Peter in their weakness are put before us today, one to betray, the other to deny. So close to Jesus and yet capable of losing him.

No other celebrations, except funeral Masses, are permitted today (see Lit. Note 8)
St Isodore, bishop and doctor of the Church is not celebrated this year.

---

5 Wednesday   **Wednesday in Holy Week**
Violet   HOURS Psalter Week 2
                  MASS Proper. Preface: Passion II
READINGS   **Is 50:4-9. Ps 68:8-10, 21-22, 31, 33-34, R/ v 14. Mt 26:14-25.** *Lect* I:379

Spy Wednesday we call it – for Judas has left his mark on our calendars. The pain of his betrayal is to be felt in the account of St Matthew's Gospel. And thirty pieces of silver goes into language currency ever since. At the end of this Lent, which has seen us trying to purify ourselves of all that is not Christian, these thirty pieces of silver come before us as a warning.

No other celebrations, except funeral Masses, are permitted today (see Lit. Note 8)
St Vincent Ferrer, priest is not celebrated this year.

| **6 Thursday** | **HOLY THURSDAY** |
| | **Morning** |

Violet   HOURS Readings: Ants and Pss may be taken from Friday Week 3

Morning Prayer and Day Hour: Psalter Week 2

White   The CHRISM MASS is the only Mass that takes place in the morning

Gloria. No Creed. Preface: Priesthood

READINGS *Lect* I:382

Is 61:1-3, 6, 8-9. This passage is seen as Jesus' own description of his mission. It serves to highlight the vocation of those who follow him in priestly ministry. The priests of the Lord are to bring comfort, healing and joy.

Ps 88:21-22, 25, 27, R/ v 2. The priest's vocation is given by God in love. That love supports him always.

Apoc 1:5-8. Christ loved us and gave his life for us. Through that redeeming act we have become a community that shares his kingly and priestly identity.

Lk 4:16-21. Christ uses the text of Isaiah to tell his hearers that the words are now an actual event before them. The priest shares in Christ's ministry, has received the same Spirit, is anointed for service.

'This Mass, which the bishop concelebrates with his college of presbyters and at which he consecrates the holy chrism and blesses the other oils, manifests the communion of the presbyters with their bishop.

The holy chrism consecrated by the bishop is used to anoint the newly baptised, to seal the candidates for confirmation, and to anoint the hands of presbyters and the heads of bishops at their ordination, as well as in rites of anointing pertaining to the dedication of churches and altars. The oil of catechumens is used in the preparation of the catechumens for their baptism. The oil of the sick is used to bring comfort and support to the sick in their infirmity.

Presbyters are brought together and concelebrate this Mass as witnesses and co-operators with their bishop in the consecration of the chrism because they share in the sacred office of the bishop in building up, sanctifying and ruling the people of God. This Mass is therefore a clear expression of the unity of the priesthood and sacrifice of Christ, which continue to be present in the Church.

To show the unity of the college of presbyters, the presbyters who concelebrate with the bishop should come from different parts of the diocese.

Presbyters who take part, but for some reason do not concelebrate, may receive Communion under both kinds.

If it is difficult for the clergy and the people to assemble with the bishop on Holy Thursday morning, the blessing of oils may be held on an earlier day, near Easter, with the celebration of the proper Chrism Mass.

Because of its meaning and pastoral importance in the life of the diocese, the Chrism Mass should be celebrated as a stational Mass in the cathedral church, or, for pastoral reasons, in another church.' (*Ceremonial of Bishops*)

During today and the Sacred Triduum all other celebrations, even funeral Masses, are prohibited. For the Liturgy of the Dead, see Liturgical Note 10.

THE EASTER TRIDUUM

The Fathers of the Church saw this celebration as a unitive commemoration: St Augustine spoke of 'the most holy triduum of the crucified, buried and risen Lord'. Over Friday, Saturday and Sunday we celebrate a single, indivisible mystery. The Easter Triduum begins with the evening Mass of the Lord's Supper, reaches its high point in the Easter Vigil, and closes with Evening Prayer on Easter Sunday (*UNLYC*, 18–19).

Christ redeemed us all and gave perfect glory to God principally through his paschal mystery: dying he destroyed our death and rising he restored our life. Therefore the Easter Triduum of the passion and resurrection of Christ is the culmination of the entire liturgical year. Thus the solemnity of Easter has the same kind of pre-eminence in the liturgical year that Sunday has in the week.

The celebration of the paschal mystery is not simply a recalling of past events in history. It is a sacramental celebration that renders present and actualises the saving power of Christ's death and resurrection to the Church.

Active participation
For the celebration of the Easter Triduum, a sufficient number of ministers and assistants should be prepared for their role. The faithful should be instructed on the meaning of each part of the celebration so that they can take part more fully and fruitfully. The chants for the people are of special importance for their participation and should not be lightly omitted.

Where the number of participants and ministers is so small that the celebrations of the Easter Triduum cannot be carried out with the requisite solemnity, such groups of the faithful should assemble in a larger church. It is fitting that small religious communities should participate in neighbouring principal churches.

The Paschal Fast
The Easter Fast is sacred on the first two days of the Triduum, in which, according to ancient tradition, the Church fasts 'because the Spouse has been taken away' (*Mk* 2:19-20).

Good Friday is a day of fasting and abstinence; it is also recommended that Holy Saturday be so observed, 'so that the Church, with uplifted and welcoming heart, be ready to celebrate the joys of the Sunday of the resurrection' (*Sacrosanctum Concilium*, 110).

The Liturgy of the Hours during the Easter Triduum
The Office is proper for each day.

On Good Friday and Holy Saturday, the Office of Readings should be celebrated publicly with the people before Morning Prayer, as far as this is possible.

Evening Prayer is not said by those who attend the Evening Mass on Holy Thursday or the Commemoration of the passion on Good Friday.

The Easter Vigil takes the place of the Office of Readings. Morning Prayer for Easter Sunday is said by all.

It is fitting that Evening Prayer of Easter Sunday be celebrated in a more solemn way to mark the ending of the Triduum and to commemorate the occasions when the Lord showed himself to his disciples.

THE EASTER TRIDUUM

6 Thursday   **HOLY THURSDAY**
                    Evening Mass of the Lord's Supper
White   MASS Proper. Gloria. No Creed. Preface: Eucharist I
                    In the Roman Canon, proper forms
READINGS   **Ex 12:1-8, 11-14. Ps 115:12-13, 15-18, R/ cf. 1 Cor
                    10:16. 1 Cor 11:23-26. Jn 13:1-15.** *Lect* I:387

The scripture readings this evening direct our minds at the opening of the great paschal celebration to the meaning of what we celebrate. We are entering into this mystery is such a way that when we break bread and share the cup this evening we once more proclaim the death of the Lord.

Evening Mass of the Lord's Supper should be celebrated with the full participation of the whole community, with all the priests concelebrating. The pastoral reasons that permit another Mass should be seriously considered before breaking the unity of the celebration.

The hearing of confessions should not take place during Mass; the faithful should be encouraged to approach the sacrament earlier in Lent.

At the Evening Mass, the tabernacle should be entirely empty; a sufficient amount of bread should be consecrated at this Mass for the Communion of all on this day and tomorrow.

Bells may be rung during the *Gloria* and are not rung again until the Paschal Vigil.

'With this Mass, celebrated in the evening of the Thursday in Holy Week, the Church begins the sacred Easter Triduum and devotes itself to the remembrance of the Last Supper. At this supper on the night he was betrayed, the Lord Jesus, loving those who were his own in the world even to the end, offered his body and blood to the Father under the appearances of bread and wine, gave them to the apostles to eat and drink, then enjoined the apostles and their successors in the priesthood to offer them in turn.

This Mass is, first of all, the memorial of the institution of the Eucharist, that is, of the memorial of the Lord's Passover, by which under sacramental signs he perpetuated among us the sacrifice of the New Law. The Mass of the Lord's Supper is also the memorial of the institution of the priesthood, by which Christ's mission and sacrifice are perpetuated in the world. In addition, this Mass is the memorial of that love by which the Lord loved us even to death. The bishop should see to it that all these considerations are suitably presented to the faithful through the ministry of the word so that by their devotion they may be able to deepen their grasp of such great mysteries and reflect them more faithfully in the conduct of their lives.' (*Ceremonial of Bishops*, 298)

EVENING PRAYER is omitted by those who attend the Evening Mass.
Solemn adoration of the Blessed Sacrament should end at midnight.
After the Evening Mass the altar is stripped privately, and crucifixes, if not removed from the church, are veiled.
Night Prayer 2 of Sunday.

THE EASTER TRIDUUM

Celebrating the Evening Mass of the Lord's Supper

Unity of the Celebration
The Mass of the Lord's Supper is celebrated in the evening, at a time more convenient for the full participation of the whole local community. All priests may concelebrate, even if they have already celebrated. Where pastoral considerations require it, the local ordinary may permit another Mass to be celebrated, but not for the benefit of private persons or small groups, or to the detriment of the main Mass. All Masses without the participation of the people are forbidden on this day.

The Mandatum
The gospel account of the Mandatum is actualised when the rite is carried out. The tradition of the washing of the feet should be maintained, and its proper significance explained. Gifts for the poor, especially those collected during Lent as the fruit of penance, may be presented in the procession of gifts.

The Sick and Infirm
It is appropriate that the Eucharist be borne directly from the altar by the deacons or acolytes or extraordinary ministers at the moment of Communion, for the sick and infirm who must communicate at home, so that in this way they may be more closely united to the celebrating church.

Place of Repose
For the reservation of the Blessed Sacrament that will be distributed in Communion on Good Friday, a place should be prepared and adorned in such a way as to be conducive to prayer and meditation. The Blessed Sacrament should be reserved in a closed tabernacle or pyx. When the tabernacle is located in a chapel separated from the central part of the church, it is appropriate to prepare there the place of repose or adoration. The faithful should be encouraged to spend some period of time there during the night before the Blessed Sacrament. This adoration may be accompanied by the reading of some part of the Gospel of St John, chapters 13–17. From midnight onwards the adoration should be made without solemnity, for the day of the Lord's passion has begun. After Mass the altar should be stripped. It is fitting that any crosses in the church be covered with a red or purple veil. Lamps should not be lit before the images of saints.

The Lectionary for the Easter Triduum
On Holy Thursday at the evening Mass the readings direct attention to the supper preceding Christ's departure. On Good Friday the liturgical service has as its centre John's narrative of the passion of him who was portrayed in Isaiah as the Servant of God and who became the one High Priest by offering himself to the Father. On the holy night of the Easter Vigil there are seven Old Testament readings recalling the wonderful works of God in the history of salvation. The New Testament readings announce the resurrection and speak of baptism as the sacrament of Christ's resurrection. On Easter Day, the gospel reading is from John on the finding of the empty tomb, or the Easter Vigil gospel may be used. In the evening Luke's story of the disciples on the road to Emmaus may be used.

THE EASTER TRIDUUM

7 Friday   **GOOD FRIDAY**
                      Day of Fast and Abstinence
Red   HOURS Proper

The OFFICE OF READINGS and MORNING PRAYER should, if possible, be celebrated publicly and with the participation of the people.

Red   **Celebration of the Lord's Passion**. Proper

This celebration takes place in the afternoon, about three o'clock, unless pastoral reasons suggest a later hour. The celebration consists of three parts: Liturgy of the Word, veneration of the Cross, and Holy Communion (*Ceremonial of Bishops*, 313).
READINGS *Lect* I:390

Is 52:13-53:12. This servant song, applied to Christ, gives a horrifying account of his sufferings, and the cause of them – our sins.

Ps 30:2, 6, 12-13, 15-17, 25, R/ Lk 23:46. A lament for the sufferings of the just one, and an expression of trust in God who is faithful.

Heb 4:14-16, 5:7-9. Christ embraced our human state and lived through our hardships. Because he was a man without sin God heard him, and all the human race as well on his behalf.

Jn 18:1-19:42. St John's account of the passion is more reflective and theological. He emphasises Jesus' obedience to the Father's will. The kingship of Jesus is asserted: the crucifixion is a victory, the hour of death is also the hour of triumph. 'Christ gives his life, he is 'lifted up' on the Cross, but willingly, and only in order to enter into his glory, a glory that is made visible even in this world to the confusion of unbelievers and ending in the defeat of Satan once and for all.' (*New Jerusalem Bible*)

After the proclamation of the passion, a homily should be given, at the end of which the faithful may be invited to spend a short time in meditation.

'On this day, when 'Christ our paschal lamb was sacrificed', what had long been promised in signs and figures was at last revealed and brought to fulfilment. The true lamb replaced the symbolic lamb, and the many offerings of the past gave way to the single sacrifice of Christ.

The wonderful works of God among the people of the Old Testament were a prelude to the work of Christ the Lord. He achieved his task of redeeming humanity and giving perfect glory to God, principally by the paschal mystery of his blessed Passion, Resurrection from the dead, and glorious ascension, whereby dying he destroyed our death and rising he restored our life (Preface of Easter). For it was from the side of Christ as he slept the sleep of death upon the Cross that there came forth the sublime sacrament of the whole Church.

In contemplating the Cross of its Lord and Bridegroom, the Church commemorates its own origin and its mission to extend to all peoples the blessed effects of Christ's Passion that it celebrates on this day in a spirit of thanksgiving for his marvellous gift.' (*Ceremonial of Bishops*, 312)

St John Baptist de la Salle, priest is not celebrated this year.

Killala Today is the anniversary of the episcopal ordination of Most Rev. John Fleming, 7 April 2002.

EVENING PRAYER is omitted by those who attend the Celebration of the Lord's Passion.

Night Prayer 2 of Sunday.

THE EASTER TRIDUUM

The Celebration of Good Friday

On this day when 'Christ our passover was sacrificed' (1 Cor 5:7), the Church meditates on the passion of her Lord and Spouse, venerates the Cross, commemorates her origin from the side of Christ on the Cross, and intercedes for the salvation of the whole world. On this day, in accordance with ancient tradition, the Church does not celebrate Eucharist; Holy Communion is distributed to the faithful during the celebration of the Lord's passion alone, though it may be brought at any time of the day to the sick who cannot take part in the celebration.

Day of Penance

Good Friday is a day of penance to be observed as of obligation in the whole Church, and indeed through abstinence and fasting. All celebration of the sacraments on this day is strictly prohibited, except for the sacraments of penance and anointing of the sick. Funerals are to be celebrated without singing, music or tolling of bells.

Times of Celebrations

The Office of Readings and Morning Prayer should take place in the morning. The Celebration of the Lord's Passion is to take place in the afternoon, around three o'clock. For pastoral reasons, in order to allow the faithful to assemble more easily, another time may be chosen, such as shortly after midday, or in the late evening, but not later than nine o'clock.

Celebration of the Lord's Passion

The order for the celebration of the Lord's passion, which stems from an ancient tradition of the Church, should be observed faithfully and religiously. The priest and ministers proceed to the altar in silence and without any singing. If any words of introduction are to be said, they should be pronounced before the ministers enter. The rite of prostration should be strictly observed as it signifies human abasement and the grief of the Church. The general intercessions are to follow the wording and form handed down by ancient tradition, maintaining the full range of intentions.

Veneration of the Cross

For the veneration of the Cross, let a cross be used that is of appropriate size and beauty. The rite should be carried out with the splendour worthy of the mystery of our salvation. After each sung invitation and response, the celebrant holds the raised Cross for a period of respectful silence. The Cross is to be presented to each of the faithful individually for their veneration, since the personal veneration of the Cross is a most important feature in this celebration, and only when necessitated by the large numbers of faithful present should the rite of veneration be made simultaneously by all present. Only one cross should be used for the veneration, as this contributes to the full symbolism of the rite. After the celebration, an appropriate place (for example, the chapel of repose used for reservation of the Eucharist on Holy Thursday) can be prepared, and there the Lord's Cross is placed with four candles, so that the faithful may venerate and kiss it, and spend some time in meditation.

Popular Devotions

Devotions, such as the Way of the Cross and Prayer around the Cross, are not to be neglected. The texts and songs should be appropriate to the spirit of this day. Such devotions should be assigned to a time of the day that makes it quite clear that the liturgical celebration by its very nature far surpasses them in importance (*Sacrosanctum Concilium*, 13).

APRIL 2023

8 Saturday   HOLY SATURDAY
Violet   LITURGY OF THE HOURS Proper

It is highly recommended that on this day the OFFICE OF READINGS and MORNING PRAYER be celebrated with the participation of the people. Where this cannot be done, there should be some celebration of the word of God, or some act of devotion suited to the mystery celebrated on this day.

Night Prayer 2 of Sunday is said only by those who do not attend the Paschal Vigil.

> 'Let the paschal fast be kept sacred. Let it be observed everywhere on Good Friday and, where possible, prolonged throughout Holy Saturday, as a way of coming to the joys of the Sunday of the resurrection with uplifted and welcoming heart' (*Sacrosanctum Concilium*, 110).

On **Holy Saturday** the Church is as it were at the Lord's tomb, meditating on his passion and death, and on his descent into hell, and awaiting his resurrection with prayer and fasting. The image of Christ crucified or lying in the tomb, or the descent into hell, which mystery Holy Saturday recalls, as also an image of the Sorrowful Virgin Mary can be placed in the church for the veneration of the faithful.

On this day the Church abstains strictly from the celebration of the Sacrifice of the Mass. Holy Communion may be given only in the form of Viaticum. The celebration of marriages is forbidden, as also the celebration of other sacraments, except penance and anointing of the sick.

The faithful are to be instructed on the special character of Holy Saturday. Festive customs and traditions associated with this day on account of the former practice of anticipating the celebration of Easter on Holy Saturday should be reserved for Easter night and the day that follows.

By means of a more intensive pastoral care and a deeper spiritual effort, all who celebrate the Easter feasts will by the Lord's grace experience their effect in their daily lives.

Announcing the Easter Vigil
In announcements concerning the Easter Vigil the participation of the faithful should be promoted; care should be taken to present it not as the concluding period of Holy Saturday, but rather it should be stressed that the Easter Vigil is celebrated 'during Easter night and that it is one single act of worship. The faithful who are absent from their parish on vacation should be urged to participate in the liturgy of the place where they happen to be'.

> #### Time of Celebration
> 'The entire celebration of the Easter Vigil takes place at night. It should not begin before nightfall; it should end before daybreak on Sunday' (*Ceremonial of Bishops*, 333). This rule is to be taken according to its strictest sense. Reprehensible are those abuses and practices which have crept in in many places whereby the Easter Vigil is celebrated at the time of day that it is customary to celebrate anticipated Sunday Masses' (*Paschale solemnitatis*, 78). Sunset on Saturday, 8 April 2023 in Ireland may be calculated as 20.10/20.25. Darkness can be calculated as about forty-five minutes to an hour after sunset.

THE EASTER TRIDUUM
THE EASTER VIGIL

This is the night when the Church keeps vigil, waiting for the resurrection of the Lord, and celebrates the sacraments of Christian Initiation.

The Passover Vigil, in which the Hebrews kept watch for the Lord's Passover which was to free them from slavery to Pharaoh, prefigured the true Pasch of Christ that was to come. For the resurrection of Christ, in which he 'broke the chains of death and rose triumphant from the grave', is the foundation of our faith and hope, and through baptism and confirmation we are inserted into the paschal mystery of Christ, dying, buried and raised with him, and with him we shall also reign.

The full meaning of this Vigil is a waiting for the coming of the Lord.

The Paschal Candle, for effective symbolism must be made of wax, never be artificial, be renewed each year, be only one in number, and be of sufficiently large size so that it may evoke the truth that Christ is the Light of the World. The Paschal Candle has its proper place either by the ambo or by the altar and should be lit at least in all the more solemn liturgical celebrations until Pentecost Sunday, whether at Mass or at Morning and Evening Prayer.

After the Easter season, the Candle should be kept with honour in the baptistery and it should not otherwise be lit or placed in the sanctuary outside the Easter season.

Baptismal Promises

The Sunday assembly commits us to an inner renewal of our baptismal promises, which are in a sense implicit in the recitation of the Creed and are an explicit part of the liturgy of the Easter Vigil and whenever baptism is celebrated during Mass. In this context, the proclamation of the Word in the Sunday Eucharist celebration takes on the solemn tone found in the Old Testament at moments when the covenant was renewed, when the law was proclaimed and the community of Israel was called – like the people in the desert at the foot of Mount Sinai (see *Ex* 19:7-8, 24:3-7) – to repeat its 'yes', renewing its decision to be faithful to God and to obey his commandments. In speaking his word, God awaits our response: a response which Christ has already made for us with his 'Amen' and which echoes in us through the Holy Spirit so that what we hear may involve us at the deepest level (*Dies Domini*, 41).

A Fifty-Day Celebration

The celebration of Easter is prolonged throughout the Easter season. The fifty days from Easter Sunday to Pentecost Sunday are celebrated as one feast day, the 'Great Sunday'.

The Sundays of Easter have precedence over all feasts of the Lord and over all solemnities.

During Easter time, pastors should instruct the faithful on the meaning of the Church's precept concerning the reception of Holy Communion during this period (*CIC, Can.* 920). It is highly recommended that Communion be brought frequently to the sick also, especially during the Easter octave.

The custom of blessing houses at Easter gives an opportunity for exercising a pastoral ministry. The pastor should go to each house for the purpose of undertaking a pastoral visitation. He will speak with each family and pray with them using texts from the Book of Blessings. In larger cities, consideration should be given to the gathering of several families for a common celebration of the blessing for all.

EASTER SUNDAY

THE RESURRECTION OF THE LORD

White **THE EASTER VIGIL**

In accordance with ancient tradition, this night is one of vigil for the Lord. St Augustine called it the 'mother of all vigils'. The Gospel of St Luke (12:35 ff.) reminds the faithful to have their lamps burning ready, awaiting their master's return, so that when he arrives he will find them wide awake and will seat them at his table.

There are **four parts to the Rite**:

SERVICE OF LIGHT

The new fire should be blessed outside the church, and its flames should be such that they genuinely dispel the darkness and light up the night. During the procession into the church, there is no reason why to each response 'Thanks be to God' there should not be added some acclamation in honour of Christ. All present should hold candles to which the light of the **Paschal Candle** is gradually passed. A cantor may sing the *Exsultet*, or **Easter Proclamation**, if no deacon or celebrant can do so. The Proclamation may be adapted by inserting acclamations from the people.

LITURGY OF THE WORD

In the **Readings** from Sacred Scripture, the Church 'beginning with Moses and all the Prophets' explains Christ's paschal mystery. This is 'the fundamental element of the Easter Vigil'. Consequently, wherever this is possible all the readings should be read, in order that the character of the Easter Vigil, which demands the time necessary, be respected at all costs. The reading from *Exodus* ch. 14 with its canticle must never be omitted. It will be helpful to introduce the people to the meaning of each reading by means of a brief introduction, given by the priest himself or by a deacon. Each reading is followed by **the singing of a psalm**, for which melodies should be provided that foster the people's participation and devotion. Great care must be taken that trivial songs do not take the place of the psalms. The resurrection of the Lord is proclaimed from the **Gospel** as the high point of the whole Liturgy of the Word. After the gospel, a **homily** is to be given, no matter how brief.

LITURGY OF BAPTISM

In the baptismal liturgy, Christ's resurrection and ours is celebrated. This is given full expression when the **Christian initiation** of adults is held or at least the baptism of infants. Through the sprinkling with blessed water and the **renewal of baptismal vows**, the faithful recall the baptism they have received.

LITURGY OF THE EUCHARIST

MASS Proper. Gloria. No Creed. Preface: Easter I. Proper forms in Roman Canon. This most solemn and joyful celebration fulfils the Sunday obligation. Priests who celebrate or concelebrate the Mass at night may celebrate or concelebrate the second Mass of Easter Sunday.

The celebration of the **Eucharist** is in the fullest sense the Easter Sacrament, that is to say, the commemoration of the sacrifice of the Cross and the presence of the Risen Christ, the completion of Christian initiation, and the foretaste of the eternal pasch. Great care must be taken that it is not celebrated in haste; all the rites and words must be given their full force. It is fitting that in the Communion of the Easter Vigil full expression be given to the symbolism of the Eucharist, namely, by consuming the Eucharist under the species of both bread and wine.

EASTER SUNDAY: THE RESURRECTION OF THE LORD
THE EASTER VIGIL READINGS

I Genesis 1:1-2:2 (shorter form 1:1, 26-31). *About creation. Lect* I:399
Psalm 103 *or* 32
God saw all that he had made, and indeed it was very good.
The understanding of baptism as our new creation in the image of God makes this first reading appropriate on this night. This is a proclamation to the catechumens and the already baptised of God's creative work at all times.
II Genesis 22:1-18 (shorter form 1-2, 9-13, 15-18). *About Abraham's sacrifice.*
Lect I:403
Psalm 15
The sacrifice of Abraham, our father in faith.
The Isaac story has been seen by Christians from the beginning as a type of Christ's sacrifice. The carrying of the wood represents the Cross, and his reprieve from death is seen as a kind of resurrection.
III Exodus 14:15-15:1. *About the passage through the Sea. Lect* I:405
Psalm from **Exodus 15**
The Israelites went on dry ground right through the sea.
This is the most important reading of the night. The crossing of the sea is the type of Christ's death and resurrection, and of the Christian's journey in baptism through dying and rising with Christ.
IV Isaiah 54:5-14. *About the new Jerusalem. Lect* I:407
Psalm 29
With everlasting love I will have compassion on you, says the Lord, your Redeemer.
This passage in which Deutero-Isaiah speaks of the return from exile, has several pictures. In the exodus God had taken Israel as a bride; in the exile he had rejected her, but only for a moment; in his compassion he brings her back. Christ's compassion for his Church is seen in his death and resurrection. The new kingdom is rebuilt with precious stones, the Church shines forth in splendour.
V Isaiah 55:1-11. *About salvation freely offered to all. Lect* I:408
Psalm from **Isaiah 12**
Incline your ear, and come to me; listen, so that you may live. I will make with you an everlasting covenant.
The Easter Eucharist this night is a foretaste of the eschatological banquet to which all are invited, and to which all Lenten preparation has been directed. This is why God's word has gone out and has not returned empty.
VI Baruch 3:9-15, 32-4:4. *About the fountain of wisdom. Lect* I:410
Psalm 18
Walk towards the shining of her light.
The images of Egyptian captivity and Babylonian exile are used tonight to speak to us of alienation from God. We are called to return to him from the land of our enemies, to enter into the full life of the Church.
VII Ezekiel 36:16-28. *About a new heart and a new spirit. Lect* I:412
Psalm 41 (or if Baptism takes place, Psalm from **Isaiah 12 *or* Psalm 50)**
I shall pour clean water over you and you will be cleansed; I shall give you a new heart, and put a new spirit in you.
Exile was a punishment for Israel's sin; return demands purification, new heart, new spirit. This is achieved for the Christian through baptism, in which new birth and a new spirit is achieved through Christ's death and resurrection.
VIII Romans 6:3-11. *About the new life through baptism. Lect* I:414 **Psalm 117**
This reading prepares us for the celebration and renewal of baptismal vows. In union with Christ we imitate his death and rising. We go from death to life, from darkness to light, from captivity to freedom, from the old way of life to the new.
Alleluia, alleluia, alleluia!
IX Matthew 28:1-10. *He has risen from the dead and now he is going before you into Galilee. Lect* I:415

(Taken from *In the Light of Christ: The Old Testament Readings for the Easter Vigil.* Commentaries by Brian Magee CM, Anne F. Kelly, Andrew McGrady, Anne Looney and Donal Neary SJ, Veritas, 1994).

THE EASTER SEASON

9 Sunday   **EASTER DAY OF THE LORD'S RESURRECTION**
Solemnity with Octave

White ✠   HOURS Proper. The Office of Readings is omitted by those who have attended the Easter Vigil. If celebrated – Te Deum.
MASS on Easter Day. Proper. Gloria. Sequence. Creed.
Preface: Easter I. In the Roman Canon, proper forms

READINGS   **Acts 10:34, 37-43. Ps 117:1-2, 16-17, 22-23, R/ v 24. Col 3:1-4 or 1 Cor 5:6-8. Jn 20:1-9.** Lect I:417

The gospel from the Easter Vigil, **Matthew 28:1-10.** *Lect I:415 may be used at the Day Mass as an alternative.*

'Christ is risen, alleluia!' This is the ancient Christian greeting on this day of great joy and happiness for all. 'Easter is not simply one feast among others, but the "Feast of feasts". The mystery of the resurrection, in which Christ crushed death, permeates with its powerful energy our old time, until all is subjected to him' (CCC, 1169).

Evening Mass: Gospel: **Lk 24:13-35.** *Lect I:428 may be used as an alternative.*

The penitential rite may take the form of sprinkling with water blessed at the Vigil. The Rite of Renewal of Baptismal Promises is desirable after the homily.

It is fitting that EVENING PRAYER should be celebrated in a more solemn manner to mark the close of the Easter Triduum and to commemorate the apparitions in which our Lord showed himself to his disciples (*GILH*, 213).

Night Prayer 1 or 2 of Sunday is used at choice throughout the Octave.

No other celebrations, not even funeral Masses, are permitted today (see Lit. Note 8)

Clonfert Today is the anniversary of the episcopal ordination of Most Rev. John Kirby, 9 April 1988.

EASTER TIME

The celebration of Easter is prolonged throughout the Easter season. The fifty days from Easter Sunday to Pentecost Sunday are celebrated as one feast day, the 'great Sunday'.

The Sundays of this season are regarded as Sundays of Easter and are so termed; they have precedence over all feasts of the Lord and over all solemnities. Solemnities that fall on one of these Sundays are anticipated on the Saturday. Celebrations in honour of the Blessed Virgin Mary or the saints that fall during the week may not be transferred to one of these Sundays.

For adults who have received Christian initiation during the Easter Vigil, the whole of this period is given over to mystagogical catechesis. Therefore, wherever there are neophytes, the prescriptions of the *Rite of Christian Initiation of Adults* should be observed. Intercession should be made in the Eucharistic Prayer for the newly baptised through the Easter octave in all places.

Throughout the Easter season, the neophytes should be assigned their own special place among the faithful. All neophytes should endeavour to participate at Mass along with their godparents. In the homily and, according to local circumstances, in the General Intercessions, mention should be made of them. Some celebration should be held to conclude the period of mystagogical catechesis on or about Pentecost Sunday, depending upon local custom. It is also appropriate that children receive their first Communion on one or other of the Sundays of Easter.

During Easter time, pastors should instruct the faithful who have been already initiated into the Eucharist on the meaning of the Church's precept concerning the reception of Holy Communion during this period. It is highly recommended that Communion also be brought to the sick, especially during the Easter octave.

Where there is the custom of blessing houses in celebration of the resurrection, this blessing is to be imparted after the Solemnity of Easter and not before, by the parish priest or other priest or deacon delegated by him. This is an opportunity for exercising a pastoral ministry. The parish priest should go to each house for the purpose of undertaking a pastoral visitation of each family. There, he will speak with the residents and spend a few moments with them in prayer, using texts to be found in the Book of Blessings. In larger cities, consideration should be given to the gathering of several families for a common celebration of the blessing for all.

According to the differing circumstances of places and peoples, there are found a number of popular practices linked to celebrations of the Easter season, which in some instances attract greater numbers of the people than the sacred liturgy itself. These practices are not in any way to be undervalued, for they are often well adapted to the religious mentality of the faithful. Let episcopal conferences and local ordinaries, therefore, see to it that practices of this kind, which seem to nourish popular piety, be harmonised in the best way possible with the sacred liturgy, be imbued more distinctly with the spirit of the liturgy, be in some way derived from it, and lead the people to it.

This sacred period of fifty days concludes with Pentecost Sunday, when the gift of the Holy Spirit to the apostles, the beginnings of the Church, and the start of its mission to all tongues and peoples and nations are commemorated.

Encouragement should be given to the prolonged celebration of Mass in the form of a Vigil, whose character is not baptismal as in the Easter Vigil, but is one of urgent prayer, after the example of the apostles and disciples, who persevered together in prayer with Mary, the Mother of Jesus, as they awaited the Holy Spirit.

'It is proper to the paschal festivity that the whole Church rejoices at the forgiveness of sins, which is not only for those who are reborn in holy baptism, but also for those who have long been numbered among the adopted children' (St Leo the Great). By means of a more intensive pastoral care and a deeper spiritual effort, all who celebrate the Easter feasts will, by the Lord's grace, experience their effect in their daily lives.

Congregation for Divine Worship, *Paschale solemnitatis*,
letter on the preparation and celebration of the Easter feasts, 100–8

---

10 Monday	**EASTER MONDAY**
White	HOURS Proper. Te Deum
	MASS Proper. Gloria. Preface: Easter 1. Sequence optional. In the Roman Canon, proper forms
READINGS	**Acts 2:14, 22-33. Ps 15:1-2, 5, 7-11, R/ v 1. Mt 28:8-15.** *Lect* I:423

The women clasp the feet of the real body of the risen Lord who is thus identified with the earthly Jesus. But they are not to cling on in signs of love. His appearances are for the purpose of sending them on mission, to tell others.

No other celebrations, except funeral Masses, are permitted today (see Lit. Note 8)

Ardagh and Clonmacnois Today is the anniversary of the episcopal ordination of Most Rev. Colm O'Reilly, 10 April 1983.

---

11 Tuesday   **EASTER TUESDAY**
White   HOURS Proper. Te Deum
                        MASS Proper. Gloria. Preface: Easter 1. Sequence optional. In
                        the Roman Canon, proper forms
READINGS   **Acts 2:36-41. Ps 32:4-5, 18-20, 22, R/ v 5. Jn 20:11-
                        18.** *Lect* I:425

Mary Magdalene is told that the old relationship is now changed, she is not to
cling on, for Jesus has to return to the Father, to fulfil what he had been sent to
do.
No other celebrations, except funeral Masses, are permitted today (see Lit. Note 8)
St Stanislaus, bishop and martyr is not celebrated this year.

---

12 Wednesday EASTER WEDNESDAY
White   HOURS Proper. Te Deum
                        MASS Proper. Gloria. Preface: Easter 1. Sequence optional. In
                        the Roman Canon, proper forms
READINGS   **Acts 3:1-10. Ps 104:1-4, 6-9, R/ v 3. Lk 24:13-35.**
                        Lect I:427

Two disillusioned followers who cannot understand are met by someone who
opens their minds and hearts by showing how God's word can give meaning to
their lives. Invited to share their table, he takes bread, blesses it, breaks it and
gives it to them, and they know the Lord Jesus in that fourfold action. With joy they
go back to tell the good news.
No other celebrations, except funeral Masses, are permitted today (see Lit. Note 8)
Waterford and Lismore Today is the anniversary of the episcopal ordination
of Most Rev. Alphonsus Cullinan, 12 April 2015.

---

13 Thursday   **EASTER THURSDAY**
White   HOURS Proper. Te Deum
                        MASS Proper. Gloria. Preface: Easter I. Sequence optional. In
                        the Roman Canon, proper forms
READINGS   **Acts 3:11-26. Ps 8:2, 5-9, R/ v 2. Lk 24:35-48.** *Lect*
                        I:430

'Immediately they touched him, and through this contact with his flesh and spirit,
they believed' (Ignatius of Antioch). And Jesus, though in his risen body he did not
need food, shows them the courtesy of sharing their food.
No other celebrations, except funeral Masses, are permitted today (see Lit. Note 8)
St Martin I, pope and martyr is not celebrated this year.

14 Friday
White

EASTER FRIDAY
HOURS Proper. Te Deum
MASS Proper. Gloria. Preface: Easter 1. Sequence optional. In the Roman Canon, proper forms

READINGS **Acts 4:1-12. Ps 117:1-2, 4, 22-27, R/ v 22. Jn 21:1-14.** Lect I:432

The appearance at the lakeside – perhaps on a Sunday morning after a Sabbath rest from work – has echoes of the meals that Jesus shared during his earthly life. It recalls the sign of the Eucharist in the multiplication of the loaves and fishes.
No other celebrations, except funeral Masses, are permitted today (see Lit. Note 8)
Limerick Today is the anniversary of the episcopal ordination of Most Rev. Brendan Leahy, 14 April 2013.

---

15 Saturday
White

EASTER SATURDAY
HOURS Proper. Te Deum
MASS Proper. Gloria. Preface: Easter 1. Sequence optional. In the Roman Canon, proper forms

READINGS **Acts 4:13-21. Ps 117:1, 14-21, R/ v 21. Mk 16:9-15.** Lect I:435

The news of the resurrection brings belief or incredulity. Jesus has to reproach his disciples for being so slow to believe. They are to go out with the good news, and the response to their preaching will be again belief or unbelief. Only those who believe will be saved.
No other celebrations, except funeral Masses, are permitted today (see Lit. Note 8)

Active participation

'Filled as We are with a most ardent desire to see the true Christian spirit flourish in every respect and be preserved by all the faithful, we deem it necessary to provide before anything else for the sanctity and dignity of the temple, in which the faithful assemble for no other object than that of acquiring this spirit from its foremost and indispensable font, which is the active participation [partecipazione attiva] in the most holy mysteries and in the public and solemn prayer of the Church.'

Pope Pius X, *Tra le sollecitudini*
(*Motu proprio* on Sacred Music, 22 November 1903)

APRIL 2023

16 Sunday	**SECOND SUNDAY OF EASTER**
	Divine Mercy Sunday
White ✠	HOURS Proper. Te Deum
	MASS Proper. Gloria. Creed. Preface: Easter I. In the Roman Canon, proper forms
READINGS	**Acts 2:42-47. Ps 117:2-4, 13-15, 22-24, R/ v 1. 1 Pt 1:3-9. Jn 20:19-31.** Lect I:438

The struggle for faith experienced by Thomas leads us to think on the meaning of faith in the risen Christ. We do not depend on physical experience of Christ but know his presence in keeping God's commandments and as a gathered community, in the hearing of the word and in sacramental signs. So the Christian community is a thankful one, always blessing God for a sure hope through the resurrection of Christ.

No other celebrations, not even funeral Masses, are permitted today (see Lit. Note 8)

---

17 Monday	**2nd Week of Easter**
White	HOURS Psalter Week 2
	MASS Proper. Preface: Easter I–V
READINGS	**Acts 4:23-31. Ps 2:1-9, R/ cf. v 13. Jn 3:1-8.** Lect I:447

Jesus is the light. That light led Nicodemus to faith in Jesus as more than a wonder-worker and teacher of the law. Enlightened by Christ the disciples prayed, and were all filled with the Holy Spirit and began to proclaim the word of God boldly.

---

18 Tuesday	**2nd Week of Easter**
White	HOURS Psalter Week 2
	MASS Proper. Preface: Easter I–V
White	Optional memorial of **St Laserian, bishop**
Leighlin	**St Laserian, bishop** Feast
READINGS	**Acts 4:32-37. Ps 91:1-2, 5, R/ v 1. Jn 3:7-15.** Lect I:449

Jesus is the perfect revealer of God whose revelation reaches its climax in his exaltation on the cross. Faith is an active response to Jesus.

St Laserian, see *The Irish Calendar*, p. 186.

Limerick Today is the anniversary of the episcopal ordination of Most Rev. Donal Murray, 18 April 1982.

---

19 Wednesday 2nd Week of Easter
White   HOURS Psalter Week 2
           MASS Proper. Preface: Easter I–V
READINGS   **Acts 5:17-26. Ps 33:2-9, R/ v 7. Jn 3:16-21.** *Lect* I:452
God's love calls for a response of faith in Jesus. This faith results in making the truth part of one's living. To refuse faith is to be self-condemned.

---

20 Thursday   2nd Week of Easter
White   HOURS Psalter Week 2
           MASS Proper. Preface: Easter I–V
READINGS   **Acts 5:27-33. Ps 33:2, 9, 17-20, R/ v 7. Jn 3:31-36.**
           Lect I:454
St Peter speaking before the officials says clearly that the apostles are the authentic witnesses to the events which are God's Spirit at work.

---

21 Friday   2nd Week of Easter
White   HOURS Psalter Week 2
           MASS Proper. Preface: Easter I–V
White   Optional memorial of **St Anselm, bishop and doctor of the Church**
READINGS   **Acts 5:34-42. Ps 26:1, 4, 13-14, R/ v cf. v 4. Jn 6:1-15.** *Lect* I:456
Jesus communicates his life-giving power through his living word and the gift of his own life in the eucharistic bread.
St Anselm from Lombardy joined the monastic school at Bec in Normandy in 1059 under the direction of Lanfranc whom he succeeded as Archbishop of Canterbury. He was exiled twice and died in 1109.
Derry   **Dedication of the Cathedral** (see *Lit. Note 12*)
Armagh Today is the anniversary of the episcopal ordination of Most Rev. Eamon Martin, 21 April 2013.

---

22 Saturday   2nd Week of Easter
White   HOURS Psalter Week 2
           MASS Proper. Preface: Easter I–V
READINGS   **Acts 6:1-7. Ps 32:1-2, 4-5, 18-19, R/ v 22. Jn 6:16-21.** *Lect* I:459
The Church continues to grow and the apostles re-order the ministries to cope with different needs. The Spirit works in the Church, and brings peace.
Dublin Today is the anniversary of the episcopal ordination of Most Rev. Eamonn Walsh, 22 April 1990.

APRIL 2023

23 Sunday   THIRD SUNDAY OF EASTER
White ✠   HOURS Proper. Te Deum. Psalter Week 3
                 MASS Proper. Gloria. Creed. Preface: Easter I–V
READINGS   **Acts 2:14, 22-33. Ps 15:1-2, 5, 7-11, R/ v 11. 1 Pt 1:17-21. Lk 13-35.** *Lect* I:461

The gospel story contains a wealth of teaching on the meaning of the Eucharist as a celebration of the presence of the Risen Lord. Christ takes, blesses, breaks and gives the bread to his disciples and is known to them in the action. It is in the context of two or three gathered in his name that they come to faith. It is he who opens their minds and hearts explaining their doubts in the light of Sacred Scripture. And it is on the first day of the week, the Lord's Day, that the Lord of Days walks with them in the cool of the evening.

No other celebrations, not even funeral Masses, are permitted today (see Lit. Note 8)
St George, martyr and **St Adalbert of Prague, bishop and martyr** are not celebrated this year.
Ferns Today is the anniversary of the episcopal ordination of Most Rev. Denis Brennan, 23 April 1990.

---

24 Monday   3rd Week of Easter
White   HOURS Psalter Week 3
                 MASS Proper. Preface: Easter I–V
Red   Optional memorial of **St Fidelis of Sigmaringen, priest and martyr**
READINGS   **Acts 6:8-15. Ps 118:23-24, 26-27, 29-30, R/ v 1. Jn 6:22-29.** *Lect* I:472

Stephen, filled with grace and power, witnesses to Christ, becomes a threat to the synagogue and is arrested. Jesus tells the people to look beyond the bread they eat to the mystery, and to seek him in faith.
St Fidelis of Sigmaringen, 1578–1622, a Capuchin who preached to the Calvinists in Switzerland, where he was killed by a group of extremists.

---

25 Tuesday   ST MARK, EVANGELIST   Feast
Red   HOURS Proper. Te Deum. Psalter Week 3 at Day Hour
                  MASS Proper. Gloria. Preface: Apostles II
READINGS   **1 Pet 5:5-14. Ps 88:2-3, 6-7, 16-17, R/ cf. v 2. Mk 16:15-20.** *Lect* II:1005

St Mark was closely connected with the preaching of Ss Peter, Paul, and Barnabas. His Gospel was probably written at Rome when he was with Paul, and is traditionally viewed as representing St Peter's approach to the preaching of the good news. Later tradition has him as an interpreter for St Peter. His symbol is a winged lion.
No Masses for the dead, except funeral Masses, are permitted today (see Lit. Note 8)

---

26 Wednesday 3rd Week of Easter
White   HOURS Psalter Week 3
                 MASS Proper. Preface: Easter I–V
READINGS   **Acts 8:1-8. Ps 65, 1-7, R/ v 1. Jn 6:35-40.** *Lect* I:476
The persecution of the Church in Jerusalem under Saul sends the Christians to preach the good news elsewhere.

---

27 Thursday   **3rd Week of Easter**
White   HOURS Psalter Week 3
                  MASS Proper. Preface: Easter I–V
White   Optional memorial of **St Asicus, bishop**
Elphin   **St Asicus, bishop**   Feast
READINGS   **Acts 8:26-40. Ps 65:8-9, 16-17, 20, R/ v 1. Jn 6:44-51.** *Lect* I:479

The Ethiopian official was humble enough to ask to have the scriptures explained to him. Philip's opening up of the word of God brought the man to faith and baptism. We also ought to search the scriptures daily.
St Asicus, bishop see *The Irish Calendar*, p. 186.

---

28 Friday   **3rd Week of Easter**
White   HOURS Psalter Week 3
                 MASS Proper. Preface: Easter I–V
Red   Optional memorial of **St Peter Chanel, priest and martyr**
White   Optional memorial of **St Louis Marie Grignion de Montfort, priest**
READINGS   **Acts 9:1-20. Ps 116, R/ Mk 16:15. Jn 6:52-59.** *Lect* I:481

The conversion of St Paul comes through his meeting with the risen Lord on the Road to Damascus. It is the same risen Lord who gives himself to believers in the Eucharist in a personal communion. That communion is a pledge of an eternal communion with Jesus and the Father.
St Peter Chanel, 1803–41, is honoured as the first martyr of the Church in Oceania.
St Louis Marie Grignion de Montfort, 1673–1716, was a priest whose calling was to preach missions and to care for the sick and the poor. His writings concern Mary's role in the mystery of salvation. He strongly promoted the praying of the rosary.

---

29 Saturday   ST CATHERINE OF SIENA, VIRGIN AND DOCTOR OF THE CHURCH, PATRON OF EUROPE   .   Feast
White   HOURS Proper. Psalter Week 3 at Day Hour
                  MASS Proper. Gloria. Preface: Virgins and Religious
READINGS   **1 Jn 1:5-2:2. Ps 102:1-4, 8-9, 13-14, 17-18, R/ v 1. Mt 11:25-30.** *Lect* II:1009

St Catherine of Siena, 1347–80, humble and dauntless Dominican tertiary, who brought peace to her native Siena, to Italy, and to fourteenth-century Europe, spent all her energies on the Church, being able to achieve the pope's return from Avignon to Rome. She is remembered also as a mystic and reformer of religious life. Proclaimed doctor of the Church in 1970 and patron of Europe in 2000.
No Masses for the dead, except funeral Masses, are permitted today (see Lit. Note 8)
Cork and Ross Today is the anniversary of the episcopal ordination of Most Rev. John Buckley, 29 April 1984.
Derry Today is the anniversary of the episcopal ordination of Most Rev. Donal McKeown, 29 April 2001.
White   FIRST EVENING PRAYER of **Fourth Sunday of Easter**

APRIL/MAY 2023

30 Sunday   **FOURTH SUNDAY OF EASTER**
                 Day of Prayer for Vocations
White ✠   HOURS Proper. Te Deum. Psalter Week 4
                 MASS Proper Gloria. Creed. Preface: Easter I–V
READINGS   **Acts 2:14, 36-41. Ps 22:1-6, R/ v 1. 1 Pt 2:20-25. Jn
                 10:1-10.** *Lect* I:487

This is Good Shepherd Sunday, a day of special prayer for vocations to the work of service in the Church. There is the enduring command of Christ to his Church to go out and preach to all people. There is need for people of faith to respond to that command, people who are prepared to dedicate their lives to this work for the sake of the gospel.

No other celebrations, not even funeral Masses, are permitted today (see Lit. Note 8)

St Pius V, pope is not celebrated this year.

MAY 2023

1 Monday   **4th Week of Easter**
White   HOURS Psalter Week 4
                 MASS Proper. Preface: Easter I–V
White   Optional memorial of **St Joseph the Worker**
READINGS   **Acts 11:1-18. Pss 41:2-3, 42:3-4, R/ cf. Ps 41:3. Jn
                 10:11-18.** *Lect* I:496

'The Church is, accordingly, a sheepfold, the sole and necessary gateway to which is Christ. It is also the flock, of which God himself foretold that he would be the shepherd, and whose sheep, even though governed by human shepherds, are unfailingly nourished and led by Christ himself, the Good Shepherd, Prince of Shepherds, who gave his life for his sheep' (*Lumen Gentium*, 6).

**St Joseph the Worker: Gn 1:26-2:3 or Col 3:14-15, 17, 23-24. Ps
89:2-4, 12-14, 16, R/ v 17. Mt 13:54-58.** *Lect* II:1013

The feast, instituted by Pope Pius XII in 1955, proposes the example and intercession of St Joseph as worker and patron of workers. On this date many countries celebrate the dignity of human labour.

---

2 Tuesday   **4th Week of Easter**
                 St Athanasius, bishop and doctor of the Church
                                                                    Memorial
White   HOURS of the memorial. Psalter Week 4
                 MASS of the memorial. Preface: Easter I–V or of the Saint
READINGS   **Acts 11:19-26. Ps 86:1-7, R/ Ps 116:1. Jn 10:22-30.**
                 Lect I:499

At Antioch the good news is first preached to the pagans and the disciples are first called 'Christians'. Those who receive Jesus as their shepherd receive his protection and the gift of eternal life.

St Athanasius. Born at Alexandria around 295, he fought ceaselessly against the Arian heresy, defending the true and equal divinity of Christ. As a result, he had to endure much tribulation and he was several times sent into exile.

---

3 Wednesday SS PHILIP AND JAMES, APOSTLES Feast
Red HOURS Proper. Psalter Week 4 at Day Hour
MASS Proper. Gloria. Preface of the Apostles I–II
READINGS **1 Cor 15:1-8. Ps 18:2-5, R/ v 5. Jn 14:6-14.** *Lect* II:1017

St Philip asks to see and, having seen, he tells the good news to others. He was born at Bethsaida. Formerly a disciple of John the Baptist, he became a follower of Christ. **St James**, the son of Alphaeus and a cousin of the Lord, ruled the Church at Jerusalem, wrote an Epistle, and led a life of penance. He converted many of the people of Jerusalem to the faith and was martyred in the year 62.
No Masses for the dead, except funeral Masses, are permitted today (see Lit. Note 8)

---

4 Thursday **4th Week of Easter**
White HOURS Psalter Week 4
MASS Proper. Preface: Easter I–V
White Optional memorial of **St Conleth, bishop**
Kildare **St Conleth, bishop** Feast
READINGS **Acts 13:13-25. Ps 88:2-3, 21-22, 25, 27, R/ cf. v 2. Jn 13:16-20.** *Lect* I:503

Sharing in the life and dignity of Jesus means also sharing in his self-giving and humble service of others.
St Conleth see *The Irish Calendar,* p. 186.

---

5 Friday **4th Week of Easter**
White HOURS Psalter Week 4
MASS Proper. Preface: Easter I–V
White Optional memorial of **Bl. Edmund Rice, religious**
READINGS **Acts 13:26-33. Ps 2:6-11, R/ v 7. Jn 14:1-6.** *Lect* I:505

'I am the Way, the Truth and the Life.' Jesus encourages peace in our hearts in times of trouble. There remains for us a place of rest in his Father's house. Following him who is the Way, we come to the Father.
Bl. Edmund Rice see *The Irish Calendar,* p. 187.

---

6 Saturday **4th Week of Easter**
White HOURS Psalter Week 4
MASS Proper. Preface: Easter I–V
READINGS **Acts 13:44-52. Ps 97:1-4, R/ v 3. Jn 14:7-14.** *Lect* I:508

Prayer in the name of Jesus, animated by the Spirit, will lead us to think and desire as he does.

MAY 2023

7 Sunday **FIFTH SUNDAY OF EASTER**
White ✠ HOURS Proper. Te Deum. Psalter Week 1
MASS Proper Gloria. Creed. Preface: Easter I–V
READINGS **Acts 6:1-7. Ps 32:1-2, 4-5, 18-19, R/ v 22. 1 Pt 2:4-9. Jn 14:1-12.** *Lect* I:511

No one can come to the Father except through Christ. The Church must work so that all peoples may come to the Father. Working together in love, all God's people can build up the kingdom in the name of the Lord Jesus Christ, our High Priest.
No other celebrations, not even funeral Masses, are permitted today (see Lit. Note 8)

---

8 Monday **5th Week of Easter**
White HOURS Psalter Week 1
MASS Proper. Preface: Easter I–V
In some places Optional memorial of **Bl. John Sullivan, priest** (see Collect, p. 183)
READINGS **Acts 14:5-18. Ps 113B:1-4, 15-16, R/ v 1. Jn 14:21-26.** *Lect* I:519

The apostle Jude is puzzled and asks, 'What is this all about?' A very human and common question. It is then he is given the promise of the Advocate, the Holy Spirit, who will be the solver of problems, the one who answers our questions. This searching has to be done in love – to those who love, Christ will show himself.
Bl. John Sullivan see *The Irish Calendar*, p. 187.

---

9 Tuesday **5th Week of Easter**
White HOURS Psalter Week 1
MASS Proper. Preface: Easter I–V
READINGS **Acts 14:19-28. Ps 144:10-13, 21, R/ cf. v 12. Jn 14:27-31.** *Lect* I:522

'As witnesses of the Risen One, the apostles – and Peter in particular – remain the foundation stones of his Church' (CCC, 642).

---

10 Wednesday 5th Week of Easter
White HOURS Psalter Week 1
MASS Proper. Preface: Easter I–V
White Optional memorial of **St Comgall, abbot**
White Optional memorial of **St John of Ávila, priest and doctor of the Church**
READINGS **Acts 15:1-6. Ps 121:1-5, R/ cf. v 1. Jn 15:1-8.** *Lect* I:524

The apostles and teachers come together in search of unity of faith. The branches must remain part of the vine so that life will flow to them and they will bear fruit.
St Comgall see *The Irish Calendar*, p. 187.
St John of Ávila, 1499–1569. Priest, honoured as apostle of Andalusia, renowned for his preaching and his quest for the renewal of Christian life.

---

11 Thursday   **5th Week of Easter**
White   HOURS Psalter Week 1
   MASS Proper. Preface: Easter I–V
READINGS   **Acts 15:7-21. Ps 95:1-3, 10, R/ cf. v 3. Jn 15:9-11.**
   Lect I:526

Jesus loves his disciples with that same gift of love with which the Father loves him. Genuine love means attending to the needs and weaknesses of others.

---

12 Friday   **5th Week of Easter**
White   HOURS Psalter Week 1
   MASS Proper. Preface: Easter I–V
Red   Optional memorial of **Ss Nereus and Achilleus, martyrs**
Red   Optional memorial of **St Pancras, martyr**
READINGS   **Acts 15:22-31. Ps 56:8-12, R/ v 10. Jn 15:12-17.** *Lect* I:528

Jesus tells his disciples that the world will fail to understand them and so persecute them. The followers of Jesus will get the same treatment as he received. But they must have courage and go out with the good news to others.

Ss Nereus and Achilleus were martyred in 304 under Diocletian. They were Roman soldiers who, on conversion, refused further military service.

St Pancras as a boy of fourteen suffered at the same time and was martyred in Rome in 304.

---

13 Saturday   **5th Week of Easter**
White   HOURS Psalter Week 1
   MASS Proper. Preface: Easter I–V
White   Optional memorial of **Our Lady of Fatima**
READINGS   **Acts 16:1-10. Ps 99:1-3, 5, R/ v 1. Jn 15:18-21.** *Lect* I:531

The conflict between the believer and the world is part of the Christian's inheritance. The disciple cannot expect other than what his Master also received. It is better to be persecuted for doing right than simply to conform to the ways of the world.

Our Lady of Fatima: Is 61:9-11. Ps 44:11-12, 14-17, R/ v 11. Lk 11:27-28. *Lect* II:1431, 1426, 1448. The apparitions to the three children of Fatima took place in the summer of 1917, beginning on 13 May when the 'Lady' asked them to pray for sinners and an end to the World War. In the final apparition on 13 October, the 'Lady' identified herself as Our Lady of the Rosary and called for prayer and conversion.

MAY 2023

14 Sunday **SIXTH SUNDAY OF EASTER**
White ✠ HOURS Proper. Te Deum. Psalter Week 2
MASS Proper Gloria. Creed. Preface: Easter I–V
READINGS **Acts 8:5-8, 14-17. Ps 65:1-7, 16, 20, R/ v 1. 1 Pt 3:15-18. Jn 14:15-21.** *Lect* I:534.

Through baptism and confirmation we have been given the Holy Spirit, that same Spirit who gave Christ the victory over the world. This Advocate is our support in the difficulties of life. The Spirit of truth convinces us of the meaning and value of the Christian way.

The second reading and gospel of the Seventh Sunday of Easter may be used with the first reading and psalm of the Sixth Sunday (as above): **Acts 8:5-8, 14-17. Ps 65:1-7, 16, 20, R/ v 1.** *Lect* I:534. **1 Pt 4:13-16. Jn 17:1-11.** *Lect* 568
No other celebrations, not even funeral Masses, are permitted today (see Lit. Note 8)
St Matthias, apostle is not celebrated this year.

---

15 Monday **6th Week of Easter**
White HOURS Psalter Week 2
MASS Proper. Preface: Easter I–V
White Optional memorial of **St Carthage, bishop**
**Waterford
and Lismore** **St Carthage, bishop** Feast
READINGS **Acts 16:11-15. Ps 149:1-6, 9, R/ v 4. Jn 15:26-16:4.** *Lect* I:542

Jesus understands the fear of his disciples as they face the world. The Spirit of truth is with us to help us to speak up for our faith in the face of opposition, ridicule or indifference.
St Carthage see *The Irish Calendar*, p. 187.
Down and Connor Today is the anniversary of the episcopal ordination of Most Rev. Patrick Walsh and Most Rev. Anthony Farquhar, 15 May 1983.

---

16 Tuesday **6th Week of Easter**
White HOURS Psalter Week 2
MASS Proper. Preface: Easter I–V
White Optional memorial of **St Brendan, abbot**
Clonfert **St Brendan, abbot** Feast
Kerry **St Brendan, abbot** Feast
READINGS **Acts 16:22-34. Ps 137:1-3, 7-8, R/ v 7. Jn 16:5-11.** *Lect* I:544

'God is Love' and love is his first gift, containing all others. Because we are dead or at least wounded by sin, the first effect of the gift of love is the forgiveness of our sins. The communion of the Holy Spirit in the Church restores to the baptised the divine likeness lost through sin (CCC, 733–4).
St Brendan see *The Irish Calendar*, p. 187.

17 Wednesday 6th Week of Easter
White   HOURS Psalter Week 2

MASS Proper. Preface: Easter I–V

READINGS   **Acts 17:15, 22-18:1. Ps 148:1-2, 11-14. Jn 16:12-15.**
Lect I:546

St Paul preached to the citizens of Athens about their unknown God, but they preferred to think about it all at a later time. The Spirit continues with the Church, helping us to interpret the signs of the times. We must be always ready to listen.

---

18 Thursday   6th Week of Easter
HOURS Psalter Week 2

MASS Proper. Preface: Easter I–V

Red   Optional memorial of **St John I, pope and martyr**

READINGS   **Acts 18:1-8. Ps 97:1-4, R/ cf. v 2. Jn 16:16-20.** *Lect*
I:560

St Paul gives the example of missionary work, devoting all his time to preaching. As a result a great many Corinthians embrace the faith. 'Faith comes from hearing.'

St John I was the first Bishop of Rome to visit Constantinople. He was involved in Arian controversies and imprisoned at Ravenna, where he died in 526.

---

19 Friday   6th Week of Easter
White   HOURS Psalter Week 2

MASS Proper. Preface: Easter I–V

READINGS   **Acts 18:9-18. Ps 46:2-7, R/ v 8. Jn 16:20-23.** *Lect*
I:562

'On the day of Pentecost when the seven weeks of Easter had come to an end, Christ's Passover is fulfilled in the outpouring of the Holy Spirit, manifested, given and communicated as a divine person: of his fullness, Christ, the Lord, pours out the Spirit in abundance' (CCC, 731).

Ardagh and Clonmacnois   **Dedication of the Cathedral** (see *Lit. Note 12*)

---

20 Saturday   6th Week of Easter
White   HOURS Psalter Week 2

MASS Proper. Preface: Easter I–V

White   Optional memorial of **St Bernardine of Siena, priest**

READINGS   **Acts 18:23-28. Ps 46:2-3, 8-10, R/ v 8. Jn 16:23-28.**
Lect I:564

The conflict between the believer and the world is part of the Christian's inheritance. The disciple cannot expect other than what his Master also received. It is better to be persecuted for doing right than simply to conform to the ways of the world.

St Bernardine, born 1380. As a young man he took charge of a hospital in Siena during a plague. Then he became a Franciscan, travelled through Italy, preaching with great success. He promoted devotion to the Holy Name and to St Joseph. He died in 1444.

FIRST EVENING PRAYER of the **Ascension**

MAY 2023

21 Sunday   **THE ASCENSION OF THE LORD**   Solemnity
World Communications Day
White ✠   HOURS Proper. Te Deum.
MASS Proper. Gloria. Creed. Preface: Ascension I–II. In the
Roman Canon, proper form
READINGS   **Acts 1:1-11. Ps 46:2-3, 6-9, R/ v 6. Eph 1:17-23. Mt
28:16-20.** *Lect* I:549

'**The Ascension of Christ** means our own salvation as well; where the glorious
Head has gone before, the body is called to follow in hope. Let us therefore exult,
beloved, as is fitting, and let us rejoice in devout thanksgiving. For on this day not
only have we been confirmed in our possession of paradise, but we have even
entered heaven in the person of Christ; through his grace we have regained far
more than we had lost through the devil's hatred' (St Leo the Great, Sermon 73:4).
No other celebrations, not even funeral Masses, are permitted today (see Lit. Note 8)
The week of prayer for the coming of the Holy Spirit recalls the waiting in prayer
of the disciples with Mary.
Ss Christopher Magallánes, priest and Companions, martyrs are not
celebrated this year.

---

22 Monday   **7th Week of Easter**
White   HOURS Psalter Week 3
MASS Proper. Preface: Easter I–V/Ascension I–II
White   Optional memorial of **St Rita of Cascia, religious**
READINGS   **Acts 19:1-8. Ps 67:2-7, R/ v 33. Jn 16:29-33.** *Lect*
I:576

Jesus understands the fear of his disciples as they face the world. The Spirit of
truth is with us to help speak up for our faith in the face of opposition, ridicule or
indifference.
St Rita of Cascia, 1386–1457, was married for eighteen years. Her husband,
an ill-tempered and abusive man, was murdered. Later Rita entered the
Augustinian convent in Cascia and spent forty years in prayer and charity, and
working for peace in the region.

---

23 Tuesday   **7th Week of Easter**
White   HOURS Psalter Week 3
MASS Proper. Preface: Easter I–V/Ascension I–II
READINGS   **Acts 20:17-27. Ps 67:10-11, 20-21, R/ v 33. Jn 17:1-
11.** *Lect* I:578

'Through the Holy Spirit we are restored to paradise, led back to the kingdom of
heaven and adopted as children, given confidence to call God 'Father' and to
share in Christ's grace, called children of light and given a share in eternal glory'
(St Basil).

---

24 Wednesday 7th Week of Easter
World Day of Prayer for the Church in China

White   HOURS Psalter Week 3

MASS Proper. Preface: Easter I–V/Ascension I–II

READINGS **Acts 20:28-38. Ps 67:29-30, 33-36, R/ v 33. Jn 17:11-19.** *Lect* I:580

St Paul warns the Ephesians to be on their guard against the false teachers.

In a Letter written to the faithful of the Catholic Church in China in May 2007, Pope Benedict XVI expressed the hope that today, the memorial of Our Lady Help of Christians who is venerated with such devotion at the Marian shrine of Sheshan in Shanghai, would become a day of prayer for the Church in China.

Our Lady of Sheshan, sustain all those in China,
who, amid their daily trails, continue to believe, to hope, to love.
May they never be afraid to speak of Jesus to the world,
and of the world to Jesus.
In the statue overlooking the Shrine you lift your Son on high,
offering him to the world with open arms in a gesture of love.
Help Catholics always to be credible witnesses to this love,
ever clinging to the rock of Peter on which the Church is built.
Mother of China and all Asia, pray for us, now and for ever. Amen!
          from the prayer written by Pope Benedict XVI

---

25 Thursday   7th Week of Easter

White   HOURS Psalter Week 3

MASS Proper. Preface: Easter I–V/Ascension I–II

White   Optional memorial of **St Bede the Venerable, priest and doctor of the Church**

White   Optional memorial of **St Gregory VII, pope**

White   Optional memorial of **St Mary Magdalene de' Pazzi, virgin**

READINGS **Acts 22:30, 23:6-11. Ps 15:1-2, 5, 7-11, R/ v 1. Jn 17:20-26.** *Lect* I:583

Jesus prays for the gift of unity among his followers – a unity that will mirror the unity of the Trinity.

St Bede, 673–735, monk of Jarrow, historian and biblical commentator. Patron of scholars.

St Gregory VII, c. 1025–1085, Hildebrand of Tuscany was a Cluniac monk in Rome who, on becoming pope, worked for reform and died in exile at Salerno.

St Mary Magdalene de' Pazzi, 1566–1607, a Carmelite in Florence, offered her life for the spiritual renewal of the Church.

---

26 Friday   **7th Week of Easter**
                    St Philip Neri, priest   Memorial
White   HOURS of the memorial. Psalter Week 3
                    MASS of the memorial. Preface: Easter I–V/Ascension I–II or of
                    the Saint
READINGS   **Acts 25:13-21. Ps 102:1-2, 11-12, 19-20, R/ v 19. Jn
                    21:15-19.** Lect I:585

Paul is now on his way to Rome to meet his death there. Jesus foretells Peter's last
days which will also be in Rome.
St Philip Neri, 1515–1595, founded the Congregation of the Oratory to foster
good preaching and to promote holiness of priestly life.

---

27 Saturday   **7th Week of Easter**
White   HOURS Psalter Week 3
                    MASS Proper. Preface: Easter I–V/Ascension I–II
White   Optional memorial of **St Augustine of Canterbury, bishop**
READINGS   **Acts 28:16-20, 30-31. Ps 10:4-5, 7, R/ cf. v 7. Jn
                    21:20-25.** Lect I:588

St Paul teaches the truth about Jesus until the end. St John's Gospel reminds us at
the end that much more happened and was said than is written in the books.
St Augustine of Canterbury was a monk in Rome when sent by Pope
Gregory the Great to preach to the English. He set up his see at Canterbury and
had much success in converting the south of England.

---

27 Saturday   **SOLEMNITY OF PENTECOST**
The Fifty Days of Easter conclude with the celebration of Pentecost Sunday.
Red ✠   EVENING MASS of the Vigil. Proper. Gloria. Creed
                    Preface: Pentecost. In the Roman Canon, proper form
READINGS   **Gn 11:1-9 or Ex 19:3-8, 16-20 or Ez 37:1-14 or Jl
                    3:1-5. Ps 103:1-2, 24, 27-30, 35, R/ cf. v 30. Rm
                    8:22-27. Jn 7:37-39.** Lect I:596
                    FIRST EVENING PRAYER: Proper
                    Night Prayer 1 of Sunday
*It is appropriate to celebrate the Vigil with an extended Liturgy of the Word at the
Evening Mass, using the readings above with the addition of Responsorial Psalms
and Prayers after the Readings as in RM, pp. 315–18.*

28 Sunday   **PENTECOST SUNDAY**
Red ✠   HOURS Proper. Te Deum
     MASS Proper Gloria. Sequence. Creed. Preface: Pentecost. In
     the Roman Canon, proper forms

READINGS   **Acts 2:1-11. Ps 103:1, 24, 29-31, 34, R/ cf. v 30. 1
Cor 12:3-7, 12-13. Jn 20:19-23.** Lect I:601
     EVENING PRAYER of Pentecost

'The Church was made manifest to the world on the day of Pentecost by the
outpouring of the Holy Spirit. The gift of the Spirit ushers in a new era in the
dispensation of the mystery – the age of the Church, during which Christ manifests,
makes present and communicates his work of salvation through the liturgy of his
Church "until he comes"' (CCC, 1076).

No other celebrations, not even funeral Masses, are permitted today (see Lit. Note 8)
St Boniface, bishop and martyr is not celebrated this year.

*At the end of the Easter season, the Paschal Candle should be kept in the
baptistery. It is lit during baptisms and from it the candles of the newly baptised
are lighted. At funerals the Easter Candle should be placed near the coffin, to
signify that Christian death is a true Passover.*

Ars Celebrandi

The priest lives his characteristic participation in the celebration in virtue of the gift
received in the sacrament of Holy Orders, and this is expressed precisely in
presiding. Like all the roles he is called to carry out, this is not primarily a duty
assigned to him by the community but is rather a consequence of the outpouring
of the Holy Spirit received in ordination which equips him for such a task. The
priest also is formed by his presiding in the celebrating assembly.

For this service to be well done – indeed, with art! – it is of fundamental
importance that the priest have a keen awareness of being, through God's mercy,
a particular presence of the risen Lord. The ordained minister is himself one of the
types of presence of the Lord which render the Christian assembly unique, different
from any other assembly. (cf. SC, 7) This fact gives 'sacramental' weight (in the
broad sense) to all the gestures and words of the one presiding. The assembly has
the right to be able to feel in those gestures and words the desire that the Lord has,
today as at the Last Supper, to eat the Passover with us. So, the risen Lord is in the
leading role, and not our own immaturities, assuming roles and behaviours which
are simply not appropriate. The priest himself should be overpowered by this desire
for communion that the Lord has toward each person. It is as if he were placed in
the middle between Jesus' burning heart of love and the heart of each of the
faithful, which is the object of the Lord's love. To preside at Eucharist is to be
plunged into the furnace of God's love. When we are given to understand this
reality, or even just to intuit something of it, we certainly would no longer need a
Directory that would impose the proper behaviour. If we have need of that, then it
is because *of the hardness of our hearts*. The highest norm, and therefore the most
demanding, is the reality itself of the eucharistic celebration, which selects words,
gestures, feelings that will make us understand whether or not our use of these are
at the level of the reality they serve. It is obvious that this cannot be improvised. It is
an art. It requires application on the part of the priest, an assiduous tending to the
fire of the love of the Lord that he came to ignite on the earth. (Lk 12:49)

Pope Francis, *Desiderio Desideravi*, 56–57

ORDINARY TIME

Ordinary Time resumes this year with Week 8

READINGS Sunday Cycle A/Weekday Cycle 1   Psalter Week 4

Volume III of the Divine Office is used from today

29 Monday   **8th Week in Ordinary Time**
               The Blessed Virgin Mary, Mother of the Church
                                                    Memorial
White   HOURS of the memorial. Psalter Week 4
               MASS *RM*, Votive Mass 10B, p. 1252. Preface: Blessed Virgin
               Mary. (Collect see p. 181)
READINGS   **Gn 3:9-15, 20.** *Lect* II:1421 **or Acts 1:12-14.** *Lect* II:1434.
               Ps 87:1-2, 3, 5, 6-7, R/ v 3. Jn 19:25-34. (Gospel from
               St John's Passion: *Lect* I:397 beginning '*Near the cross of Jesus
               stood his mother*', ending I:398 '*and immediately there came
               out blood and water*'; cf. *Lect* II:1449)

Mary, Mother of the Church. From the cross Jesus entrusted Mary to his
disciples as their mother and entrusted his disciples to Mary as her children. Mary,
present with the disciples at Pentecost, prayed with them as the Holy Spirit
descended. Mary has never ceased to take motherly care of the pilgrim Church on
earth.

St Paul VI, pope is not celebrated this year.

---

30 Tuesday   **8th Week in Ordinary Time**
Green   HOURS Psalter Week 4. MASS of choice
READINGS   **Eccles (Sir) 35:1-12. Ps 49:5-8, 14, 23, R/ v 23. Mk
               10:28-31.** *Lect* II:96

Generosity in the service of the Lord is rewarded. Token sacrifices are not enough,
there has to be a complete giving, with cheerful heart. Leaving everything to
follow Christ brings its own reward.

---

31 Wednesday THE VISITATION OF THE BLESSED VIRGIN MARY   Feast
White   HOURS Proper. Te Deum. Psalter Week 4 at Day Hour
               MASS Proper. Gloria. Preface: BVM I–II
READINGS   **Zeph 3:14-18 or Rm 12:9-16. Ps Is 12:2-6, R/ v 6. Lk
               1:39-56.** *Lect* II:1040

The Visitation of the Blessed Virgin Mary. Today's liturgy recalls the
'Blessed Virgin Mary carrying her Son within her' and visiting Elizabeth to offer
charitable assistance and to proclaim the mercy of God the Saviour (*Marialis
Cultus*).
No Masses for the dead, except funeral Masses, are permitted today (see Lit. Note 8)

---

1 Thursday   **8th Week in Ordinary Time**
               St Justin, martyr   Memorial
Red   HOURS of the memorial. Psalter Week 3
               MASS of the memorial. Preface: Common or of the Saint
READINGS   **Eccles (Sir) 42:15-25. Ps 32:2-9, R/ v 6. Mk 10:46-52.** *Lect* II:100

The words spoken in the account of the cure of the blind man, Bartimaeus, are prayers and reflections for our own needs and expressions of faith.

St Justin was born in the Holy Land and settled in Rome. He became a Christian and is remembered for his defence of Christian belief and practice. He was martyred c. 165.

---

2 Friday   **8th Week in Ordinary Time**
Green   HOURS Psalter Week 4. MASS of choice
Red   Optional memorial of **Ss Marcellinus and Peter, martyrs**
READINGS   **Eccles (Sir) 44:1, 9-13. Ps 149:1-6, 9, R/ v 4. Mk 11:11-26.** *Lect* II:103

Praise is due for our ancestors in the faith in whom the Lord takes delight. The Church cherishes the memory of the holy men and women whose generosity in the service of Christ has enriched us.

Ss Marcellinus and Peter, Roman clergy, martyred under Diocletian in 304.

---

3 Saturday **8th Week in Ordinary Time**
               St Kevin, abbot   Memorial
Dublin   **St Kevin, abbot**   Feast
White   HOURS of the memorial. Psalter Week 3
               MASS of the memorial. Preface: Common or the Saint
READINGS   **Eccles (Sir) 51:12-20. Ps 18:8-11, R/ v 9. Mk 11:27-33.** *Lect* II:105

True wisdom is to be found in keeping the law of God. Searching for the will of God is an occupation for a lifetime.

St Kevin, see *The Irish Calendar*, p. 187.

White   FIRST EVENING PRAYER of **Trinity Sunday**

JUNE 2023

4 Sunday   **THE MOST HOLY TRINITY**   Solemnity
White ✠   HOURS Proper (Vol III p.7). Te Deum
    Psalter Week 1 at Day Hour
    MASS Proper (*RM* p. 361). Gloria. Creed. Preface: Trinity
READINGS   **Ex 34:4-6, 8-9. Ps Dn 3:52-56, R/ v 52. 2 Cor 13:11-13. Jn 3:16-18.** *Lect* I:611

The relationships in the **Holy Trinity** are relationships of love. The reflection on this mystery today is not in terms of philosophy but of Christian living. The unity and harmony of the life in the Trinity is to be the aim of each community. Where love is, there God is. God's revelation of this inner life is for our salvation – a gift given in love. Our response can only be one of glory and praise.

'In the Church one God is preached, who is "above all things and through all things and in all things". Yes, certainly, "above all things" as the Father, the first principle and origin; and truly "through all things", that is through the Word, and finally "in all things" in the Holy Spirit' (St Athanasius in Office of Readings).

No other celebrations, not even funeral Masses, are permitted today (see Lit. Note 8)

Ss Charles Lwanga and Companions, martyrs are not celebrated this year.

---

5 Monday   **9th Week in Ordinary Time**
    St Boniface, bishop and martyr   Memorial
Red   HOURS of the memorial. Psalter Week 1
    MASS of the memorial. Preface: Common or of the Saint
READINGS   **Tob 1:3, 2:1-8. Ps 111:1-6, R/ v 1. Mk 12:1-12.** *Lect* II:107

Tobit is exiled at Nineveh with his tribe of Naphtali after the fall of Israel. The Book of Tobit calls for a renewal of faith at a difficult time for the people who fear that God has abandoned them. It stresses community and family solidarity in times of trouble, the maintenance of the purity of religious belief in the midst of pagan ways of life, the mediation of God through angels, and the importance of Israel for the salvation of other nations.

St Boniface, c. 675–754, was born at Crediton in Devonshire and educated in monastery schools in England. He went as a missionary to Germany. He founded monasteries in Bavaria, including Fulda in 735.

---

6 Tuesday   **9th Week in Ordinary Time**
Green   HOURS Psalter Week 1. MASS of choice
White   Optional memorial of **St Norbert, bishop**
White   Optional memorial of **St Jarlath, bishop**
Tuam   **St Jarlath, bishop**
READINGS   **Tob 2:9-14. Ps 111:1-2, 7-9, R/ cf. v 7. Mk 12:13-17.** *Lect* II:110

Tobit is blinded but does not blame God. He seeks always to be just and honest.

St Norbert, 1080–1134, Archbishop of Magdeburg, founder of the Norbertine Canons.

St Jarlath see *The Irish Calendar*, p. 187.

7 Wednesday   9th Week in Ordinary Time
Green   HOURS Psalter Week 1. MASS of choice
White   Optional memorial of **St Colman, bishop**
Dromore   **St Colman, bishop**   Feast
READINGS   **Tob 3:1-11, 16-17. Ps 24:2-9, R/ v 1. Mk 12:18-27.**
                   Lect II:112

Tobit gives an example of prayer in the home, and Sarah has recourse also to the Lord. Their prayer finds favour before the Lord.
St Colman see *The Irish Calendar*, p. 187.

---

8 Thursday   9th Week in Ordinary Time
Green   HOURS Psalter Week 1. MASS of choice
READINGS   **Tob 6:10-11, 7:1, 9-14, 8:4-9. Ps 127:1-5, R/ cf. v 1.**
                   Mk 12:28-34. *Lect* II:115

Tobias, Tobit's son, goes off to find a bride, guided by the angel Raphael. In Raguel's home he accepts Sarah as his bride. She had had seven husbands one after another killed by the demon, Asmodeus. They pray with the best of intentions for God's protection.

---

9 Friday   ST COLUMBA (COLUM CILLE), ABBOT AND MISSIONARY
                    SECONDARY PATRON OF IRELAND   Feast
White   HOURS Proper. (Divine Office, III p. 444*) Te Deum. Psalter
                    Week 1 at Day Hour
                    MASS Proper. Gloria. Preface: Proper
Derry   **St Columba, abbot and missionary**   Feast
Raphoe   **St Columba, abbot and missionary**   Feast
READINGS   **Rm 12:1-2, 9-13 or 2 Cor 5:14-21. Ps 33:2-3, 10-11,**
                    12-13, 14-15, R/ v 11. Mt 8:18-27 or Mt 19:27-29.
                    National Proper
No Masses for the dead, except funeral Masses, are permitted today (see Lit. Note 8)
St Columba (Colum Cille) see *The Irish Calendar*, p. 188.

---

10 Saturday   9th Week in Ordinary Time
Green   HOURS Psalter Week 1. MASS of choice
White   Optional memorial of **St Ephrem, deacon and doctor of
                   the Church** (see Collect, p. 180)
White/Green   Saturday Mass of the **Blessed Virgin Mary**
READINGS   **Tob 12:1, 5-15, 20. Ps Tob 13:2, 6-8, R/ v 1. Mk
                   12:38-44.** *Lect* II:121

Tobias has married without misfortune, returned home and cured his father's blindness. Raphael reveals who he is, and tells how prayer with fasting and almsgiving are always efficacious.
St Ephrem the Syrian, c. 306–373, was a native of Nisibis in Mesopotamia, and became a monk and deacon near Edessa in modern Turkey. He wrote commentaries on scripture and several hymns which were later included in the liturgy, he defended the faith against Arianism and encouraged devotion to Our Lady.
White   FIRST EVENING PRAYER of the **Body and Blood of Christ**

JUNE 2023

11 Sunday — THE MOST HOLY BODY AND BLOOD OF CHRIST

(Corpus Christi)   Solemnity

White ✠ | HOURS Proper. Te Deum. Psalter Week 1 at Day Hour

MASS Proper (RM p. 365). Gloria. Sequence optional. Creed
Preface: Eucharist I–II

READINGS **Deut 8:2-3, 14-16. Ps 147:12-15, 19-20, R/ v 12. 1 Cor 10:16-17. Jn 6:51-58.** *Lect* I:617

'From this feast of **Corpus Christi** have originated many practices of eucharistic devotion that, under the inspiration of divine grace, have increased from day to day and that the Catholic Church uses eagerly to show ever greater homage to Christ, to thank him for so great a gift and to implore his mercy' (Pope St Paul VI). *No other celebrations, not even funeral Masses, are permitted today (see Lit. Note 8)* **St Barnabas, apostle** is not celebrated this year.

---

12 Monday — 10th Week in Ordinary Time

Green | HOURS Psalter Week 2. MASS of choice

READINGS **2 Cor 1:1-7. Ps 33:2-, R/ v 9. Mt 5:1-12.** *Lect* II:124

This letter of Paul provides an inspiring example of a person committed to and concerned for his community. Paul draws on his understanding of Christ and its implications for his life and, therefore, also for his readers.

---

13 Tuesday — 10th Week in Ordinary Time

St Anthony of Padua, priest and doctor of the Church Memorial

White | HOURS of the memorial. Psalter Week 2

MASS of the memorial. Preface: Common or of the Saint

READINGS **2 Cor 1:18-22. Ps 118:129-133, 135, R/ v 135. Mt 5:13-16.** *Lect* II:126

Both readings emphasise the positive nature of Christian living, in the words of the gospel, being the salt of the earth and the light of the world.

---

14 Wednesday — 10th Week in Ordinary Time

Green | HOURS Psalter Week 2. MASS of choice

White | Optional memorial of **St Davnet, virgin**

READINGS **2 Cor 3:4-11. Ps 98:5-9, R/ v 9. Mt 5:17-19.** *Lect* II:128

The life of a Christian is marked by faith and service.

St Davnet see *The Irish Calendar*, p. 188.

---

15 Thursday **10th Week in Ordinary Time**
Green HOURS Psalter Week 2. MASS of choice
READINGS **2 Cor 3:15-4:1, 3-6. Ps 84:9-14, R/ cf. v 10. Mt 5:20-26.** *Lect* II:130

The Old Law brought death, the New Covenant brings freedom from death. As Christians we see here by faith, advancing in perfection until we see Christ as he is.

FIRST EVENING PRAYER of the **Sacred Heart**

---

16 Friday **THE MOST SACRED HEART OF JESUS** Solemnity
World Day of Prayer for Priests
White HOURS Proper. Te Deum. Complementary Psalms at Day Hour
MASS Proper (**RM** p. 368). Gloria. Creed. Preface: Proper
READINGS **Deut 7:6-11. Ps 102:1-4, 6-8, 10, R/ v 17. 1 Jn 4:7-16. Mt 11:25-30.** *Lect* I:628

The Sacred Heart of Jesus. 'Understood in the light of the scriptures, the term "Sacred Heart of Jesus" denotes the entire entire mystery of Christ: Son of God, uncreated wisdom, infinite charity, principle of the salvation and sanctification of humankind' (*Directory on Popular Piety and Liturgy*, 166).
No Masses for the dead, except funeral Masses, are permitted today (see Lit. Note 8)
Raphoe **Dedication of the Cathedral** (see *Lit. Note 12*)
EVENING PRAYER of the Sacred Heart

---

17 Saturday **10th Week in Ordinary Time**
The Immaculate Heart of the Blessed Virgin Mary
Memorial
White HOURS of the memorial. Psalter Week 2
MASS of the memorial. Preface: Blesssed Virgin Mary
READINGS **Is 61:9-11. Ps 1 Sm 2:1, 4-8, R/ cf. v 1. Lk 2:41-51.** *Lect* II:1043

'The Church celebrates the liturgical memorial of the **Immaculate Heart of Mary** the day after the Solemnity of the Sacred Heart of Jesus. The contiguity of both celebrations is in itself a liturgical sign of their close connection: the *mysterium* of the Heart of Jesus is projected onto and reverberates in the Heart of his Mother, who is also one of his followers and a disciple. (*Directory on Popular Piety and Liturgy*, 174).

JUNE 2023

18 Sunday — ELEVENTH SUNDAY IN ORDINARY TIME
Green ✠
HOURS Proper. Te Deum. Psalter Week 3
MASS Proper. Gloria. Creed. Preface: Sundays I–VIII

READINGS **Ex 19:2-6. Ps 99:2-3, 5, R/ v 3. Rm 5:6-11. Mt 9:36–10:8.** *Lect* I:666

Jesus sees the need for labourers in the harvest. His choice of the Twelve is for the puspose of going out to seek the lost sheep, to cure and to heal. It is a total vocation for them, a dedication freely given..
No Masses for the dead, except funeral Masses, are permitted today (see Lit. Note 8)

---

19 Monday — 11th Week in Ordinary Time
Green   HOURS Psalter Week 3. MASS of choice
White   Optional memorial of **St Romuald, abbot**
Cashel and
Emly   Optional memorial of **Bl. Dermot O'Hurley, bishop, and Companions, martyrs**

READINGS **2 Cor 6:1-10. Ps 97:1-4, R/ v 2. Mt 5:38-42.** *Lect* II:136

Let us prove ourselves to be servants of God by living in the way that Christ has taught. Paul himself shows by his way of life that he is a servant following Christ who came only to serve.

St Romuald was a monk who lived a life of strict penance and solitude. He established many monasteries, most notably at Camaldoli in Tuscany. He died in 1027.
Bl. Dermot O'Hurley and Companions see *The Irish Calendar*, p. 188.
Limerick   Dedication of the Cathedral (see *Lit. Note 12*)

---

20 Tuesday — 11th Week in Ordinary Time
The Irish Martyrs   Memorial
Red   HOURS of the memorial. Psalter Week 3
MASS of the memorial. Preface: Common or Martyrs

READINGS **2 Cor 8:1-9. Ps 145:2, 5-9, R/ v 2. Mt 5:43-48.** *Lect* II:138

Christ became poor for our sakes that we might become rich. The more we grow in love so much the more we become perfect as God is perfect.
The Irish Martyrs see *The Irish Calendar*, p. 188.

---

21 Wednesday 11th Week in Ordinary Time
St Aloysius Gonzaga, religious Memorial

White   HOURS of the memorial, Psalter Week 3.
                     MASS of the memorial. Preface: Common or of the Saint
READINGS   **2 Cor 9:6-11. Ps 111:1-4, 9, R/ v 1. Mt 6:1-6, 16-18.**
                     Lect II:140

God who provides seed for the sower and bread for food gives ungrudgingly. God loves a cheerful giver. He sees all that is done in secret and will bestow his reward.

St Aloysius Gonzaga joined the Jesuits. As a model novice he worked in the plague hospital and caught the fever, dying in 1591 at the age of twenty-three. Patron of youth.

---

22 Thursday   11th Week in Ordinary Time
Green   HOURS Psalter Week 3. MASS of choice
White   Optional memorial of **St Paulinus of Nola, bishop**
Red   Optional memorial of **Ss John Fisher, bishop and Thomas More, martyrs**
READINGS   **2 Cor 11:1-11. Ps 110:1-4, 7-8, R/ v 7. Mt 6:7-15.**
                     Lect II:142

The Lord's Prayer shows us that many words are not necessary. In it we praise God's glory, and ask for our human needs: 'provision, pardon and protection'.

St Paulinus, 355–431, bishop of Nola in the Campania.

St John Fisher, 1469–1535, as Vice-chancellor, built Christ's and St John's Colleges, Cambridge. Bishop of Rochester. His love of truth brought about his death. **St Thomas More**, 1478–1535, the first commoner to be Lord Chancellor of England, suffered martyrdom also under Henry VIII. Patron of lawyers and those in public life.

Cashel and Emly   **Dedication of the Cathedral** (see *Lit. Note 12*)

---

23 Friday   **11th Week in Ordinary Time**
Green   HOURS Psalter Week 3. MASS of choice
READINGS   **2 Cor 11:18, 21-30. Ps 33:2-7, R/ cf. v 18. Mt 6:19-23.** Lect I:144

Paul gave example in his own life by unselfishly serving his disciples. He has suffered much for them and his concern for them is his daily burden. They are his treasure, close to his heart.

FIRST EVENING PRAYER of **Nativity of St John the Baptist**

White   Evening MASS of the Vigil of the Solemnity Proper. Gloria. Creed. Preface: Proper
READINGS   **Jer 1:4-10. Ps 70:1-6, 15, 17, R/ v 6. 1 Pet 1:8-12. Lk 1:5-17.** Lect I:973 or II:1070

---

24 Saturday   **THE NATIVITY OF ST JOHN THE BAPTIST**   Solemnity
White   HOURS Proper. Te Deum. Complementary Psalms at Day Hour
MASS Proper. Gloria. Creed. Preface: Proper
READINGS   **Is 49:1-6. Ps 138:1-3, 13-15, R/ v 14. Acts 13:22-26. Lk 1:57-66, 80.** Lect I:976 or II:1073

We rejoice at the coming of **St John the Baptist**, a man of self-denial, integrity of life and purpose, and an uncompromising prophetic voice. John means 'The Lord has shown favour'. This feast relates to the summer solstice, when the days begin to grow shorter, recalling John's words, 'He must increase, but I must decrease.'

No Masses for the dead, except funeral Masses, are permitted today (see Lit. Note 8)
EVENING PRAYER of the Solemnity

St John the Baptist, the son of Zachary and Elizabeth, straddles both Old and New Testaments. His parents were reckoned as 'just before God' (Lk 1:6). John the Baptist is a major figure in the history of salvation. While in his mother's womb, he recognised the Saviour (cf. Lk 1:39-45); his birth was accompanied by great signs (cf. Lk 1:57-66); he retired to the desert where he led a life of austerity and penance (cf. Lk 1:80; Mt 3:4); 'Prophet of the Most High' (Lk 1:76), the word of God descended on him (Lk 3:2); 'he went through the whole of the Jordan district proclaiming a baptism of repentance for the forgiveness of sins' (Lk 3:3); like the new Elijah, humble and strong, he prepared his people to receive the Lord (cf. Lk 1:17); in accordance with God's saving plan, he baptised the Saviour of the World in the waters of the Jordan (cf. Mt 3:13-16); to his disciples, he showed that Jesus was 'the Lamb of God' (Jn 1:29), 'the Son of God' (Jn 1:34), the Bridegroom of the new messianic community (cf. Jn 3:28-30); he was imprisoned and decapitated by Herod for his heroic witness to the truth (cf. Mk 6:14-29), thereby becoming the Precursor of the Lord's own violent death, as he had been in his prodigious birth and prophetic preaching. Jesus praised him by attributing to him the glorious phrase 'of all children born to women, there is no one greater than John' (Lk 7:28).

Directory on Popular Piety and the Liturgy, 224

Silence in Worship

Silence is an important element in all communication. It is particularly important to allow for silence as a part of the dialogue between God and the community of faith. It allows for the voice of the Holy Spirit to be heard in the hearts of the people of God and to enable them to unite personal prayer more closely with the word of God and the public voice of the Church (*GILH,* 202; *Letter on Eucharistic Prayers* [*EP*], 18). During liturgical silence all respond in their own way, recollecting themselves, pondering what has been heard, petitioning and praising God in their inmost spirit (*EP,* 18).

Liturgical silence is not merely an absence of words, a pause, or an interlude. It is a stillness, a quieting of spirits, a making of time and leisure to hear, assimilate, and respond. Any haste that hinders reflectiveness should be avoided. The dialogue between God and the community of faith taking place through the Holy Spirit requires intervals of silence, suited to the assembly, so that all can take to heart the word of God and respond to it in prayer (*Lumen Gentium,* 28; *GIRM,* 56).

At the beginning of the rite of blessing and sprinkling of water, the people pause to ask for God's blessing on the water as a sign of baptism. In the Penitential Act, they pause to remember their sinfulness and the loving-kindness of God in Christ. At the collect (opening prayer), they put themselves and their deepest needs and desires before God. After the readings and Homily, they savour God's word, ponder it in their hearts like Mary (see *Lk* 2:19), and apply it to their lives. Before Communion, they compose themselves to receive the Lord, and afterwards praise and pray to God in their hearts (*GIRM,* 45).

Liturgical silence is a corporate activity shared in by all present, by which all support and sustain each other in profound prayerful solidarity. It demands a stillness and prayerful concentration, which the priest celebrant and all ministers can help to bring about.

Structurally, liturgical silence is indispensable to the rhythm of a balanced celebration. Without periods of prayerful and reflective silence the celebration can become perfunctory in its haste or burdensome in its unrelieved sound and song.

(National Centre for Liturgy,
Celebrating the Mystery of Faith: A Guide to the Mass, Veritas Publications)

* * *

Among the ritual acts that belong to the whole assembly, silence occupies a place of absolute importance. Many times it is expressly prescribed in the rubrics. The entire eucharistic celebration is immersed in the silence which precedes its beginning, and which marks every moment of its ritual unfolding. In fact, it is present in the penitential act, after the invitation 'Let us pray,' in the Liturgy of the Word (before the readings, between the readings and after the homily), in the eucharistic prayer, after communion. Such silence is not an inner haven in which to hide oneself in some sort of intimate isolation, as if leaving the ritual form behind as a distraction. That kind of silence would contradict the essence itself of the celebration. Liturgical silence is something much grander: it is a symbol of the presence and action of the Holy Spirit who animates the entire action of the celebration. For this reason, it constitutes a point of arrival within a liturgical sequence. Precisely because it is a symbol of the Spirit, it has the power to express the Spirit's multifaceted action. In this way, going over again the moments I just mentioned, silence moves to sorrow for sin and the desire for conversion. It awakens a readiness to hear the Word and awakens prayer. It disposes us to adore the Body and Blood of Christ. It suggests to each one, in the intimacy of communion, what the Spirit would effect in our lives to conform us to the Bread broken. For all these reasons we are called to enact with extreme care the symbolic gesture of silence. Through it the Spirit gives us shape, gives us form.

Pope Francis, *Desiderio Desideravi*, 52

JUNE 2023

25 Sunday　　TWELFTH SUNDAY IN ORDINARY TIME
Green ✠　　　　HOURS Proper. Te Deum. Psalter Week 4
　　　　　　　　MASS Proper. Gloria. Creed. Preface: Sundays I–VIII
READINGS　　**Jer 20:10-13. Ps 68:8-10, 14, 17, 33-35, R/ v 14. Rm 5:12-15. Mt 10:26-33.** *Lect* I:668

The followers of Christ must have courage at all times. Christ has promised support in time of trial. Death and Imprisonment for Christ are realities for many Christians. The erosion of faith and the dechristianising of values can be frightening. But Christ says to all, 'Be not afraid.'
No Masses for the dead, except funeral Masses, are permitted today (see Lit. Note 8)

---

26 Monday　　12th Week in Ordinary Time
Green　　　　　HOURS Psalter Week 4. MASS of choice
READINGS　　**Gn 12:1-9. Ps 32:12-13, 18-20, 22, R/ v 12. Mt 7:1-5.** *Lect* II:149

'Following in the footsteps of the prophets and John the Baptist, Jesus announced the judgement of the Last Day In his preaching. Then will the conduct of each one and the secrets of the heart be brought to light. Then will the culpable unbelief that counted the offer of God's grace as nothing be condemned. Our attitude to our neighbour will disclose acceptance or refusal of grace and divine love' (CCC, 678).

---

27 Tuesday　　12th Week in Ordinary Time
Green　　　　　HOURS Psalter Week 4. MASS of choice
White　　　　　Optional memorial of **St Cyril of Alexandria, bishop and doctor of the Church**
READINGS　　**Gn 13:2, 5-18. Ps 14:2-5, R/ v 1. Mt 7:6, 12-14.** *Lect* II:151

Abraham was one who did no wrong to his brother, but selflessly sought peace. His generosity is an example of treating others as you would like them to treat you.
St Cyril, c. 376–444, patriarch of Alexandria, fought against Nestorianism at the Council of Ephesus, 431, which proclaimed Mary the Mother of God.

---

28 Wednesday 12th Week in Ordinary Time
St Irenaeus, bishop and martyr Memorial

Red HOURS of the memorial. Psalter Week 4
MASS of the memorial. Preface: Common or of the Saint

READINGS **Gn 15:1-12, 17-18. Ps 104:1-4, 6-9, R/ v 8. Mt 7:15-20.** Lect II:153

The ritual sacrifices that mark the making of a covenant may seem strange to us. How much more wonderful is God's taking us to himself in an everlasting covenant of love. Let the hearts that seek the Lord rejoice.

St Irenaeus lived just after the time of the apostles and knew those who had seen and talked with them. He became Bishop of Lyons, the largest trading centre in Gaul. The note of moderation, the desire to win people to Christianity by love rather than by fear, was apparent in all of Irenaeus' work.

FIRST EVENING PRAYER of **Ss Peter and Paul**

Red Evening MASS of the Vigil of the Solemnity Proper. Gloria. Creed. Preface: Proper

READINGS **Acts 3:1-10. Ps 18:2-5, R/ v 5. Gal 1:11-20. Jn 21:15-19.** Lect I:979 or II:1079

---

29 Thursday **SS PETER AND PAUL, APOSTLES** Solemnity
Red HOURS Proper. Te Deum. Complementary Psalms at Day Hour
MASS Proper. Gloria. Creed. Preface: Proper

READINGS **Acts 12:1-11. Ps 33:2-9, R/ v 5, alt R/ v 8. 2 Tm 4:6-8, 17-18. Mt 16:13-19.** Lect I:981 or II:1082

Ss Peter and Paul. On the day traditionally considered in pagan Rome to be its foundation day by Romulus, we celebrate the twin founders of the Church in Rome. St Peter died by crucifixion and St Paul by beheading between 64–7.

EVENING PRAYER of Ss Peter and Paul

No Masses for the dead, except funeral Masses, are permitted today (see Lit. Note 8)

Down and Connor Today is the anniversary of the episcopal ordination of Most Rev. Noel Treanor, 29 June 2008.

---

30 Friday **12th Week in Ordinary Time**
Green HOURS Psalter Week 4. MASS of choice

Red Optional memorial of **The First Martyrs of the Holy Roman Church**

READINGS **Gn 17:1, 9-10, 15-22. Ps 127:1-5, R/ v 4. Mt 8:1-4.** Lect II:158

Circumcision is given as a sign of the covenant; and Abraham is to be the father of many peoples.

The First Martyrs of Rome, in addition to Ss Peter and Paul, died under Nero in the year 64.

Ferns **Dedication of the Cathedral** (see *Lit. Note 12*)

Cork and Ross Today is the anniversary of the episcopal ordination of Most Rev. Fintan Gavin, 30 June 2019.

JULY 2023

1 Saturday	**12th Week in Ordinary Time**
	St Oliver Plunkett, bishop and martyr Memorial
Red	HOURS of the memorial. Psalter Week 1.
	MASS of the memorial. Preface: Common or of the Saint
Armagh	**St Oliver Plunkett, bishop and martyr** Feast
Meath	**St Oliver Plunkett, bishop and martyr** Feast
READINGS	**Gn 18:1-15. Ps Lk 1:46-50, 53-55, R/ cf. v 54. Mt 8:5-17.** Lect II:160

Both Abraham and Sarah are amazed at the promise. But is anything too wonderful for God? Jesus rejoices in the faith of the centurion and shows his power over sickness and disease.

St Oliver Plunkett see *The Irish Calendar*, p. 188.

Elphin   **Dedication of the Cathedral** (see *Lit. Note 12*)

THE SUNDAY EUCHARIST

It is true that, in itself, the Sunday Eucharist is no different from the Eucharist celebrated on other days, nor can it be separated from liturgical and sacramental life as a whole. By its very nature, the Eucharist is an epiphany of the Church; and this is most powerfully expressed when the diocesan community gathers in prayer with its Pastor: 'The Church appears with special clarity when the holy People of God, all of them, are actively and fully sharing in the same liturgical celebrations – especially when it is the same Eucharist – sharing one prayer at one altar, at which the bishop is presiding, surrounded by his presbyters and his ministers' (SC, 41). This relationship with the bishop and with the entire Church community is inherent in every Eucharistic celebration, even when the bishop does not preside, regardless of the day of the week on which it is celebrated. The mention of the bishop in the Eucharistic Prayer is the indication of this.

But because of its special solemnity and the obligatory presence of the community, and because it is celebrated 'on the day when Christ conquered death and gave us a share in his immortal life', the Sunday Eucharist expresses with greater emphasis its inherent ecclesial dimension. It becomes the paradigm for other Eucharistic celebrations. Each community, gathering all its members for the 'breaking of the bread', becomes the place where the mystery of the Church is concretely made present. In celebrating the Eucharist, the community opens itself to communion with the universal Church, imploring the Father to 'remember the Church throughout the world' and make her grow in the unity of all the faithful with the pope and with the pastors of the particular Churches, until love is brought to perfection.

Therefore, the *dies Domini* is also the *dies Ecclesiae*. This is why on the pastoral level the community aspect of the Sunday celebration should be particularly stressed. As I have noted elsewhere, among the many activities of a parish, 'none is as vital or as community-forming as the Sunday celebration of the Lord's Day and his Eucharist'. Mindful of this, the Second Vatican Council recalled that efforts must be made to ensure that there is 'within the parish, a lively sense of community, in the first place through the community celebration of Sunday Mass' (SC, 42). Subsequent liturgical directives made the same point, asking that on Sundays and holydays the Eucharistic celebrations held normally in other churches and chapels be co-ordinated with the celebration in the parish church, in order 'to foster the sense of the Church community, which is nourished and expressed in a particular way by the community celebration on Sunday, whether around the bishop, especially in the Cathedral, or in the parish assembly, in which the pastor represents the bishop' (*Euch. Mysterium*).

The Sunday assembly is the privileged place of unity: it is the setting for the celebration of the *sacramentum unitatis* which profoundly marks the Church as a people gathered 'by' and 'in' the unity of the Father, of the Son and of the Holy Spirit (St Cyprian; *LG*, 4; *SC*, 26). For Christian families, the Sunday assembly is one of the most outstanding expressions of their identity and their 'ministry' as 'domestic churches', when parents share with their children at the one Table of the word and of the Bread of Life. We do well to recall in this regard that it is first of all the parents who must teach their children to participate in Sunday Mass; they are assisted in this by catechists, who are to see to it that initiation into the Mass is made a part of the formation imparted to the children entrusted to their care, explaining the important reasons behind the obligatory nature of the precept. When circumstances suggest it, the celebration of Masses for Children, in keeping with the provisions of the liturgical norms, can also help in this regard.

At Sunday Masses in parishes, insofar as parishes are 'Eucharistic communities', it is normal to find different groups, movements, associations and even the smaller religious communities present in the parish. This allows everyone to experience in common what they share most deeply, beyond the particular spiritual paths which, by discernment of Church authority, legitimately distinguish them. This is why on Sunday, the day of gathering, small group Masses are not to be encouraged: it is not only a question of ensuring that parish assemblies are not without the necessary ministry of priests, but also of ensuring that the life and unity of the Church community are fully safeguarded and promoted. Authorisation of possible and clearly restricted exceptions to this general guideline will depend upon the wise discernment of the pastors of the particular churches, in view of special needs in the area of formation and pastoral care, and keeping in mind the good of individuals or groups – especially the benefits which such exceptions may bring to the entire Christian community.

As the Church journeys through time, the reference to Christ's Resurrection and the weekly recurrence of this solemn memorial help to remind us of *the pilgrim and eschatological character of the People of God*. Sunday after Sunday the Church moves towards the final 'Lord's Day', that Sunday which knows no end. The expectation of Christ's coming is inscribed in the very mystery of the Church (cf. *LG* 48–51) and is evidenced in every Eucharistic celebration. But, with its specific remembrance of the glory of the Risen Christ, the Lord's Day recalls with greater intensity the future glory of his 'return'. This makes Sunday the day on which the Church, showing forth more clearly her identity as 'Bride', anticipates in some sense the eschatological reality of the heavenly Jerusalem. Gathering her children into the Eucharistic assembly and teaching them to wait for the 'divine Bridegroom', she engages in a kind of 'exercise of desire' (St Augustine), receiving a foretaste of the joy of the new heavens and new earth, when the holy city, the new Jerusalem, will come down from God, 'prepared as a bride adorned for her husband' (*Rv* 21:2).

Viewed in this way, Sunday is not only the day of faith, but is also *the day of Christian hope*. To share in 'the Lord's Supper' is to anticipate the eschatological feast of the 'marriage of the Lamb' (*Rv* 19:9). Celebrating this memorial of Christ, risen and ascended into heaven, the Christian community waits 'in joyful hope for the coming of our Saviour, Jesus Christ'. Renewed and nourished by this intense weekly rhythm, Christian hope becomes the leaven and the light of human hope. This is why the Prayer of the Faithful responds not only to the needs of the particular Christian community but also to those of all humanity; and the Church, coming together for the Eucharistic celebration, shows to the world that she makes her own 'the joys and hopes, the sorrows and anxieties of people today, especially of the poor and all those who suffer' (*GetS*, 1). With the offering of the Sunday Eucharist, the Church crowns the witness which her children strive to offer every day of the week by proclaiming the Gospel and practising charity in the world of work and in all the many tasks of life; thus she shows forth more plainly her identity 'as a sacrament, or sign and instrument of intimate union with God and of the unity of the entire human race' (*LG*, 1).

Pope St John Paul II,
Dies Domini, Keeping the Lord's Day Holy, 34–8 (1998)

JULY 2023

2 Sunday   **THIRTEENTH SUNDAY IN ORDINARY TIME**
Green ✠   HOURS Proper. Te Deum. Psalter Week 1
MASS Proper. Gloria. Creed. Preface: Sundays I–VIII
READINGS   **2 Kg 4:8-11, 14-16. Ps 88:2-3, 16-19, R/ v 2. Rm 6:3-4, 8-11. Mt 10:37-42.** Lect I:671

Those whom Christ sends are to be received in his name. This is more than hospitality. It means openness to the other and to the message. Each member of the Church has received a mission so we must accept each other in a spirit of faith and love. Those who Christ sends in an apostolic or prophetic ministry are to be listened to, whatever our natural feelings about them may be.
No Masses for the dead, except funeral Masses, are permitted today (see Lit. Note 8)

---

3 Monday   ST THOMAS, APOSTLE   Feast
Red   HOURS Proper. Te Deum. Psalter Week 1 at Day Hour
MASS Proper. Gloria. Preface: Apostles I–II
READINGS   **Eph 2:19-22. Ps 116, R/ Mk 16:15. Jn 20:24-29.** Lect II:1087

St Thomas is said to have preached the gospel in India where he was martyred. The faith that led him to know Christ in his wounds also sent him to the farthest places to preach Christ.
No Masses for the dead, except funeral Masses, are permitted today (see Lit. Note 8)

---

4 Tuesday   **13th Week in Ordinary Time**
Green   HOURS Psalter Week 1. MASS of choice
White   Optional memorial of **St Elizabeth of Portugal**
READINGS   **Gn 19:15-29. Ps 25:2-3, 9-12, R/ v 3. Mt 8:23-27.** Lect I:165

A weakness of faith gives rise to fear. Jesus calls his disciples to greater faith. Lot's wife in her fear did not trust God's word.
St Elizabeth of Portugal, 1271–1336, of the House of Aragon, had an unhappy marriage with the King of Portugal. She persevered in prayer and good works, and as a widow lived in poverty as a Franciscan tertiary.

5 Wednesday **13th Week in Ordinary Time**
Green HOURS Psalter Week 1. MASS of choice
White Optional memorial of **St Anthoy Zaccaria, priest**
READINGS **Gn 21: 5, 8-20. Ps 33:7-8, 10-13, R/ v 7. Mt 8:28-34.** *Lect* II:167

Abraham's faith is stressed in this version of the story of Hagar's child. The power of Jesus over evil is stressed in the strange gospel story. That power he gives to us: we must not reject him as the people did through fear.

St Anthony Zaccaria, 1502–39, was a medical doctor before becoming a priest in Milan. He founded the Barnabites.

---

6 Thursday **13th Week in Ordinary Time**
Green HOURS Psalter Week 1. MASS of choice
Red Optional memorial of **St Maria Goretti, virgin and martyr**
White Optional memorial of **St Moninne, virgin**
READINGS **Gn 22:1-19. Ps 114:1-6, 8-9, R/ v 9. Mt 9:1-8.** *Lect* II:169

The sacrifice of our father Abraham. In being prepared to sacrifice his son Isaac, Abraham's faith is tested. He is proved loyal and faithful and is rewarded with the promise of many descendants who will become a great nation.

St Maria Goretti, 1890-1902, stabbed to death in defence of her virtue.

St Moninne of Killeavy see *The Irish Calendar*, p. 188.

---

7 Friday **13th Week in Ordinary Time**
Green HOURS Psalter Week 1. MASS of choice
White Optional memorial of **St Maelruain, bishop and abbot**
READINGS **Gn 23:1-4, 19, 24:1-8, 62-67. Ps 105:1-5, R/ v 1. Mt 9:9-13.** *Lect* II:172

Isaac loved Rebekah and so was consoled for the loss of his mother. God's love for us is without end and is the cause of our joy and consolation. In Christ we see the fullness of that love.

St Maelruain see *The Irish Calendar*, p. 189

---

8 Saturday **13th Week in Ordinary Time**
Green HOURS Psalter Week 1. MASS of choice
Red Optional memorial of St Kilian, bishop and martyr
White/Green Saturday Mass of the **Blessed Virgin Mary**
READINGS **Gn 27:1-5, 15-29. Ps 134:1-6, R/ v 3. Mt 9:14-17.** *Lect* II:175

The mysterious ways of God are seen in the supplanting of Esau by Jacob. 'The Lord does whatever he wills.' His ways are not our ways.

St Kilian see *The Irish Calendar*, p. 189.

JULY 2023

9 Sunday   **FOURTEENTH SUNDAY IN ORDINARY TIME**
Green ✠   HOURS Proper. Te Deum. Psalter Week 2
     MASS Proper. Gloria. Creed. Preface: Sundays I–VIII
READINGS   **Zec 9:9-10. Ps 144:1-2, 8-11, 13-14, R/ v 1. Rm 8:9, 11-13. Mt 11:25-30.** Lect I:673

To know the Father and the Son we must become pupils in the school of Christ. The way of Christ is one of humility and gentleness. Intellectual pride and arrogance are not to be seen in the Christian. The teachings of Christ are to be learnt with humility and in prayer.

No Masses for the dead, except funeral Masses, are permitted today (see Lit. Note 8)
Ss Augustine Zhao Rong and Companions are not celebrated this year.

---

10 Monday   **14th Week in Ordinary Time**
Green   HOURS Psalter Week 2. MASS of choice
READINGS   **Gn 28:10-22. Ps 90:1-4, 14-1, R/ cf. b 2. Mt 9:18-26.** Lect II:178

God confirms the blessing given by Isaac to Jacob. God's faithfulness to his promise is shown in the protection that is to be given to Jacob.

---

11 Tuesday   ST BENEDICT, ABBOT, PATRON OF EUROPE   Feast
White   HOURS Proper. Te Deum. Psalter Week 2 at Day Hour
     MASS Proper. Gloria. Preface: Saint
READINGS   **Prov 2:1-9. Ps 33:2-11, R/ v 2. Mt 19:27-29.** Lect II:1095

St Benedict, c. 480–547, after living as a hermit at Subiaco, founded the monastery of Monte Cassino. His Rule, observed by Benedictines and Cistercians, is distinguished by its wisdom and balance and those who lived by it did much to shape the Europe of today. Named patron of Europe in 1964.

No Masses for the dead, except funeral Masses, are permitted today (see Lit. Note 8)

---

12 Wednesday 14th Week in Ordinary Time
Green   HOURS Psalter Week 2. MASS of choice
READINGS   **Gn 41:55-57, 42:5-7, 17-24. Ps 32:2-3, 10-11, 18-1, R/ v 22. Mt 10:1-7.** Lect II:182

The story of Joseph and his brothers has led to the situation where the brothers begin to repent. God's goodness in preserving them in time of famine is a further sign of his providential protection.

---

13 Thursday   **14th Week in Ordinary Time**
Green   HOURS Psalter Week 2. MASS of choice
White   Optional memorial of **St Henry**
READINGS   **Gn 44:18-21, 23-29, 45:1-5. Ps 104:16-21, R/ v 5. Mt 10-7-15.** Lect II:184

Joseph reveals himself to his brothers and forgives them. Joseph has received plenty at the hand of God without charge, and he makes return generously.

St Henry, 973–1024, Duke of Bavaria and later emperor. A just ruler, humble man of prayer and reformer of the Church.

Elphin Today is the anniversary of the episcopal ordination of Most Rev. Kevin Doran, 13 July 2014.

---

14 Friday   **14th Week in Ordinary Time**
Green   HOURS Psalter Week 2. MASS of choice
White   Optional memorial of **St Camillus de Lellis, priest**
READINGS   **Gn 46:1-7, 28-30. Ps 36:3-4, 18-19, 27-28, 39-4, R/ v 39. Mt 10:16-23.** Lect II:187

The final purposes of God will be worked out when he makes of Israel a great people in Egypt. They are destined to return to Canaan.

St Camillus de Lellis, 1550–1614, rough-tempered and a gambler in his early life as a soldier, he was converted at the age of twenty-five. Guided by St Philip Neri, he became a priest and worked for the sick with two companions. His Servants of the Sick prospered and founded hospitals especially where others would not go. Patron of nurses, hospitals and the sick.

---

15 Saturday   **14th Week in Ordinary Time**
    St Bonaventure, bishop and doctor of the Church
    Memorial
White   HOURS Psalter Week 2. MASS of choice
READINGS   **Gn 49:29-33, 50:15-26. Ps 104:1-4, 6-7, R/ Ps 68:33. Mt 10:24-33.** Lect II:189

The Church's liturgy has retained certain elements of the worship of the Old Covenant as integral and irreplaceable. She has adopted them as her own: notably, reading the Old Testament, praying the psalms and above all, recalling the saving events which have their fulfilment in the mystery of Christ – promise and covenant, Exodus and Passover, kingdom and temple, exile and return (see CCC, 1093).

St Bonaventure, 1221–74, born in Tuscany, Minister General of the Franciscans, Cardinal Archbishop of Albano, theologian of the Council of Lyons.

JULY 2023

16 Sunday   FIFTEENTH SUNDAY IN ORDINARY TIME
Green ✠   HOURS Proper. Te Deum. Psalter Week 3
            MASS Proper. Gloria. Creed. Preface: Sundays I–VIII
READINGS   **Is 55:10-11. Ps 64:10-14, R/ Lk 8:8. Rm 8:18-23. Mt 13:1-23** (shorter form 13:1-9). *Lect I:675*

We must have faith in the power of God's word. It is the instrument by which God effects his purpose. It does not work automatically, but grows in a soil of faith and prayer. We have to be concerned about teaching, preaching and praying the word and to work to ensure a receptive soil.

No Masses for the dead, except funeral Masses, are permitted today (see Lit. Note 8)
Our Lady of Mount Carmel is not celebrated this year.

---

17 Monday   15th Week in Ordinary Time
Green   HOURS Psalter Week 3. MASS of choice
READINGS   **Ex 1:8-14, 22. Ps 123, R/ v 8. Mt 10:34-11:1.** *Lect II:192*

The people of Israel are oppressed by Pharaoh. Christ warns his disciples that their fate will be to suffer opposition. In all our difficulties, our help is in the name of the Lord.

---

18 Tuesday   15th Week in Ordinary Time
Green   HOURS Psalter Week 3. MASS of choice
READINGS   **Ex 2:1-15. Ps 68:3, 14, 30-31, 33-34, R/ cf. v 33. Mt 11:20-24.** *Lect II:194*

St Matthew's Gospel sees in Christ the new Israel and the new Moses. Like Israel Christ was baptised through the water and tested in the desert. Like Israel's great lawgiver, Moses, he gave the new law on the Mount.

---

19 Wednesday 15th Week in Ordinary Time
Green   HOURS Psalter Week 3. MASS of choice
READINGS   **Ex 3:1-6, 9-12. Ps 102:1-4, 6- 7, R/ v 8. Mt 11:25-27.** *Lect II:196*

God reveals himself to Moses and gives him a mission. Jesus is to bring a great revelation of the Father to all who are open to receive his word.

---

20 Thursday **15th Week in Ordinary Time**
Green HOURS Psalter Week 3. MASS of choice
Red Optional memorial of **St Apollinaris, bishop and martyr**
READINGS **Ex 3:13-20. Ps 104:1, 5, 8-9, 24-27, R/ v 8. Mt 11:28-30.** *Lect* II:198

Moses protests his ability to carry out God's tasks for him. He is given Aaron as a helper. No task that God gives us is impossible to bear – his burden is light.

St Apollinaris in the second century preached the gospel in the region of Ravenna. He was Bishop of Classis where he suffered martyrdom.

Armagh **Dedication of the Cathedral** (see *Lit. Note 12*)

---

21 Friday **15th Week in Ordinary Time**
Green HOURS Psalter Week 3. MASS of choice
White Optional memorial of **St Lawrence of Brindisi, priest and doctor of the Church**
READINGS **Ex 11:10-12,14. Ps 115:12-13, 15-18, R/ v 13. Mt 12:1-8.** *Lect* II:200

Familiarity with the Passover ritual is a good background for deeper appreciation of the meaning of the Mass in the Christian life.

St Lawrence of Brindisi, 1559–1619, Capuchin who preached the Counter-Reformation. He led German armies against the Turks in Hungary and gained peace for the people of Naples.

Dromore **Dedication of the Cathedral** (see *Lit. Note 12*)

Kerry Today is the anniversary of the episcopal ordination of Most Rev. Raymond Browne, 21 July 2013.

Armagh Today is the anniversary of the episcopal ordination of Most Rev. Michael Router, 21 July 2019.

---

22 Saturday ST MARY MAGDALENE Feast
White HOURS Proper. Te Deum. Psalter Week 3 at Day Hour
 MASS Proper. Gloria. Preface: Proper
READINGS **Song 3:1-4 or 2 Cor. 5:14-17. Ps 62:2-6, 8-9, R/ v 2. Jn 20:1-2, 11-18.** *Lect* II:1108

St Mary Magdalene stood by the Cross of Jesus; with two other women she discovered the empty tomb; she was granted an appearance of the Risen Lord early the same day, from which incident she has been described as 'the apostle to the apostles'. The Gospels give no warrant for identifying her with the 'woman who was a sinner' who anointed Christ's feet (Lk 7:37) or with Mary the sister of Martha who also anointed him (Jn 12:3).

No Masses for the dead, except funeral Masses, are permitted today (see Lit. Note 8)
Green FIRST EVENING PRAYER of **Sunday**

JULY 2023

23 Sunday   **SIXTEENTH SUNDAY IN ORDINARY TIME**
World Day of Grandparents and the Elderly

Green ✠   HOURS Proper. Te Deum. Psalter Week 4
MASS Proper. Gloria. Creed. Preface: Sundays I–VIII

READINGS   **Wis 12:13, 16-19. Ps 85:5-6, 9-10, 15-16, R/ v 5. Rm 8:26-27. Mt 13:24-43** (shorter form 13:24-30)**.** Lect I:679

'You have given us the good hope that after sin you will grant repentance.' That God allows evil to flourish along with the good has always been a problem to those who know of God. In this the patience of God contrasts with the impatience of humans. The kingdom grows like the yeast spreading through the dough. The Day of the Lord will reveal all. Meanwhile we wait in hope, and pray to remain faithful.

No Masses for the dead, except funeral Masses, are permitted today (see Lit. Note 8)

St Bridget of Sweden, religious, patron of Europe is not celebrated this year.

Prayer for Grandparents

Written by Pope Emeritus Benedict XVI in 2008 for the Catholic Grandparents Association

Lord Jesus,
you were born of the Virgin Mary,
the daughter of Saints Joachim and Anne.
Look with love on grandparents the world over.
Protect them! They are a source of enrichment
for families, for the Church and for all of society.
Support them! As they grow older,
may they continue to be for their families
strong pillars of Gospel faith, guardians of noble domestic ideals,
living treasuries of sound religious traditions.
Make them teachers of wisdom and courage,
that they may pass on to future generations the fruits
of their mature human and spiritual experience.
Lord Jesus,
help families and society to value the presence and roles of grandparents.
May they never be ignored or excluded,
but always encounter respect and love.
Help them to live serenely and to feel welcomed
in all the years of life which you give them.
Mary, Mother of all the living,
keep grandparents constantly in your care,
accompany them on their earthly pilgrimage,
and by your prayers, grant that all families
may one day be reunited in our heavenly homeland,
where you await all humanity for the great
embrace of life without end. Amen.

24 Monday **16th Week in Ordinary Time**
Green HOURS Psalter Week 4. MASS of choice
White Optional memorial of **St Sharbel Makhlūf, priest**
White Optional memorial of **St Declan, bishop**

Waterford and
Lismore **St Declan, bishop** Feast
READINGS **Ex 14:5-18. Ps Ex 15:1-6, R/ v 1. Mt 12:38-42.** *Lect* II:205

This week the readings from Exodus tell the story of the passing through the Red Sea, the manna in the desert, and the making of the covenant.

St Sharbel Makhlūf became a monk at the monastery of St Maron at Annaya and was ordained in 1859. He became a hermit from 1875 until his death in 1898. He was much sought after for counsel and blessing and had a great personal devotion to the Blessed Sacrament.

St Declan see *The Irish Calendar*, p. 189.

---

25 Tuesday ST JAMES, APOSTLE Feast
Red HOURS Proper. Te Deum. Psalter Week 4 at Day Hour
MASS Proper. Gloria. Preface: Apostles I–II
READINGS **2 Cor 4:7-15. Ps 125, R/ v 5. Mt 20:20-28.** *Lect* II:1113

St James, son of Zebedee and brother of John, called the Greater. He was put to death by Herod Agrippa about the year 44, being the first of the Apostles to die for Christ. His shrine is at Compostella in Spain.

No Masses for the dead, except funeral Masses, are permitted today (see Lit. Note 8)

Waterford and Lismore Today is the anniversary of the episcopal ordination of Most Rev. William Lee, 25 July 1993.

Clogher Today is the anniversary of the episcopal ordination of Most Rev. Liam MacDaid, 25 July 2010.

---

26 Wednesday 16th Week in Ordinary Time
Ss Joachim and Anne, parents of the Blessed Virgin
Mary Memorial
Green HOURS Psalter Week 4. MASS of choice
READINGS **Ex 16:1-5, 9-15. Ps 77:18-19, 23-28, R/ v 24. Mt 13:1-9.** *Lect* II:209

The Lord gave them bread from heaven, mere mortals ate the bread of angels. The Eucharist is the nourishment for the Christian life; we must prepare worthily to receive the food of life.

Ss Joachim and Anne (or Anna). Traditionally named parents of the Blessed Virgin Mary and grandparents of the Lord. The earliest reference to their names is the second-century apocryphal Gospel of James. Their feasts were celebrated separately until joined together in the Calendar reform of 1969. St Anne is patron of Canada, women in labour, miners, cabinet-makers and home-makers.

27 Thursday   **16th Week in Ordinary Time**
Green   HOURS Psalter Week 4. MASS of choice
READINGS   **Ex 19:1-2, 9-11, 16-20. Ps Dn 3:52-56, R/ v 52. Mt 13:10-17.** *Lect* II:211

Moses is called up to the mountain as God manifests himself in terrifying splendour. Jesus reveals the mysteries of the kingdom to his disciples in parables.

---

28 Friday   **16th Week in Ordinary Time**
Green   HOURS Psalter Week 4. MASS of choice
READINGS   **Ex 20:1-17. Ps 18:8-11, R/ Jn 6:68. Mt 13:18-23.** *Lect* II:213

The commandments are given to Moses on the mountain. Jesus wants us to let his word take deep root in our lives.

---

29 Saturday   **16th Week in Ordinary Time**
                  Ss Martha, Mary and Lazarus   Memorial
White   HOURS of the memorial. Psalter Week 1
                  MASS of the memorial. Preface: Common or of the Saint (Collect, p. 183)
READINGS   **1 Jn 4:7-16. Ps 33:2-11. Jn 11:19-27 or Lk 10:38-42.** Lect II:1117

Ss Martha, Mary and Lazarus welcomed Jesus as a family friend. Martha generously offered him hospitality, Mary listened attentively to his words, and Lazarus promptly emerged from the tomb at the command of the One who humiliated death.

BAPTISM

Let the grace of your baptism bear fruit in a path of holiness. Let everything be open to God; turn to him in every situation. Do not be dismayed, for the power of the Holy Spirit enables you to do this, and holiness, in the end, is the fruit of the Holy Spirit in your life (cf. *Gal* 5:22–23). When you feel the temptation to dwell on your own weakness, raise your eyes to Christ crucified and say: 'Lord, I am a poor sinner, but you can work the miracle of making me a little bit better'. In the Church, holy yet made up of sinners, you will find everything you need to grow towards holiness. The Lord has bestowed on the Church the gifts of scripture, the sacraments, holy places, living communities, the witness of the saints and a multifaceted beauty that proceeds from God's love, 'like a bride bedecked with jewels' (*Is* 61:10).

Pope Francis, *Gaudete et Exsultate*, 15

JULY 2023

30 Sunday   SEVENTEENTH SUNDAY IN ORDINARY TIME

Green ✠   HOURS Proper. Te Deum. Psalter Week 1

MASS Proper. Gloria. Creed. Preface: Sundays I–VIII

READINGS   **1 Kg 3:5, 7-12. Ps 118:57, 72, 76-77, 127-130, R/ v 97. Rm 8:28-30. Mt 13:44-52** (shorter form 13:44-46)**.** *Lect* I:682

Listening to the word of God enables us to acquire true wisdom. By it we learn where our true good lies, that it means more than silver and gold. This wisdom helps us to make the right choices in our search for the real treasure. We ought to pray for the ability to make the positive, radical decision for the Kingdom. Jesus asks us all, 'Have you understood all this?'

No Masses for the dead, except funeral Masses, are permitted today (see Lit. Note 8)

St Peter Chrysologus, bishop and doctor of the Church is not celebrated this year.

---

31 Monday   17th Week in Ordinary Time
St Ignatius of Loyola, priest   Memorial

White   HOURS of the memorial. Psalter Week 1

MASS of the memorial. Preface: Common or of the Saint

READINGS   **Ex 32:15-24, 30-34. Ps 105:19-23, R/ v 1. Mt 13:31-35.** *Lect* II:218

The people commit sin by making themselves an idol of gold.

St Ignatius of Loyola, 1491–1556, from the north of Spain, founded the Society of Jesus. By the time of his death, the Society had spread widely and had over one thousand members. His great theme was the service of God and God's greater glory. The experience of his conversion led to his writing of the Spiritual Exercises.

We may not even be aware of it, but every time we go to Mass, the first reason is that we are drawn there by his desire for us. For our part, the possible response – which is also the most demanding asceticism – is, as always, that surrender to this love, that letting ourselves be drawn by him.

Pope Francis, *Desiderio Desideravi*, 6

AUGUST 2023

1 Tuesday   **17th Week in Ordinary Time**
St Alphonsus Liguori, bishop and doctor of the Church Memorial

White   HOURS of the memorial. Psalter Week 1
MASS of the memorial. Preface: Common or of the Saint

READINGS   **Ex 33:7-11, 34:5-9, 28. Ps 102:6-1, R/ v 8. Mt 13:36-43.** *Lect* II:220

The Lord reveals himself as a God of tenderness and compassion. Moses speaks with God, face to face, on behalf of the people.

St Alphonsus Liguori, 1696–1787, founder of the Redemptorist Congregation, taught much on moral theology and the spiritual life. He is remembered as a popular preacher and influential writer of theology.

---

2 Wednesday   **17th Week in Ordinary Time**
Green   HOURS Psalter Week 1. MASS of choice
White   Optional memorial of **St Eusebius of Vercelli, bishop**
White   Optional memorial of **St Peter Julian Eymard, priest**
READINGS   **Ex 34:29-35. Ps 98: 5-7, 9, R/ cf. v 9. Mt 13:44-46.** *Lect* II:223

Moses comes down the mountain and his face reflects the holiness of God.

St Eusebius of Vercelli is renowned for his preaching against Arianism.

St Peter Julian Eymard,1811–68, a fervent disciple of the Eucharistic Mystery, established the Blessed Sacrament Fathers and, with the help of Marguerite Guillot, the Servants of the Blessed Sacrament.

The Indulgence of St Mary of the Portiuncula. On 2 August, or on another day determined by the Ordinary for the convenience of the people, a plenary indulgence may be acquired in parish churches. The practices prescribed for the obtaining of the indulgence are a devout visit to the church and the recitation there of the Our Father and Creed, and in addition a sacramental confession, Holy Communion and prayer for the intentions of the Supreme Pontiff. This indulgence may be acquired only once. The visit may be made from noon the previous day until midnight of the day itself.

**World Youth Day takes place 1–6 August 2023
in Lisbon, Portugal**

Christ is alive! He is our hope, and in a wonderful way he brings youth to our world, and everything he touches becomes young, new, full of life. The very first words, then, that I would like to say to every young Christian are these: Christ is alive and he wants you to be alive!

Pope Francis, *Christus Vivit*

3 Thursday **17th Week in Ordinary Time**
Green HOURS Psalter Week 1. MASS of choice
READINGS **Ex 40:16-21, 34-38. Ps 83:3-6, 8, 11, R/ v 2. Mt 13:47-53.** Lect II:225

The cloud covered the Tent of Meeting and the glory of the Lord filled the tabernacle. How lovely is your dwelling place, Lord, God of Hosts. In the Sunday meeting Christ is present to the assembly, in his word and in the Eucharist.

---

4 Friday **17th Week in Ordinary Time**
  St John Mary Vianney, priest Memorial
White HOURS of the memorial. Psalter Week 1
  MASS of the memorial. Preface: Common or of the Saint
READINGS **Lev 23:1, 4-11, 15-16, 27, 34-37. Ps 80:3-6, 10-1, R/ v 2. Mt 13:54-58.** Lect II:227

Jewish festivals: Passover, celebrates the Exodus event. At Pentecost, seven weeks later, is celebrated Shavuot, God's gift of the Torah as a guide to life. Jewish New Year is Rosh Hashanah, 15 September 2023 (5784), beginning at sunset the previous evening; a period of penance concluding with the feast of Yom Kippur or Day of Atonement. 24 September 2023; Sukkot, the feast of tents, 29 September 2023, a harvest celebration of God's generous gifts of nature and our creation. Hanukkah, Feast of Lights, first day begins evening 7 December 2023.

St John Vianney, 1786–1859, had to contend with poverty, military service and his own intellectual shortcomings in order to become a priest. In 1817 he was sent to care for the people of Ars, a small, obscure French village. The marvellous gift of the unlearned priest for seeing into the depths of the soul brought the world to Ars. From 1830 on, the curé averaged twelve to sixteen hours a day in the confessional. Patron of priests.

Kildare and Leighlin Today is the anniversary of the episcopal ordination of Most Rev. Denis Nulty, 4 August 2013.

---

5 Saturday **17th Week in Ordinary Time**
Green HOURS Psalter Week 1. MASS of choice
White Optional memorial of The **Dedication of the Basilica of St Mary Major**
White/Green Saturday Mass of the **Blessed Virgin Mary**
READINGS **Lev 25:1, 8-17. Ps 66:2-3, 5, 7-8, R/ v 4. Mt 14:1-12.** Lect II:229

Let none of you wrong his neighbour in the year of Jubilee. A year of renewal in which past debts are annulled.

St Mary Major: Apoc 21:1-5. Ps Jdt 13:18-19, R/ 15:9. Lk 11:27-28. Lect II:1129

The basilica was built by Pope Sixtus III after the Council of Ephesus (431). It is the first church in the West named in honour of the Mother of God.

FIRST EVENING PRAYER of the **Transfiguration**

AUGUST 2023

6 Sunday   THE TRANSFIGURATION OF THE LORD   Feast
White ✠   HOURS Proper. Te Deum. Psalter Week 2 at Day Hour
                  MASS Proper. Gloria. Creed. Preface: Proper
READINGS   **Dn 7:9-10, 13-14. Ps. 96:1-2, 5-6, 9, R/ vv 1, 9. 2 Pt
                  1:16-19. Mt 17:1-9.** Lect I:984 or II:1131

The Transfiguration. The Cross requires the exodus of Jesus, his death, resurrection and glorification. The disciples have to realise that he must depart, just as they are now prepared for his going up to Jerusalem to die.
No Masses for the dead, except funeral Masses, are permitted today (see Lit. Note 8)
Raphoe Today is the anniversary of the episcopal ordination of Most Rev. Alan McGuckian, SJ, 6 August 2017.

---

7 Monday   **18th Week in Ordinary Time**
Green   HOURS Psalter Week 2. MASS of choice
Red   Optional memorial of **Ss Sixtus II, pope, and
               Companions, martyrs**
White   Optional memorial of **St Cajetan, priest**
READINGS   **Num 11:4-15. Ps 80:12-17, R/ v 2. Mt 14:13-21.** Lect
                  II:232

'A better knowledge of the Jewish people's faith and religious life as professed and lived even now can help our better understanding of certain aspects of Christian liturgy. The relationship between Jewish liturgy and Christian liturgy, but also their differences in content, are particularly evident in the great feasts of the liturgical year, such as Passover' (CCC, 1096).
St Sixtus II, pope, and his four deacon companions were put to death in 258.
St Cajetan, 1480–1547, founded the Theatines to renew sacramental life in the Church.

---

8 Tuesday   **18th Week in Ordinary Time**
                       St Dominic, priest   Memorial
White   HOURS of the memorial. Psalter Week 2
                  MASS of the memorial. Preface: Common or of the Saint
READINGS   **Num 12:1-13.Ps 50:3-7, 12-13, R/ cf. v 3. Mt 14:22-
                  36.** Lect II:235

Miriam is punished for opposing Moses' authority. God has placed him in a special position with the Israelites.
St Dominic, 1170–1221, a Spaniard who founded the Order of Preachers (Dominicans) to counteract the Albigensian heresy.

9 Wednesday ST TERESA BENEDICTA OF THE CROSS (EDITH STEIN)
VIRGIN AND MARTYR, PATRON OF EUROPE Feast
Red HOURS Proper. Te Deum. Psalter Week 2 at Day Hour
MASS Proper. Gloria. Preface: Martyrs I–II
READINGS **Hos 2:16-17, 21-22. Ps 44:11-12, 14-17, R/ v 11, alt R/ Mt 25:6. Mt 25:1-13.** *Lect* II:1518 and 1524

St Teresa Benedicta of the Cross (Edith Stein), born 1891 at Breslau (now Wroclaw, Poland), the youngest of seven children of a Jewish family. A brilliant student, she gained her doctorate in philosophy at twenty-five. Became a Catholic in 1922 and a Carmelite nun. Both Jewish and Catholic, she fled to Holland when the Nazis came to power but she was captured and sent to Auschwitz where she died in its gas chamber on 9 August 1942.

No Masses for the dead, except funeral Masses, are permitted today (see Lit. Note 8)

St Nathy, bishop and **St Felim, bishop** are not celebrated this year, except

Achonry **St Nathy, bishop** Feast
Kilmore **St Felim, bishop** Feast

St Nathy see *The Irish Calendar*, p. 189.
St Felim see *The Irish Calendar*, p. 189.

---

10 Thursday ST LAWRENCE, DEACON AND MARTYR Feast
Red HOURS Proper. Te Deum. Psalter Week 2 at Day Hour
MASS Proper. Gloria. Creed. Preface: Martyrs I–II
READINGS **2 Cor 9:6-10. Ps 111:1-2, 5-9, R/ v 5. Jn 12:24-26.** *Lect* II:1141

St Lawrence, died 258, is seen as the cheerful giver since he was one of the seven deacons of the Roman Church in charge of the material needs of the faithful. Gifted with a sense of humour, he met his death cheerfully on a gridiron. From earliest times seen not only as a patron saint of the poor, but also of cooks.

No Masses for the dead, except funeral Masses, are permitted today (see Lit. Note 8)

---

11 Friday **18th Week in Ordinary Time**
St Clare, virgin Memorial
White HOURS of the memorial. Psalter Week 2
MASS of the memorial. Preface: Common or of the Saint
READINGS **Deut 4:32-40. Ps 76:12-16, 21, R/ v 12. Mt 16:24-28.** *Lect* II:243

The people are called to wonder at the nearness of God to them, and so to keep the commandments as tokens of love.

St Clare, born at Assisi in 1193, died 1253. She followed Saint Francis in his life of poverty and was founder and ruler of the Poor Clares. She led an austere life, abounding in works of piety and charity. Patron of television.

---

12 Saturday	**18th Week in Ordinary Time**	
Green	HOURS Psalter Week 2. MASS of choice	
White	Optional memorial of **St Jane Frances de Chantal, religious**	
White	Optional memorial of **St Lelia, virgin**	
White	Optional memorial of **St Attracta, virgin**	
White	Optional memorial of **St Muredach, bishop**	
White/Green	Saturday Mass of the **Blessed Virgin Mary**	
Achonry	**St Attracta, virgin**	Feast
Killala	**St Muredach, bishop**	Feast
READINGS	**Deut 6:4-13. Ps 17:2-4, 47, 51, R/ v 2. Mt 17:14-20.** *Lect* II:245	

'A better knowledge of the Jewish people's faith and religious life as professed and lived even now can help our better understanding of certain aspects of Christian liturgy. The relationship between Jewish liturgy and Christian liturgy, but also their differences in content, are particularly evident In the great feasts of the liturgical year, such as Passover' (CCC, 1096).

St Jane Frances de Chantal, 1572–1641, at the age of twenty married Baron de Chantal but after nine years she was left a widow with four children. Her friendship with St Francis de Sales led to the foundation of the Congregation of the Visitation.

St Muredach see *The Irish Calendar*, p. 189.

St Attracta see *The Irish Calendar*, p. 189.

St Lelia see *The Irish Calendar*, p. 189.

Cloyne	**Dedication of the Cathedral** (see *Lit. Note 12*)
Killala	**Dedication of the Cathedral** (see *Lit. Note 12*)

Eucharist – directing us to be stewards of creation

It is in the Eucharist that all that has been created finds its greatest exaltation. Grace, which tends to manifest itself tangibly, found unsurpassable expression when God himself became man and gave himself as food for his creatures. The Lord, in the culmination of the mystery of the Incarnation, chose to reach our intimate depths through a fragment of matter. He comes not from above, but from within, he comes that we might find him in this world of ours. In the Eucharist, fullness is already achieved; it is the living centre of the universe, the overflowing core of love and of inexhaustible life. Joined to the incarnate Son, present in the Eucharist, the whole cosmos gives thanks to God. Indeed the Eucharist is itself an act of cosmic love: 'Yes, cosmic! Because even when it is celebrated on the humble altar of a country church, the Eucharist is always in some way celebrated on the altar of the world' (St John Paul II, *Ecclesia de Eucharistia*, 8). The Eucharist joins heaven and earth; it embraces and penetrates all creation. The world which came forth from God's hands returns to him in blessed and undivided adoration: in the bread of the Eucharist, 'creation is projected towards divinisation, towards the holy wedding feast, towards unification with the Creator himself' (Benedict XVI, Homily, 15 June 2006). Thus, the Eucharist is also a source of light and motivation for our concerns for the environment, directing us to be stewards of all creation.

Pope Francis, *Laudato Si'*, 236

Liturgical Formation

We can not forget, first of all, that the liturgy is life that forms, not an idea to be learned. It is useful in this regard to remember that reality is more important than the idea (see Apostolic Exhortation *Evangelii gaudium*, 231–233). And it is good therefore, in the liturgy as in other areas of ecclesial life, not to end up favouring sterile ideological polarisations, which often arise when, considering our own ideas valid for all contexts, we tend to adopt an attitude of perennial dialectic towards who does not share them. Thus, starting perhaps from the desire to react to some insecurities in the current context, we risk then falling back into a past that no longer exists or of escaping into a presumed future. The starting point is instead to recognise the reality of the sacred liturgy, a living treasure that can not be reduced to tastes, recipes and currents, but which should be welcomed with docility and promoted with love, as irreplaceable nourishment for the organic growth of the People of God. The liturgy is not 'the field of do-it-yourself', but the epiphany of ecclesial communion. Therefore, 'we', and not 'I', resounds in prayers and gestures; the real community, not the ideal subject. When we look back to nostalgic past tendencies or wish to impose them again, there is the risk of placing the part before the whole, the 'I' before the People of God, the abstract before the concrete, ideology before communion and, fundamentally, the worldly before the spiritual.

The Liturgical Formation of the People of God

The task that awaits us is indeed essentially that of spreading among the People of God the splendour of the living mystery of the Lord, who makes himself manifest in the liturgy. Speaking of liturgical formation in the People of God means first and foremost being aware of the indispensable role the liturgy holds in the Church and for the Church. And then, concretely helping the People of God to interiorise better the prayer of the Church, to love it as an experience of encounter with the Lord and with brothers and sisters who, in the light of this, rediscover its content and observe its rites.

Liturgy and Mystagogy

Since the liturgy is an experience extended to the conversion of life through the assimilation of the Lord's way of thinking and behaving, liturgical formation can not be limited to simply offering knowledge – this is a mistake – though necessary, in liturgical books, nor even to protect the dutiful fulfilment of the ritual disciplines. In order for the liturgy to fulfil its formative and transforming function, it is necessary that the pastors and the laity be introduced to their meaning and symbolic language, including art, song and music in the service of the mystery celebrated, even silence. The Catechism of the Catholic Church itself adopts the mystagogical way to illustrate the liturgy, valuing its prayers and signs. Mystagogy: this is a suitable way to enter the mystery of the liturgy, in the living encounter with the crucified and risen Lord. Mystagogy means discovering the new life we have received in the People of God through the sacraments, and continually rediscovering the beauty of renewing it.

Pope Francis addressing the plenary of the
Congregation for Divine Worship and the Discipline of the Sacraments
14 February 2019

AUGUST 2023

13 Sunday   **NINETEENTH SUNDAY IN ORDINARY TIME**
Green ✠   HOURS Proper. Te Deum. Psalter Week 3
               MASS Proper. Gloria. Creed. Preface: Sundays I–VIII
READINGS   **1 Kg 19:9, 11-13. Ps 84:9-14, R/ v 8. Rm 9:1-5. Mt 14:22-33.** *Lect* I:688

For Elijah, the Lord was not in the mighty wind but in the gentle breeze. Peter's faith fails in the face of the force of the wind on the sea. 'Lord! Save me' is a prayer for all in times of fear and opposition.
No Masses for the dead, except funeral Masses, are permitted today (see Lit. Note 8)
Ss Pontian, pope, and Hippolytus, priest, martyrs and **St Fachtna, bishop** are not celebrated this year, except
Ross   **St Fachtha, bishop**   This year as Solemnity
St Fachtna see *The Irish Calendar*, p. 189.

---

14 Monday   **19th Week in Ordinary Time**
               St Maximilian Kolbe, priest and martyr   Memorial
Red   HOURS of the memorial. Psalter Week 3
               MASS of the memorial. Preface: Common or of the Saint
READINGS   **Deut 10:12-22. Ps 147:12-15, 19-20, R/ v 12. Mt 17:22-27.** *Lect* II:247

Look for justice for the poor. Give hospitality to strangers.
St Maximilian Kolbe, 1894–1941, a Conventual Franciscan who worked in the apostolate of the press in Poland and Japan, and died in Auschwitz.

White   FIRST EVENING PRAYER of the **Assumption**
               Evening MASS of the Vigil of the Assumption Proper. Gloria. Creed. Preface: Proper
READINGS   **1 Chr 15:3-4,15-16, 16:1-2. Ps 131:6-7, 9-10, 13-14, R/ v 8. 1 Cor 15:54-57. Lk 11:27-28.** *Lect* I:992 or II:1146

---

15 Tuesday   **THE ASSUMPTION OF THE BLESSED VIRGIN MARY**
                                                            Solemnity
White ✠   HOURS Proper. Te Deum. Complementary Psalms at Day Hour
               MASS Proper. Gloria. Creed. Preface: Proper
READINGS   **Apoc 11:19, 12:1-6, 10. Ps 44:10-12, 16, R/ v 10. 1 Cor 15:20-26. Lk 1:39-56.** *Lect* I:994 or II:1148

'The **Assumption of Mary** honours the fullness of blessedness that was her destiny, the glorification of her immaculate soul and virginal body that completely conformed her to the risen Christ. This is a celebration that offers to the Church and to all humanity an exemplar and a consoling message, teaching us the fulfilment of our highest hopes. Their own future glorification is happily in store for all those whom Christ has made his own brothers and sisters by taking on their flesh and blood' (*Marialis Cultus*). Patronal Day of France, India, Malta, Paraguay.
No Masses for the dead, not even funeral Masses, are permitted today (see Lit. Note 8)
Galway   **Dedication of the Cathedral** (see *Lit. Note 12*)

---

16 Wednesday 19th Week in Ordinary Time
Green   HOURS Psalter Week 3. MASS of choice
White   Optional memorial of **St Stephen of Hungary**
READINGS   **Deut 34:1-12. Ps 65:1-3, 5, 16-17, R/ cf. vv 20, 9.**
                 Mt 18:15-20. Lect II:251

Jesus illustrates his teaching on forgiveness with the parable about the unjust servant.

St Stephen of Hungary, 975–1038, first King of Hungary and its patron saint, worked for the conversion of his people to Christianity.

---

17 Thursday   19th Week in Ordinary Time
                 Our Lady of Knock   Memorial
White   HOURS of the memorial. Psalter Week 3
                 MASS of the memorial. Preface: Blessed Virgin Mary
READINGS   **Jos 3:7-11, 13-17. Ps 113A:1-6. Mt 18:21-19:1.** Lect
                 II:253

'When Israel came forth from Egypt, the Jordan turned back on its course. The priests with the Ark of the Covenant led the people across the Jordan.

Our Lady of Knock READINGS: Common of the Blessed Virgin Mary Lect II:1421–1449. See The Irish Calendar, p. 189.

---

18 Friday   19th Week in Ordinary Time
Green   HOURS Psalter Week 3. MASS of choice
READINGS   **Jos 24:1-13. Ps 135:1-3, 16-18, 21-22, 24. Mt 19:3-**
                 12. Lect II:256

It is right to give God thanks and praise for all his wonderful works.

Tuam   Dedication of the Cathedral (see Lit. Note 12)

---

19 Saturday   19th Week in Ordinary Time
Green   HOURS Psalter Week 3. MASS of choice
White   Optional memorial of **St John Eudes, priest**
White/Green   Saturday Mass of the **Blessed Virgin Mary**
READINGS   **Jos 24:14-29. Ps 15:1-2, 5, 7-8, 11, R/ cf. v 5. Mt**
                 19:13-15. Lect II:258

The renewal of the Covenant at Shechem is an acknowledgement by the people of God's role in their history.

St John Eudes, 1601–80, from Normandy, France, spent a fruitful twenty years with the French Oratory, then left to found a congregation to improve the standards of the clergy through seminaries. He founded also the Sisters of Our Lady of Charity and Refuge. He was a powerful preacher and among the first to promote devotion to the Sacred Heart.

AUGUST 2023

20 Sunday   **TWENTIETH SUNDAY IN ORDINARY TIME**
Green ✠   HOURS Proper. Te Deum. Psalter Week 4
           MASS Proper. Gloria. Creed. Preface: Sundays I–VIII
READINGS   **Is 56:1, 6-7. Ps 66:2-3, 5-6, 8, R/ v 4. Rm 11:13-15, 29-32. Mt 15:21-28.** Lect I:690

There is a great mystery in the will of God that all be saved. He knows the minds and hearts of all and does not judge in a human way. We hold to the belief in the need of membership for salvation, but we do so in the light of the universality of salvation. Like the Canaanite woman we must persevere with a determined faith in seeking the truth in love, until all nations learn of God's salvation, and all peoples praise his name.

No Masses for the dead, except funeral Masses, are permitted today (see Lit. Note 8)
St Bernard, abbot and doctor of the Church is not celebrated this year.

---

21 Monday   **20th Week in Ordinary Time**
           St Pius X, pope   Memorial
White   HOURS of the memorial. Psalter Week 4
           MASS of the memorial. Preface: Common or of the Saint
READINGS   **Jg 2:11-19. Ps 105:34-37, 39-40, 43-44, R/ v 4. Mt 19:16-22.** Lect II:261

The Lord's anger flamed out against Israel because of infidelity. Despite the quality of leadership given them, they still turned away to other gods.
St Pius X, 1835–1914, Cardinal Patriarch of Venice, then Pope from 1903. Encouraged pastoral liturgy and sacramental practice, especially of frequent communion, to which he admitted young children.

---

22 Tuesday   **20th Week in Ordinary Time**
           The Queenship of the Blessed Virgin Mary   Memorial
White   HOURS of the memorial. Psalter Week 4
           MASS of the memorial. Preface: Blessed Virgin Mary
READINGS   **Is 9:1-6. Ps 112:1-8, R/ v 2. Lk 1:26-38.** Lect II:1160

The Queenship of Mary. During the Middle Ages, Mary was venerated as queen of the angels and saints. Pope Pius XII prescribed the memorial for the universal Church at the close of the Marian Year 1955. It is placed on this date to stress the connection of Mary's queenship with the Assumption.
Cork   **Dedication of the Cathedral** (see *Lit. Note 12*)
Kerry   **Dedication of the Cathedral** (see *Lit. Note 12*)

---

23 Wednesday 20th Week in Ordinary Time
Green   HOURS Psalter Week 4. MASS of choice
White   Optional memorial of **St Rose of Lima, virgin**
White   Optional memorial of **St Eugene, bishop**
Derry   **St Eugene, bishop**   Feast
READINGS   **Jg 9:6-15. Ps 20:2-, R/ v 2. Mt 20:1-16.** *Lect* II:266
Jotham tells the story of the trees seeking a king to warn the people that a king
will be either useless or dangerous. Jesus tells a story to illustrate the generosity of
God who rewards even the latecomers.
St Rose of Lima, 1586–1617, Dominican tertiary and recluse, helped the poor
and marginalised. Seen as originator of social service in Peru.
St Eugene (Eoghan) see *The Irish Calendar*, p. 189.

---

24 Thursday   ST BARTHOLOMEW, APOSTLE   Feast
Red   HOURS Proper. Te Deum. Psalter Week 4 at Day Hour
                 MASS Proper. Gloria. Preface: Apostles I–II
READINGS   **Apoc 21:9-14. Ps 144:10-13, 17-18, R/ cf. v 12. Jn
                 1:45-51.** *Lect* II:1164
St Bartholomew's name occurs in the Synoptic Gospels only in the list of
apostles. He is probably to be identified with Nathanael of Cana, whom Philip
brings to our Lord. Preached the gospel in India. Patron saint of plasterers,
tanners and leather workers.
No Masses for the dead, except funeral Masses, are permitted today (see Lit. Note 8)

---

25 Friday   **20th Week in Ordinary Time**
Green   HOURS Psalter Week 4. MASS of choice
White   Optional memorial of **St Louis of France**
White   Optional memorial of **St Joseph Calasanz, priest**
READINGS   **Ruth 1:1, 3-6, 14-16, 22. Ps 145:5-10, R/ v 2. Mt
                 22:34-40.** *Lect* II:271
'Your people shall be my people.' Ruth the Moabitess, after the death of her
husband, a man originally from Bethlehem, returns to his country with her mother-
in-law, Naomi.
St Louis, 1214–70, King of France, father of eleven children, Franciscan tertiary,
man of integrity, died in Tunisia on his second Crusade. Patron of French
monarchy and military, and of barbers.
St Joseph Calasanz, 1556–1648, founded the Piarists to run free schools.
Patron of Catholic schools.

---

26 Saturday   **20th Week in Ordinary Time**
Green   HOURS Psalter Week 4. MASS of choice
White/Green   Saturday Mass of the **Blessed Virgin Mary**
READINGS   **Ruth 2:1-3, 8-11; 4:13-17. Ps 127:1-5, R/ v 4. Mt
                 23:1-12.** *Lect* II:273
Ruth marries Boaz, a relative of her husband, by application of the law of the
levirate. From them is born Obed, grandfather of David. The story of Ruth is one
of faith in God's providential care.

AUGUST 2023

27 Sunday   **TWENTY-FIRST SUNDAY IN ORDINARY TIME**
Green ✠   HOURS Proper. Te Deum. Psalter Week 1
                MASS Proper. Gloria. Creed. Preface: Sundays I–VIII
READINGS   **Is 22:19-23. Ps 137:1-3, 6, 8, R/ v 8. Rm 11:33-36.**
                Mt 16:13-20. *Lect* I:692

Because of Peter's faith the promise is given to him. It is through faith that the Church at all times can have trust in the promise of God's protecting power. So encouraged, we can meet the difficulties and human weaknesses that are part of the Church's life. Each member must search for deeper faith through study of the scriptures and the teaching of the Church, and by more fervent prayer.
No Masses for the dead, except funeral Masses, are permitted today (see Lit. Note 8)
St Monica is not celebrated this year.

---

28 Monday   **21st Week in Ordinary Time**
                  St Augustine, bishop and doctor of the Church
                                                           Memorial
White   HOURS of the memorial. Psalter Week 1
                  MASS of the memorial. Preface: Common or of the Saint
READINGS   **1 Th 1:1-5, 8-10. Ps 149:1-6, 9, R/ v 4. Mt 23:13-22.**
                  Lect II:276

God loves us and has called us to be his people.
St Augustine, 354–430. Bishop of Hippo, where he lived with a community until his death. His theological influence has been most significant in the Church, especially on the understanding of God's grace. Patron of theologians.

---

29 Tuesday   **21st Week in Ordinary Time**
                  The Passion of St John the Baptist   Memorial
Red   HOURS Proper of the memorial. Psalter Week 1 at Day Hour
                  MASS of the memorial. Preface: Proper
READINGS   **Jer 1:17-19. Ps 70:1-6, 15, 17, R/ v 15. Mk 6:17-29.**
                  Lect II:1175

The Mass Preface lists the favours shown to **St John the Baptist** and the vocation given him. He is found worthy of the martyr's death, his last and greatest act of witness to Christ.
Cashel and Emly Today is the anniversary of the episcopal ordination of Most Rev. Kieran O'Reilly SMA, 29 August 2010.

---

30 Wednesday 21st Week in Ordinary Time

Green   HOURS Psalter Week 1. MASS of choice
White   Optional memorial of **St Fiacre, monk**
READINGS   **1 Th 2:9-13. Ps 138:7-12, R/ v 1. Mt 23:27-32.** *Lect* II:280

There is a contrast between Paul's single-minded work for the gospel, and the Pharisees who are condemned for their hypocrisy.

St Fiacre see *The Irish Calendar*, p. 190.

Meath   **Dedication of the Cathedral** (see *Lit. Note 12*)

Achonry Today is the anniversary of the episcopal ordination of Most Rev. Paul Dempsey, 30 August 2020.

---

31 Thursday 21st Week in Ordinary Time

Green   HOURS Psalter Week 1. MASS of choice
White   Optional memorial of **St Aidan of Lindisfarne, bishop and missionary**
READINGS   **1 Th 3:7-13. Ps 89:3-4, 12-14, 17, R/ v 14. Mt 24:42-51.** *Lect* II:282

Paul exhorts the community to a deeper faith which will manifest itself in a love that embraces the whole human race. Jesus calls on us to wait in readiness for his coming.

St Aidan see *The Irish Calendar*, p. 190.

The Link between Liturgy and Life

Our society favours being practical and tends to evaluate people and institutions in this light. Practicality has led to numerous inventions that have made life more humane. It also asks people to draw a closer link between theory and everyday life, urging them to be more down-to-earth.

But for some practical-minded people, religion appears to put too much emphasis on the next world rather than this one. Further, they claim that the time and effort devoted to ceremonies and otherworldly endeavours seems to have little value. They would want religion to confine itself to humanitarian deeds.

The Church has a vital role to play in shaping responsible citizens with moral character and with a willingness to contribute to the well-being of society. The liturgy and worship of the Church have much to do with these admirable goals. At divine worship, people receive the grace to help them to be formed ever more closely to Christ. The saving grace of the dying and rising of Christ are communicated to us in the Sacraments so that we might live more perfectly Christ's truth and virtues such as love, justice, mercy and compassion.

Every Mass ends with the mission to go forth and serve the Lord. This sending means that the love of God and neighbour and the moral implications of the Beatitudes and the Ten Commandments should be witnessed by the participants in everyday life. People of faith know that their liturgical experience provides a unique spiritual vision and strength for making this a better world.

The lives of the saints provide ample evidence of this truth. Saints of every age have improved healthcare and education and fostered the human dignity of the poor, the oppressed and the society at large. Saints attribute their remarkable energies to the power that comes from prayer and above all from the Sacraments, especially the Eucharist.

Irish Catholic Catechism for Adults,
Irish Episcopal Conference, Veritas, 2014, pp. 194–195

SEPTEMBER 2023

1 Friday	**21st Week in Ordinary Time**
	World Day of Prayer for the Care of Creation
Green	HOURS Psalter Week 1. MASS of choice
READINGS	**1 Th 4:1-8. Ps 96:1-2, 5-6, 10-1, R/ v 12. Mt 25:1-13.**
	Lect II:284

Paul calls for an improvement in the community's sexual ethics. Jesus reiterates his message of watchfulness.

Today, the *World Day of Prayer for the Care of Creation*, offers to individual believers and to the community a precious opportunity to renew our personal participation in this vocation as custodians of creation, raising to God our thanks for the marvellous works that He has entrusted to our care, invoking his help for the protection of creation and his mercy for the sins committed against the world in which we live. The celebration of the Day on the same date as the Orthodox Church will be a valuable opportunity to bear witness to our growing communion with our Orthodox brothers. We live in a time where all Christians are faced with identical and important challenges and we must give common replies to these in order to appear more credible and effective (Pope Francis).

---

2 Saturday	**21st Week in Ordinary Time**
Green	HOURS Psalter Week 1. MASS of choice
White/Green	Saturday Mass of the **Blessed Virgin Mary**
READINGS	**1 Th 4:9-11. Ps 97:1, 7-9, R/ v 9. Mt 25:14-30.** *Lect* II:286

Faithfulness in small things is the lesson of the parable of the talents. We all have the talent to love. Paul reminds us: let us make progress.

Clogher Today is the anniversary of the episcopal ordination of Most Rev. Joseph Duffy, 2 September 1979.

Meath Today is the anniversary of the episcopal ordination of Most Rev. Thomas Deenihan, 2 September 2018.

PROTECTING OUR COMMON HOME

13. The urgent challenge to protect our common home includes a concern to bring the whole human family together to seek a sustainable and integral development, for we know that things can change. The Creator does not abandon us; he never forsakes his loving plan or repents of having created us. Humanity still has the ability to work together in building our common home. Here I want to recognise, encourage and thank all those striving in countless ways to guarantee the protection of the home which we share. Particular appreciation is owed to those who tirelessly seek to resolve the tragic effects of environmental degradation on the lives of the world's poorest. Young people demand change. They wonder how anyone can claim to be building a better future without thinking of the environmental crisis and the sufferings of the excluded.

14. I urgently appeal, then, for a new dialogue about how we are shaping the future of our planet. We need a conversation which includes everyone, since the

environmental challenge we are undergoing, and its human roots, concern and affect us all. The worldwide ecological movement has already made considerable progress and led to the establishment of numerous organisations committed to raising awareness of these challenges. Regrettably, many efforts to seek concrete solutions to the environmental crisis have proved ineffective, not only because of powerful opposition but also because of a more general lack of interest. Obstructionist attitudes, even on the part of believers, can range from denial of the problem to indifference, nonchalant resignation or blind confidence in technical solutions. We require a new and universal solidarity. As the bishops of Southern Africa have stated: 'Everyone's talents and involvement are needed to redress the damage caused by human abuse of God's creation'. All of us can cooperate as instruments of God for the care of creation, each according to his or her own culture, experience, involvements and talents.

15. It is my hope that this Encyclical Letter, which is now added to the body of the Church's social teaching, can help us to acknowledge the appeal, immensity and urgency of the challenge we face. I will begin by briefly reviewing several aspects of the present ecological crisis, with the aim of drawing on the results of the best scientific research available today, letting them touch us deeply and provide a concrete foundation for the ethical and spiritual itinerary that follows. I will then consider some principles drawn from the Judaeo-Christian tradition which can render our commitment to the environment more coherent. I will then attempt to get to the roots of the present situation, so as to consider not only its symptoms but also its deepest causes. This will help to provide an approach to ecology which respects our unique place as human beings in this world and our relationship to our surroundings. In light of this reflection, I will advance some broader proposals for dialogue and action which would involve each of us as individuals, and also affect international policy. Finally, convinced as I am that change is impossible without motivation and a process of education, I will offer some inspired guidelines for human development to be found in the treasure of Christian spiritual experience.

16. Although each chapter will have its own subject and specific approach, it will also take up and re-examine important questions previously dealt with. This is particularly the case with a number of themes which will reappear as the Encyclical unfolds. As examples, I will point to the intimate relationship between the poor and the fragility of the planet, the conviction that everything in the world is connected, the critique of new paradigms and forms of power derived from technology, the call to seek other ways of understanding the economy and progress, the value proper to each creature, the human meaning of ecology, the need for forthright and honest debate, the serious responsibility of international and local policy, the throwaway culture and the proposal of a new lifestyle. These questions will not be dealt with once and for all, but reframed and enriched again and again.

Pope Francis, *Laudato Si'*, 13–16

SEPTEMBER 2023

3 Sunday　　**TWENTY-SECOND SUNDAY IN ORDINARY TIME**
Green ✠　　　HOURS Proper. Te Deum. Psalter Week 2
　　　　　　MASS Proper. Gloria. Creed. Preface: Sundays I–VIII
READINGS　　**Jer 20:7-9. Ps 62:2-6, 8-9, R/ v 2. Rm 12:1-2. Mt 16:21-27.** Lect I:695

As the day of resurrection, Sunday is not only a remembrance of a past event; it is a celebration of the living presence of the risen Lord in the midst of his own people. For this presence to be properly proclaimed it is important that the disciples of Christ, saved as the People of God, come together to express fully the very identity of the Church (Pope St John Paul II, *Dies Domini*, 31).

No Masses for the dead, except funeral Masses, are permitted today (see Lit. Note 8)

St Gregory the Great, pope and doctor of the Church is not celebrated this year.

---

4 Monday　　**22nd Week in Ordinary Time**
Green　　　　HOURS Psalter Week 2. MASS of choice
White　　　　Optional memorial of **St Mac Nissi, bishop**
Connor　　**St Mac Nissi, bishop**　　　　　　　　　Feast
Down　　　**St Mac Nissi, bishop**　　　　　　　　Memorial
READINGS　　**1 Th 4:13-18. Ps 95:1, 3-5, 11-13, R/ v 13. Lk 4:16-30.** Lect II:288

Paul says that physical death is no barrier to sharing in the victory of the risen Lord. We are to encourage one another to prepare in hope for the return of the Lord.

St Mac Nissi see *The Irish Calendar*, p. 190.

---

5 Tuesday　　**22nd Week in Ordinary Time**
Green　　　　HOURS Psalter Week 2. MASS of choice
READINGS　　**1 Th 5:1-6, 9-11. Ps 26:1, 4, 13-14, R/ v 13. Lk 4:31-37.** Lect II:291

We are children of the day and no longer live as in the night. Speculation about the time and place of death can be useless. We should so live as to be always ready for the coming of the Lord. Affirmation of each other will strengthen us in the faith.

Ferns Today is the anniversary of the episcopal ordination of Most Rev. Gerard Nash, 5 September 2021.

6 Wednesday   22nd Week in Ordinary Time
Green   HOURS Psalter Week 2. MASS of choice
READINGS   **Col 1:1-8. Ps 51:10-11, R/ v 10. Lk 4:38-44.** *Lect*
               II:293

St Paul writes to the Colossians to counteract heretical tendencies. He begins by praising their genuine charity, something that is not based on feelings or mood. The truth of the gospel is shown by its universal application. The Good News must be proclaimed to all places.

_____

_____

7 Thursday   22nd Week in Ordinary Time
Green   HOURS Psalter Week 2. MASS of choice
READINGS   **Col 1:9-14. Ps 97:2-6, R/ v 2. Lk 5:1-11.** *Lect* II:295

We come to God in prayer to discover his will and to request the courage to carry it out. Gratitude for the gift of salvation should be part of our prayer also.

_____

_____

8 Friday   THE NATIVITY OF THE BLESSED VIRGIN MARY   Feast
White   HOURS Proper. Te Deum. Psalter Week 2 at Day Hour
               MASS Proper. Gloria. Preface: BVM I–II
READINGS   **Mic 5:1-4 or Rm 8:28-30. Ps 12:6-7, R/ Is 61:10. Mt
               1:1-6,18-23** (shorter form 1:18-23)**.** *Lect* II:1180

We celebrate the **Nativity of the Blessed Virgin Mary**, who brought the dawn of hope and salvation to the world. She is the true Ark of the Covenant, the temple of God, because her body received the one Mediator.
No Masses for the dead, except funeral Masses, are permitted today (see Lit. Note 8)

_____

_____

9 Saturday   22nd Week in Ordinary Time
               St Ciaran, abbot   Memorial
White   HOURS of the memorial. Psalter Week 2
               MASS of the memorial. Preface: Common or of the Saint
Clonmacnois   St Ciaran, abbot   Feast
READINGS   **Col 1:21-23. Ps 53:3-4, 6, 8, R/ v 6. Lk 6:1-5.** *Lect*
               II:299

The harsh interpretation of the Sabbath commandment is criticised by Jesus. The weekly observance of Christians helps them to persevere and stand firm on the solid base of the faith as St Paul describes it.
St Ciaran see *The Irish Calendar*, p. 190.

_____

_____

SEPTEMBER 2023

10 Sunday   **TWENTY-THIRD SUNDAY IN ORDINARY TIME**
Green ✠   HOURS Proper. Te Deum. Psalter Week 3
     MASS Proper. Gloria. Creed. Preface: Sundays I–VIII
READINGS   **Ez 33:7-9. Ps 94:1-2, 6-9, R/ v 8. Rm 13:8-10. Mt 18:15-20.** *Lect* I:697

The three readings today by chance deal with the same theme of neighbourly correction. This is a difficult art and can only be exercised through genuine love and the purest of motives. We have to learn to help and to heal each other. In this we have to avoid attitudes of prying, denunciation, jealousy and informing. The spirit of the gospel which lays down a procedure must be our guide.

No Masses for the dead, except funeral Masses, are permitted today (see Lit. Note 8)

St Peter Claver, priest is not celebrated this year.

Kerry Today is the anniversary of the episcopal ordination of Most Rev. William Murphy, 10 September 1995.

---

11 Monday   **23rd Week in Ordinary Time**
Green   HOURS Psalter Week 3. MASS of choice
READINGS   **Col 1:24-2:3. Ps 61:6-7, 9, R/ v 8. Lk 6:6-11.** *Lect* II:300

Paul believes that being called to ministry is to be associated with Christ in his sufferings. His task is to preach the secret of God that the Gentiles too are to share in union with Christ, to achieve salvation and the glory of heaven.

---

12 Tuesday   **23rd Week in Ordinary Time**
Green   HOURS Psalter Week 3. MASS of choice
White   Optional memorial of **The Most Holy Name of Mary**
White   Optional memorial of **St Ailbe, bishop**
**Cashel
and Emly**   **St Ailbe, bishop**   Feast
READINGS   **Col 2:6-15. Ps 144:1-2, 8-11, R/ v 9. Lk 6:12-19.** *Lect* II:302

The whole meaning of our salvation is rooted in Christ, not in any other philosophy. We are saved from our sins not by any action other than that of entering into the very death of Christ.

The Holy Name of Mary: Gal 4:4-7 *or* **Eph 1:3-6, 11-12. Ps Lk 1:46-55. Lk 1:39-47.** *Lect* II:1438,1432,1444

This feast was included in the Roman Calendar in 1684 to celebrate the victory over the Turks at Vienna In 1683. Suppressed in the Calendar revision of 1969, it was restored as an optional memorial in 2002.

St Ailbe see *The Irish Calendar*, p. 190.

Kilmore   **Dedication of the Cathedral** (see *Lit. Note 12*)

---

13 Wednesday 23rd Week in Ordinary Time
St John Chrysostom, bishop and doctor of the Church Memorial

White HOURS of the memorial. Psalter Week 3
MASS of the memorial. Preface: Common or of the Saint

READINGS **Col 3:1-11. Ps 144:2-3, 10-13, R/ v 9. Lk 6:20-26.**
Lect II:304

'The Church's love for the poor … is a part of her constant tradition.' This love is inspired by the gospel of the Beatitudes, of the poverty of Jesus, and of his concern for the poor. Love for the poor is even one of the motives for the duty of working so as to 'be able to give to those in need'. It extends not only to material poverty but also to the many forms of cultural and religious poverty' (CCC, 2444).

St John Chrysostom, 347–407, one of the four great Greek Doctors, the 'Golden-mouthed' preacher, was Archbishop of Constantinople. He incurred much opposition and died in exile. Patron saint of preachers.

Tuam Today is the anniversary of the episcopal ordination of Most Rev. Michael Neary, 13 September 1992.

---

14 Thursday THE EXALTATION OF THE HOLY CROSS Feast
Red HOURS Proper. Te Deum. Psalter Week 3 at Day Hour
MASS Proper. Gloria. Preface: Proper or Passion I

READINGS **Num 21:4-9 *or* Phil 2:6-11. Ps 77:1-2, 34-38, R/ 7. Jn 3:13-17.** *Lect* I:996 or II:1186

The Exaltation of the Holy Cross. The discovery of the True Cross is dated to 14 September 320. On 13 September 335 the churches on Calvary were dedicated and the cross that St Helena discovered was venerated there the next day. The annual commemoration of that event has been celebrated since, in praise of the redemption won for us by Christ.

No Masses for the dead, except funeral Masses, are permitted today (see Lit. Note 8)

Prayer of St Francis of Assisi

Praised be you, my Lord, with all your creatures,
especially Sir Brother Sun,
who is the day and through whom you give us light.
And he is beautiful and radiant with great splendour;
and bears a likeness of you, Most High.
Praised be you, my Lord, through Sister Moon and the stars,
in heaven you formed them clear and precious and beautiful.
Praised be you, my Lord, through Brother Wind,
and through the air, cloudy and serene, and every kind of weather
through whom you give sustenance to your creatures.
Praised be you, my Lord, through Sister Water,
who is very useful and humble and precious and chaste.
Praised be you, my Lord, through Brother Fire,
through whom you light the night,
and he is beautiful and playful and robust and strong.

Laudato Si', 87

15 Friday　　**23rd Week in Ordinary Time**
　　　　　　　　Our Lady of Sorrows　　　　　　　Memorial
White　　　　　HOURS Proper of the memorial. Psalter Week 4 at Day Hour
　　　　　　　MASS Proper. Optional Sequence. Preface: Blessed Virgin Mary
READINGS　　**Heb 5:7-9. Ps 30:2-6, 15-16, 20, R/ v 17. Jn 19:25-27 or Lk 2:33-35.** *Lect* II:1189

Our Lady of Sorrows. Mary, standing by the cross, 'suffered intensely with her only begotten Son and united herself as his Mother to his sacrifice, consenting with love to the offering of the victim who was born of her', whom she also offered to the eternal Father (*Marialis Cultus*).

---

16 Saturday　　**23rd Week in Ordinary Time**
　　　　　　　　Ss Cornelius, pope, and Cyprian, bishop, martyrs
　　　　　　　　　　　　　　　　　　　　　　　　Memorial
Red　　　　　　HOURS of the memorial. Psalter Week 4
　　　　　　　MASS of the memorial. Preface: Common or of the Saint
READINGS　　**1 Tm 1:15-17. Ps 112:1-7, R/ v 2. Lk 6:43-49.** *Lect* II:310

Actions speak louder than words. Hearing the word of God means taking it to heart so that it changes us. And from that good heart comes forth good fruit.

St Cornelius became Pope in 251 and died in exile at Civitavecchia in 253. Patron for cattle and domestic animals. **St Cyprian**, 210–58, bishop of Carthage, teacher and preacher, martyred.

The continual rediscovery of the beauty of the liturgy is not the search for a ritual aesthetic which is content by only a careful exterior observance of a rite or is satisfied by a scrupulous observance of the rubrics. Obviously, what I am saying here does not wish in any way to approve the opposite attitude, which confuses simplicity with a careless banality, or what is essential with an ignorant superficiality, or the concreteness of ritual action with an exasperating practical functionalism.

Let us be clear here: every aspect of the celebration must be carefully tended to (space, time, gestures, words, objects, vestments, song, music…) and every rubric must be observed. Such attention would be enough to prevent robbing from the assembly what is owed to it; namely, the Paschal Mystery celebrated according to the ritual that the Church sets down. But even if the quality and the proper action of the celebration were guaranteed, that would not be enough to make our participation full.

Pope Francis, *Desiderio Desideravi*, 22–23

17 Sunday   **TWENTY-FOURTH SUNDAY IN ORDINARY TIME**
Green ✠   HOURS Proper. Te Deum. Psalter Week 4
             MASS Proper. Gloria. Creed. Preface: Sundays I–VIII
READINGS   **Eccles (Sir) 27:30-28:7. Ps 102:1-4, 9-12, R/ v 8. Rm
             14:7-9. Mt 18:21-35.** *Lect* I:699

The Christian community must be seen to be one of forgiveness and mercy. If the
Lord is compassion and love, slow to anger and rich in mercy, who are we to be
otherwise? We need to be conscious of our own weaknesses and failures so that we
may not judge others harshly. We cannot pray the Lord's Prayer with unforgiving
hearts.
No Masses for the dead, except funeral Masses, are permitted today (see Lit. Note 8)
St Robert Bellarmine, bishop and doctor of the Church and **St
Hildegard of Bingen, virgin and doctor of the Church** are not celebrated
this year.

---

18 Monday   **24th Week in Ordinary Time**
Green   HOURS Psalter Week 4. MASS of choice
READINGS   **1 Tm 2:1-8. Ps 27:2, 7-9, R/ v 6. Lk 7:1-10.** *Lect* II:312

Paul gives instructions for the good ordering of the liturgical assembly and prayer
meetings of the community. He sees himself as apostle, herald and teacher.

---

19 Tuesday   **24th Week in Ordinary Time**
Green   HOURS Psalter Week 4. MASS of choice
Red   Optional memorial of **St Januarius, bishop and martyr**
READINGS   **1 Tm 3:1-13. Ps 100:1-3, 5, 6, R/ v 2. Lk 7:11-17.**
               Lect II:314

The Letter to Timothy has called for a community of intercession for all. Now it
addresses the need for high standards in the ministerial offices of the Church.
Those of impeccable character only should be chosen.
Dromore Today is the anniversary of the episcopal ordination of Most Rev. John
McAreavey, 19 September 1999.

---

20 Wednesday 24th Week in Ordinary Time
              **Ss Andrew Kim Tae-gŏn, priest, Paul Chŏng Ha-sang,
              and Companions, martyrs**   Memorial
Red   HOURS of the memorial. Psalter Week 4
              MASS of the memorial. Preface: Common or of the Saint
READINGS   **1 Tm 3:14-16. Ps 110:1-6, R/ v 2. Lk 7:31-35.** *Lect* II:316

'Belief in the true Incarnation of the Son of God is the distinctive sign of Christian
faith: He was manifested in the flesh' (CCC, 463).
Ss Andrew Kim Tae-gŏn, the first Korean priest, **Paul Chŏng Ha-sang**, a
catechist, and 101 others were martyred during the persecutions of the Church in
Korea, 1839–67.
Kilmore Today is the anniversary of the episcopal ordination of Most Rev. Martin
Hayes, 20 September, 2020.

21 Thursday ST MATTHEW, APOSTLE AND EVANGELIST   Feast
Red   HOURS Proper. Te Deum. Psalter Week 4 at Day Hour
            MASS Proper. Gloria. Preface: Apostles I–II
READINGS   **Eph 4:1-7, 11-13. Ps 18:2-5, R/ v 5. Mt 9:9-13.** Lect
            II:1198

St Matthew, the tax collector, may also be identified with Levi, son of Alphaeus, in Mk 2:14. He is said to have been a missionary in Persia and Ethiopia. Patron of accountants, book-keepers, tax-collectors, customs officers and security guards.
No Masses for the dead, except funeral Masses, are permitted today (see Lit. Note 8)
Galway Today is the anniversary of the episcopal ordination of Most Rev. Martin Drennan, 21 September 1997.
Dublin Today is the anniversary of the episcopal ordination of Most Rev. Raymond Field, 21 September 1997.

---

22 Friday **24th Week in Ordinary Time**
Green   HOURS Psalter Week 4. MASS of choice
READINGS   **1 Tm 6:2-12. Ps 48:6-10, 17-2, R/ Mt 5:3. Lk 8:1-3.**
            Lect II:320

'The love of money is the root of all evils' and can bring people away from faith and do damage to their souls. But the person of faith avoids all that and aims to be saintly and religious. Each has to fight the good fight of faith.
Clogher   **Dedication of the Cathedral** (see Lit. Note 12)

---

23 Saturday **24th Week in Ordinary Time**
            St Pius of Pietrelcina (Padre Pio), priest   Memorial
White   HOURS of the memorial. Psalter Week 4
            MASS of the memorial. Preface: Common or of the Saint
Raphoe   **St Eunan (Adomnán) abbot**   Feast
READINGS   **1 Tm 6:13-16. Ps 99, R/ v 2. Lk 8:4-15.** Lect II:322

'Do all that you have ben told, with no faults or failures, until the Appearing of the Lord.' With a noble and generous heart become a people who take the word of God to themselves and yield a harvest through their perseverance.
St Pius of Pietrelcina (Padre Pio), died 23 September 1968. Capuchin friar, stigmatist, confessor, friend of all who suffer.
St Eunan (Adomnán) see The Irish Calendar, p. 190.

October: Mission Month
WORLD MISSION SUNDAY • 22 OCTOBER 2023

World Mission Sunday is the one Sunday of the year when the entire global Church comes together in support of mission. It is the Holy Father's annual appeal for spiritual and financial support so that the life-giving work of overseas mission and missionaries can continue. This weekend, collections will take place in every single parish where the Church is present. It is a moment of universal solidarity when each member of the Church family, regardless of location or background, play their part in supporting each other.

All offerings and donations made on World Mission Sunday become part of the Holy Father's Universal Solidarity Fund. This fund is a lifeline for struggling missionaries and the communities they serve across Africa, Asia and Latin America, where over 1,100 mission dioceses are found. These dioceses are often in remote areas devastated by war and natural disasters or where suppressed communities are just opening up to the life-saving message of Jesus Christ. As these dioceses form and grow, so do their needs. The World Mission Sunday collection offers young dioceses the financial and spiritual assistance they need to help their men, women, and children survive and thrive.

The needs of overseas dioceses vary greatly. Anything from a motorbike, so a priest can celebrate Mass in a remote village, to a community hall to allow people to gather and celebrate in safety. Or more urgently, vaccinations and medicines to protect the vulnerable.

In essence, World Mission Sunday:
- Provides Church centred infrastructure by helping communities build schools, clinics, parish halls, and churches
- Prepares the future leaders and carers of the Church by supporting the training of sisters, priests, religious brothers, and catechists
- Supports missionary programmes that protect and care for children's wellbeing by offering safe shelter, healthcare, education, and hope for the future

Missio Ireland (Pontifical Mission Societies) coordinates World Mission Sunday. We are the Holy Father's official charity for overseas mission; his chosen instrument for sharing the gospel and building the Church throughout the world. Through the generosity of parishioners and donors, we can reach out to offer aid to struggling communities helping them to grow and thrive by bringing hope to places where there is often turmoil, poverty and uncertainty. We can provide mission dioceses with the essential support they need to become self-sufficient. Working through the local bishops, churches, and missionary congregations, we ensure resources are distributed equitably and justly, based on need – local church directly helping local church! We thank people for their great generosity and kindness.

SEPTEMBER 2023

24 Sunday   **TWENTY-FIFTH SUNDAY IN ORDINARY TIME**
World Day of Migrants and Refugees

Green ✠   HOURS Proper. Te Deum. Psalter Week 1
          MASS Proper. Gloria. Creed. Preface: Sundays I–VIII

READINGS   **Is 55:6-9. Ps 144:2-3, 8-9, 17-18, R/ v 18. Phil 1:20-24, 27. Mt 20:1-16.** *Lect* I:702

The Gospel of St Matthew, directed to Jewish Christians, stresses that the pagans have also come to God's mercy and are to be accepted. As Christ came to call sinners, so the Church must accept them. God's thoughts of justice are beyond ours, his mercy cannot be measured. That is the point of the gospel story today, whatever about the details. No one can be content with his own state of sanctity and despise or judge others. God's judgement may be quite different.
No Masses for the dead, except funeral Masses, are permitted today (see Lit. Note 8)

---

25 Monday   **25th Week in Ordinary Time**
Green   HOURS Psalter Week 1. MASS of choice
White   Optional memorial of **St Finbarr, bishop**
Cork   **St Finbarr, bishop**   Feast
READINGS   **Ezra 1:1-6. Ps 125, R/ v 3. Lk 8:16-18.** *Lect* II:325

Jerusalem and the Temple were destroyed by the Babylonian armies and the real exile began in 587–6 BC. Jeremiah had prophesied throughout the exile that there would be a return to a glorious future. Cyrus, king of Persia, conquered Babylon in 539 and encouraged the exiles to return home and rebuild the temple.
St Finbarr see *The Irish Calendar*, p. 190.
Killaloe Today is the anniversary of the episcopal ordination of Most Rev. Fintan Monahan, 25 September 2016

---

26 Tuesday   **25th Week in Ordinary Time**
Green   HOURS Psalter Week 1. MASS of choice
Red   Optional memorial **of Ss Cosmas and Damian, martyrs**
READINGS   **Ezra 6:7-8, 12, 14-20. Ps 121:1-5, R/ v 1. Lk 8:19-21.** *Lect* II:327

'Semitic languages in Jesus' time did not have a precise vocabulary for a wide range of family relationships. Rather they reflected a tribal background, where members of the same tribe, clan, or family were considered brothers and sisters, no matter what their precise relationship.' The Greek terms used in the gospel may have been influenced by early Christian references phrased in Aramaic or Hebrew (cf. R.E. Brown SS, *101 Questions and Answers on the Bible*, Paulist Press, 2003).
Ss Cosmas and Damian, early martyrs in Syria, patrons of physicians. They were known as the *Anargyroi* (the holy moneyless ones) in the East, since they never took money for their medical services.

---

27 Wednesday 25th Week in Ordinary Time
St Vincent de Paul, priest Memorial
White HOURS of the memorial. Psalter Week 1
MASS of the memorial. Preface: Common or of the Saint
READINGS **Ezra 9:5-9. Ps Tob 13:2, 4, 6-8, R/ v 1. Lk 9:1-6.** Lect
II:329

The joy of the return from Exile and the building of the Second Temple are memories of God's favour for his people.

St Vincent de Paul, 1581–1660, founded the Congregation of the Mission (the Vincentians) and the Daughters of Charity (1633), the first sisters to work outside their convents in active service. He is the patron of all charitable works.

---

28 Thursday 25th Week in Ordinary Time
Green HOURS Psalter Week 1. MASS of choice
Red Optional memorial of **St Wenceslaus, martyr**
Red Optional memorial of **Ss Lawrence Ruiz and Companions, martyrs**
READINGS **Hg 1:1-8. Ps 149:1-6, 9, R/ v 4. Lk 9:7-9.** Léct II:331

The age of salvation, with the coming of the Lord and the setting up of his kingdom, is conditional on the rebuilding of the Temple.

St Wenceslaus, 907–29, Prince of Bohemia, killed by his brother. Patron of brewers.

Ss Lawrence Ruiz and Companions. During the period 1633-7 these sixteen martyrs shed their blood out of love for Christ in the city of Nagasaki, Japan.

---

29 Friday SS MICHAEL, GABRIEL AND RAPHAEL, ARCHANGELS Feast
White HOURS Proper. Te Deum. Psalter Week 1
MASS Proper. Gloria. Preface: Angels
READINGS **Dn 7:9-10, 13-14 or Apoc 12:7-12. Ps 137:1-5, R/ v 1. Jn 1:47-51.** Lect II:1205

Gabriel brought the message to Mary at the Annunciation. **Raphael** was guide to Tobias. **Michael** has been venerated as protector of Christians in general and soldiers in particular.

No Masses for the dead, except funeral Masses, are permitted today (see Lit. Note 8)

---

30 Saturday 25th Week in Ordinary Time
St Jerome, priest and doctor of the Church Memorial
White HOURS of the memorial. Psalter Week 1
MASS of the memorial. Preface: Common or of the Saint
READINGS **Zec 2:5-9, 14-15. Ps Jer 31:10-13, R/ v 10. Lk 9:43-45.** Lect II:335

The disciples find the foretelling of Christ's death puzzling. They will come to realise that through the Paschal Mystery many nations will join the Lord and he will dwell among us his people.

St Jerome, 340–420, translated the Bible into Latin, known as the Vulgate, and wrote commentaries on scripture. Patron of librarians.

OCTOBER 2023

OCTOBER 2023

1 Sunday	**TWENTY-SIXTH SUNDAY IN ORDINARY TIME**
	Day for Life
Green ✠	HOURS Proper. Te Deum. Psalter Week 2
	MASS Proper. Gloria. Creed. Preface: Sundays I–VIII
READINGS	**Ez 18:25-28. Ps 24:4-9, R/ v 6. Phil 2:1-11** (shorter form 2:1-5)**. Mt 21:28-32.** *Lect* I:705

God gives us the gift of repentance. In the parable of the two sons, Jesus holds up the example of the public sinners in his time being converted while the establishment figures refuse to listen to his message. Ezekiel reminds us that repentance is always possible, for the Lord remembers his mercy.

No Masses for the dead, except funeral Masses, are permitted today (see Lit. Note 8)

St Thérèse of the Child Jesus, virgin and doctor of the Church is not celebrated this year.

Raphoe Today is the anniversary of the episcopal ordination of Most Rev. Philip Boyce, OCD, 1 October 1995.

---

2 Monday	**26th Week in Ordinary Time**
	The Guardian Angels Memorial
White	HOURS Proper of the memorial. Psalter Week 2 at Day Hour
	MASS of the memorial. Preface: Angels
READINGS	**Ex 23:20-23. Ps 90:1-6, 10-11, R/ v 11. Mt 18:1-5, 10.** *Lect* II:1212

We venerate the **Guardian Angels**, seeking their constant protection.

Killaloe Today is the anniversary of the episcopal ordination of Most Rev. William Walsh, 2 October 1994.

---

3 Tuesday	**26th Week in Ordinary Time**
Green	HOURS Psalter Week 2. MASS of choice
White	Optional memorial of **Bl. Columba Marmion, priest**
READINGS	**Zec 8:20-23. Ps 86, R/ Zec 8:23. Lk 9:51-56.** *Lect* II:339

James and John want revenge with fire and brimstone, but Jesus has another way.

Bl. Columba Marmion see *The Irish Calendar*, p.190.

---

4 Wednesday **26th Week in Ordinary Time**
St Francis of Assisi Memorial
White HOURS of the memorial. Psalter Week 2
MASS of the memorial. Preface: Common or of the Saint
READINGS **Neh 2:1-8. Ps 136:1-6, R/v 6. Lk 9:57-62.** Lect II:341
Jesus calls us to share his life as he experiences hunger, thirst and privation.
St Francis of Assisi, 1181–1226, abandoned all things for the love of Christ,
founded the Friars Minor, and with St Clare, the Poor Clares. For the last two
years of his life he suffered the stigmata. Patron saint of ecologists.

---

5 Thursday **26th Week in Ordinary Time**
Green HOURS Psalter Week 2. MASS of choice
White Optional memorial of **St Faustina Kowalska, virgin** (see
Collect, p. 183)
READINGS **Neh 8:1-12. Ps 18:8-11, R/ v 9. Lk 10:1-12.** Lect
II:343
The assembled people are in tears as they renew their covenant with God.
'Whenever the Church, gathered by the Holy Spirit for liturgical celebration,
announces and proclaims the word of God, it has the experience of being a new
people in whom the covenant made in the past is fulfilled' (ILect, 7).
St Faustina was born in Głogowiec, near Łódz in Poland in 1905, died in
Kraków in 1938, her short life spent as a Sister of Our Lady of Mercy. Listening to
the Lord who is Love and Mercy, she understood that no human wretchedness
could measure itself against the mercy which ceaselessly pours from the heart of
Christ. She inspired the movement dedicated to proclaiming and imploring Divine
Mercy throughout the world.

Pope St Paul VI on 4 December 1963, when *Sacrosanctum Concilium*, the
Constitution on the Sacred Liturgy, was promulgated at Vatican II, quoted by Pope
Francis:

'The difficult, complex debates have had rich results. They have brought one
topic to a conclusion, the sacred liturgy. Treated before all others, in a sense it
has priority over all others for its intrinsic dignity and importance to the life of
the Church and today we will solemnly promulgate the document on the liturgy.
Our spirit, therefore, exults with true joy, for in the way things have gone we
note respect for a right scale of values and duties. God must hold first place;
prayer to him is our first duty. The liturgy is the first source of divine communion
in which God shares his own life with us. It is also the first school of the spiritual
life. The liturgy is the first gift we must make to the Christian people united to us
by faith and the fervour of their prayers. It is also a primary invitation to the
human race, so that all may now lift their mute voices in blessed and genuine
prayer and thus may experience that indescribable, regenerative power to be
found when they join us in proclaiming the praises of God and the hopes of the
human heart through Jesus Christ and in the Holy Spirit'.

Pope Francis, *Desiderio Desideravi*, 30

6 Friday **26th Week in Ordinary Time**
Children's Day of Mission Prayer
Green HOURS Psalter Week 2. MASS of choice
White Optional memorial of **St Bruno, priest**
READINGS **Bar 1:15-22. Ps 78:1-5, 8-9, R/ v 9. Lk 10:13-16.** *Lect* 346

Israel in exile is punished because of her sins in abandoning the Law given to Moses. This psalm of penitence is her confession of guilt.

St Bruno, born Cologne 1032. He became professor of theology in Rheims University and later its head. But his desire was to found a monastery where poverty, manual work, silence and worship would be the basics. He founded the Carthusians at La Grande Chartreuse, where he died in 1101.

Tuam Today is the anniversary of the episcopal ordination of Most Rev. Francis Duffy, 6 October 2013.

MISSIO
Children Helping Children

CHILDREN'S DAY OF MISSION PRAYER 2023: YOUNG PEOPLE SHARING HOPE AND SOLIDARITY WITH THE WORLD'S POOREST CHILDREN

Children's Day of Mission Prayer is celebrated on the second Friday of October each year. Its purpose is to enhance the prayer lives of children, encouraging them to pray for each other and for overseas missionaries on mission with children. This special day fosters an awareness of mission and the need to help and serve others. It is aimed at children on the whole island of Ireland, teaching professionals, priests, chaplains, religious congregations, and all those who are in ministry with children. Catholic primary schools and parishes receive a resource book, which includes a collection of prayer resources to help schools, parishes and communities celebrate mission with children. If you have not received your resource, you can download a copy from www.missio.ie

As the Holy Father's official charity for overseas mission, Missio Ireland's *Children Helping Children* supports the physical, spiritual, and emotional wellbeing of children around the world. We encourage children to pray together, for each other, and for children living in poverty and fear. We also encourage children to share whatever they can, no matter how little, to help with the material needs of their brothers and sisters. Thanks to young people living out our motto *Children Helping Children*, the Missio family can support millions of the world's poorest children every year. As a result, thousands of children's projects, led by missionaries, are supported. These missionaries, who are living out their faith through action, know the value of every donation they receive as they try to help everyone they can regardless of their backgrounds or beliefs.

To learn more about Children's Day of Mission Prayer or *Children Helping Children*, please email info@missio.ie or call Missio Ireland on +353 (0)1 4972035.

7 Saturday   **26th Week in Ordinary Time**
             Our Lady of the Rosary   Memorial
White   HOURS Proper of the memorial. Psalter Week 2 at Day Hour
             MASS of the memorial. Preface: Blessed Virgin Mary
READINGS   **Acts 1:12-14. Ps Lk 1:46-55, R/ v 49. Lk 1:26-38.**
             Lect II:1217

Our Lady of the Rosary. 'Today's celebration urges all to meditate on the mysteries of Christ, following the example of the Blessed Virgin Mary who was in a special manner associated with the incarnation, passion and glorious resurrection of the Son of God' (*Divine Office*).

Synod of Bishops in Rome

The XVI Ordinary General Assembly of the Synod of Bishops takes place in Rome, October 2023.

A synodal journey was launched by Pope Francis in October 2021 on the theme, *For a Synodal Church: Communion, Participation and Mission*.

Local Churches engaged in a two-year pathway of prayer, listening and consultation, producing a National Synthesis for the Assembly in Rome. In Ireland this phase will lead also to a National Synod, announced in March 2021, to be held within the next five years.

We stand before You, Holy Spirit,
as we gather together in Your name.

With You alone to guide us,
make Yourself at home in our hearts;
Teach us the way we must go
and how we are to pursue it.

We are weak and sinful;
do not let us promote disorder.
Do not let ignorance lead us
down the wrong path nor partiality
influence our actions.

Let us find in You our unity
so that we may journey together
to eternal life and not stray from
the way of truth and what is right.

All this we ask of You,
who are at work in every place and time,
in the communion of the Father and the Son,
forever and ever. Amen.

OCTOBER 2023

8 Sunday — TWENTY-SEVENTH SUNDAY IN ORDINARY TIME
Green ✠   HOURS Proper. Te Deum. Psalter Week 3
                 MASS Proper. Gloria. Creed. Preface: Sundays I–VIII
READINGS   **Is 5:1-7. Ps 79:9, 12-16, 19-20, R/ Is 5:7. Phil 4:6-9. Mt 21:33-43.** *Lect* I:708

Israel, God's first chosen people, did not produce the fruit expected of them. God found fault with them and the promised inheritance passed from them. The Church today must prove itself worthy of God's call by bringing forth the fruit of love and good works.

No Masses for the dead, except funeral Masses, are permitted today (see Lit. Note 8)

Ossory   Dedication of the Cathedral (see *Lit. Note 12*)

_____

_____

9 Monday — 27th Week in Ordinary Time
Green   HOURS Psalter Week 3. MASS of choice
White   Optional memorial of **St John Henry Newman, priest**
Red   Optional memorial of **Ss Denis, bishop, and Companions, martyrs**
White   Optional memorial of **St John Leonardi, priest**
READINGS   **Jon 1:1-2:1, 11. Ps Jon 2:3-5, 8, R/ v 7. Lk 10:25-37.** *Lect* II:350

Jonah's message is that there is no limit to be put on the extent of God's mercy. Jonah, who benefits from that mercy throughout the first part of the story, is the one who rebels against God's showing that mercy to others. The story speaks to all who would attempt to limit God's freedom in his dealings with others.

St Denis and Companions, Rusticus and Eleutherius were beheaded and thrown into the Seine in 258 and later buried at Montmartre. Their finest tribute is the abbey church of Saint-Denis where the kings of France are buried. Denis, the first Bishop of Paris, is one of the patrons of France.

St John Leonardi, 1541–1609, supported the reforms of Trent, published a Catechism and helped to found the Propagation of the Faith in Rome.

St John Henry Newman see *The Irish Calendar*, p. 191.

_____

_____

10 Tuesday — 27th Week in Ordinary Time
Green   HOURS Psalter Week 3. MASS of choice
READINGS   **Jon 3:1-10. Ps 129:1-4, 7-8, R/ v 3. Lk 10:38-42.** *Lect* II:353

Jonah preached repentance. The people of Nineveh renounced their evil behaviour, and God relented.

_____

_____

11 Wednesday 27th Week in Ordinary Time

Green   HOURS Psalter Week 3. MASS of choice

White   Optional memorial of **St John XXIII, pope** (see Collect, p. 182)

White   Optional memorial of **St Canice, abbot**

Kilkenny City   **St Canice, abbot**   Feast

READINGS   **Jon 4:1-11. Ps 85:3-6, 9-10, R/ v 15. Lk 11:1-4.** *Lect* II:355

Jonah in his ill-humour is told by God to have a sense of proportion. The lives of the people of Nineveh are of more account than the dead plant. We must forgive others.

St John XXIII, born in Sotto il Monte, diocese of Bergamo, 1881, taught in seminary, worked as a military chaplain in World War I, apostolic delegate in Bulgaria, later in Turkey and Greece, nuncio in Paris, Patriarch of Venice 1953, elected Pope 28 October 1958. Called the Second Vatican Council, which began on 11 October 1962. He died 3 June 1963.

READINGS   **Ez 34: 11-16. Ps 22 R/ v 1. Jn 21:15-17.** *Lect* II:1480, 1481, 1500

St Canice see *The Irish Calendar*, p.191.

---

12 Thursday 27th Week in Ordinary Time

Green   HOURS Psalter Week 3. MASS of choice

READINGS   **Mal 3:13-20. Ps 1, R/ Ps 39:5. Lk 11:5-13.** *Lect* II:357

We are asked to make a choice of God's way or the way of sinners. The choice is ours but God's judgement awaits us. The way of the wicked leads to doom, 'but for you who fear, the sun of righteousness will shine out with healing in its rays'.

---

13 Friday 27th Week in Ordinary Time

Green   HOURS Psalter Week 3. MASS of choice

READINGS   **Jl 1:13-15, 2:1-2. Ps 9:2-3, 6, 16, 8-9, R/ v 9. Lk 11:15-26.** *Lect* II:359

God will judge with justice. That judgement, because it is so searching, is to be feared. The work of the devil is to create a false security in our lives.

Galway and **Clonfert** Today is the anniversary of the episcopal ordination of Most Rev. Michael Duignan, 13 October 2019.

---

14 Saturday 27th Week in Ordinary Time

Green   HOURS Psalter Week 3. MASS of choice

Red   Optional memorial of **St Callistus I, pope and martyr**

White/Green   Saturday Mass of the **Blessed Virgin Mary**

READINGS   **Jl 4:12-21. Ps 96:1-2, 5-6, 11-1, R/ v 12. Lk 11:27-28.** *Lect* II:362

The word of God goes forth and does not return empty. It calls for repentance; for judgement is near. Happy are those who hear the word of God and keep it.

St Callistus I, after a life of slavery and imprisonment for criminal offences, was freed and became a deacon in charge of catacombs that bear his name. He became Pope in 217, opposed by Hippolytus. Died at the hands of a mob in 222.

Down and Connor   **Dedication of the Cathedral** (see *Lit. Note 12*)

OCTOBER 2023

15 Sunday   TWENTY-EIGHTH SUNDAY IN ORDINARY TIME
Green ✠   HOURS Proper. Te Deum. Psalter Week 4
               MASS Proper. Gloria. Creed. Preface: Sundays I–VIII
READINGS   **Is 25:6-10. Ps 22, R/ v 6. Phil 4:120-14, 19-20. Mt 22:1-14** (shorter form 22:1-10). *Lect* I:711

We gather to celebrate the Eucharist, which is to be a celebration in hope and joy as a foretaste of the heavenly banquet. To take part in it is a grace and a privilege. But we must wear the wedding garment of sinlessness and obedience to God's will. Many before us have been called to the feast but failed to stay.
No Masses for the dead, except funeral Masses, are permitted today (see Lit. Note 8)
St Teresa of Ávila, virgin and doctor of the Church is not celebrated this year.

---

16 Monday   28th Week in Ordinary Time
Green   HOURS Psalter Week 4. MASS of choice
White   Optional memorial of **St Hedwig, religious**
White   Optional memorial of **St Margaret Mary Alacoque, virgin**
White   Optional memorial of **St Gall, abbot and missionary**
READINGS   **Rm 1:1-7. Ps 97:1-4, R/ v 2. Lk 11:29-32.** *Lect* II:364

The Letter to the Romans gives a synthesis of Paul's theology, but not it all. The main themes headlined at the beginning are: God's free choice of his people, the relationship of faith to justification, salvation through Christ's death and resurrection, and the new covenant as fulfilment of the old.
St Hedwig, 1174–1243, wife of the Duke of Silesia, mother of seven children, some of whom caused her trouble, devoted herself to charitable works.
St Margaret Mary, 1647–90, visionary and ascetic, revived devotion to the Sacred Heart of Jesus, and was exemplary in her patience and trust.
St Gall see *The Irish Calendar*, p. 191.

---

17 Tuesday   28th Week in Ordinary Time
               St Ignatius of Antioch, bishop and martyr   Memorial
Red   HOURS of the memorial. Psalter Week 4
               MASS of the memorial. Preface: Common or of the Saint
READINGS   **Rm 1:16-25. Ps 18:2-5, R/ v 2. Lk 11:37-41.** *Lect* II:366

Faith relies on God's promises, his faithfulness to them and on his power to carry them out. The gospel reveals the power of God to make people righteous.
St Ignatius, Bishop of Antioch, died a martyr at Rome about 107. He urged Christians to unity in and through the Eucharist and around their local bishop.

18 Wednesday ST LUKE, EVANGELIST   Feast
Red   HOURS Proper. Te Deum. Psalter Week 4 at Day Hour
                         MASS Proper. Gloria. Preface: Apostles II
READINGS   **2 Tm 4:10-17. Ps 144:10-13, 17-18, R/ v 12. Lk 10:1-9.** *Lect* II:1233

St Luke was a physician from a Gentile Christian milieu. He was with St Paul on his second missionary journey and during his imprisonment in Rome. After Paul's death he is reputed to have worked in Greece. In art, he is represented by an ox. Patron of butchers, bookbinders, doctors, surgeons, artists and glassworkers.
No Masses for the dead, except funeral Masses, are permitted today (see Lit. Note 8)

19 Thursday   **28th Week in Ordinary Time**
Green   HOURS Psalter Week 4. MASS of choice
Red   Optional memorial of **Ss John de Brébeuf, Isaac Jogues, priests, and Companions, martyrs**
White   Optional memorial of **St Paul of the Cross, priest**
READINGS   **Rm 3:21-30. Ps 129:1-6, R/ v 7. Lk 11:47-54.** *Lect* II:370

Paul is clear that grace means a gift that is given absolutely freely. God takes the initiative in making us agreeable to him, only then can there be the human response.
Ss John de Brébeuf and Isaac Jogues, with their six Jesuit companions, were slain by Huron and Iroquois Indians in 1646/9.
St Paul of the Cross, 1694–1775, founded the Passionists in Rome, preaching on the passion of Christ and tending the sick, the dying and the lapsed.

20 Friday   **28th Week in Ordinary Time**
Green   HOURS Psalter Week 4. MASS of choice
READINGS   **Rm 4:1-8. Ps 31:1-2, 5, 11, R/ cf. v 7. Lk 12:1-7.** *Lect* II:372

Abraham is an example of a man justified through his faith. Jewish teaching, seeing his loyalty and steadfastness, has lauded his work, but Paul sees these works as flowing from his faith. For God, faith and uprightness are interdependent.

21 Saturday   **28th Week in Ordinary Time**
Green   HOURS Psalter Week 4. MASS of choice
White/Green   Saturday Mass of the **Blessed Virgin Mary**
READINGS   **Rm 4:13, 16-18. Ps 104:6-9, 42-43, R/ v 8. Lk 12:8-12.** *Lect* II:374

Faith is the basic requirement for salvation for all, not just for the descendants of Abraham. The promises were offered in response to faith, not as a reward for keeping the Law. Their fulfilment in Christ is accessible through faith.

OCTOBER 2023

22 Sunday — TWENTY-NINTH SUNDAY IN ORDINARY TIME
Mission Sunday

Green ✠   HOURS Proper. Te Deum. Psalter Week 1
               MASS Proper. Gloria. Creed. Preface: Sundays I–VIII
READINGS   **Is 45:1, 4-6. Ps 95:1, 3-5, 7-10, R/ v 7. 1 Th 1:1-5. Mt 22:15-21.** *Lect* I:714

God's people strive for justice, peace and salvation. Their only true happiness will be in God; apart from him, all is nothing.
No Masses for the dead, except funeral Masses, are permitted today (see Lit. Note 8)
St John Paul II, pope is not celebrated this year.

---

23 Monday — 29th Week in Ordinary Time
Green   HOURS Psalter Week 1. MASS of choice
White   Optional memorial of **St John of Capistrano, priest**
READINGS   **Rm 4:20-25. Ps Lk 1:69-75, R/ cf. v 68. Lk 12:13-21.** *Lect* II:376

Abraham's faith in God's promise never wavered. It is a model for ours. We place our faith in the mighty saviour who would free us from our sins.
St John of Capistrano, 1386–1456, studied civil and canon law and joined the Franciscan Order. A faithful servant of four popes, he attended the Council of Florence, went to Jerusalem as apostolic emissary, and, in 1451, set out on a preaching tour through the German provinces and Poland. In a battle at Belgrade he contracted fever and died there. Patron saint of jurists and military chaplains.

---

24 Tuesday — 29th Week in Ordinary Time
Green   HOURS Psalter Week 1. MASS of choice
White   Optional memorial of **St Anthony Mary Claret, bishop**
READINGS   **Rm 5:12, 15, 17-21. Ps 39:7-10, 17, R/ cf. vv 8, 9. Lk 12:35-38.** *Lect* II:378

Jesus Christ restores life to those who have inherited death through another man. The power of grace is greater than the inclination to sin.
St Anthony Mary Claret, 1807–70, founded the Claretians in Spain for missionary work. Archbishop of Santiago, Cuba, then returned as chaplain to the Queen of Spain, and built schools and museums, before being exiled with the monarchy.

---

25 Wednesday 29th Week in Ordinary Time
Green   HOURS Psalter Week 1. MASS of choice
Cork and Ross Bl. Thaddeus MacCarthy, bishop   Memorial
Cloyne   Bl. Thaddeus MacCarthy, bishop   Memorial
READINGS   **Rm 6:12-18. Ps 123, R/ v 8. Lk 12:39-48.** Lect II:380
We are still subject to natural human inclinations that can lead to sin. But Christ
has freed us from evil so as to restore us to God.
Bl. Thaddeus MacCarthy see The Irish Calendar, p. 191.
Waterford and
Lismore   Dedication of the Cathedral (see Lit. Note 12)

---

26 Thursday   29th Week in Ordinary Time
Green   HOURS Psalter Week 1. MASS of choice
READINGS   **Rm 6:19-23. Ps 1:1-4, 6, R/ Ps 39:5. Lk 12:49-53.**
                Lect II:382
The sinner earns death as the wages of sin. The Christian has been given new life,
has been sanctified, but has to live out this holiness in practice, and grow in
sanctity.

---

27 Friday   29th Week in Ordinary Time
Green   HOURS Psalter Week 1. MASS of choice
White   Optional memorial of **St Otteran, monk**
Waterford   St Otteran, monk   Feast
READINGS   **Rm 7:18-25. Ps 118:66, 68, 76-77, 93-94 R/ v 68.**
                Lk 12:54-59. Lect II:384
The powerful force of sin is such that the Christian can be torn between what is
known to be the right thing and the attraction of sin. Personal responsibility for evil
and good still remain, but the Spirit can transform the body into the likeness of the
Risen Christ in a new life of uprightness and holiness.
St Otteran see The Irish Calendar, p. 191.

---

28 Saturday   SS SIMON AND JUDE, APOSTLES   Feast
Red   HOURS Proper. Te Deum. Psalter Week 1 at Day Hour
                MASS Proper. Gloria. Preface: Apostles I–II
READINGS   **Eph 2:19-22. Ps 18:2-5, R/ v 5. Lk 6:12-19.** Lect
                II:1242
Ss Simon and Jude. The teaching of the apostles is the living gospel for all to
hear. Their authority comes from their fidelity to Christ and his message. St Jude is
patron saint of hopeless causes.
No Masses for the dead, except funeral Masses, are permitted today (see Lit. Note 8)
                FIRST EVENING PRAYER of **Thirtieth Sunday**

OCTOBER 2023

29 Sunday **THIRTIETH SUNDAY IN ORDINARY TIME**
Green ✠   HOURS Proper. Te Deum. Psalter Week 2
               MASS Proper. Gloria. Creed. Preface: Sundays I–VIII
READINGS   **Ex 22:20-26. Ps 17:2-4, 47, 51, R/ v 2. I Th 1:5-10.**
               Mt 22:34-40. *Lect* I:717

The greatest and first commandment: you must love the Lord your God with all your heart, soul and mind. The second resembles it: you must love your neighbour as yourself.
No Masses for the dead, except funeral Masses, are permitted today (see Lit. Note 8)
St Colman, bishop is not celebrated this year, except
Kilmacduagh   St Colman, bishop   This year as Solemnity
St Colman see *The Irish Calendar*, p. 191.

---

30 Monday **30th Week in Ordinary Time**
Green   HOURS Psalter Week 2. MASS of choice
READINGS   **Rm 8:12-17. Ps 67:2, 4, 6-7, 20-21, R/ v 21. Lk**
               13:10-17. *Lect* II:388

The vocation of the whole human race is to be children of God. The Spirit is the principle of divine life in us, making us into the image of the Son.

---

31 Tuesday **30th Week in Ordinary Time**
Green   HOURS Psalter Week 2. MASS of choice
Cloyne   Optional memorial of **Bl. Dominic Collins, martyr**
READINGS   **Rm 8:18-25. Ps 125, R/ v 3. Lk 13:18-21.** *Lect* II: 390

'At the very heart of Christianity is the conviction that suffering and glory are intimately related. There can be no glory without suffering. The reason for this is sin, which introduced distortion and alienation and corruption into the world. These cannot be removed without the pain of a correcting reversal of the world's direction. Paul speaks of this pain and suffering here, but he wants to begin on a positive note by stressing the coming glory as of surpassing value' (E.H. Maly, *N.T. Message* no. 9, Veritas).
Bl. Dominic Collins, see *The Irish Calendar*, p. 191.
               FIRST EVENING PRAYER of **All Saints**

ALL SOULS
Commemoration of the Faithful Departed

Belief in the resurrection of the dead is an essential part of Christian revelation. It implies a particular understanding of the ineluctable mystery of death.

Death is the end of earthy life, but 'not of our existence' (St Ambrose) since the soul is immortal. 'Our lives are measured by time, in the course of which we change, grow old and, as with all living beings on earth, death seems like the normal end of life' (CCC, 1007). Seen from the perspective of the faith, 'death is the end of man's earthly pilgrimage, of the time of grace and mercy which God offers him so as to work out his earthly life in keeping with the divine plan, and to decide his ultimate destiny' (CCC, 1013).

In one light death can seem natural, in another it can be seen as 'the wages of sin' (*Rm* 6:23). Authentically interpreting the meaning of Scripture (cf. *Jn* 2:17, 3:3, 3:19; *Wis* 1:13; *Rm* 5:12, 6:23), the Church teaches that 'death entered the world on account of man's sin' (CCC, 1008).

Jesus, the Son of God, 'born of a woman and subject to the law' (*Gal* 4:4) underwent death which is part of the human condition; despite his anguish in the face of death (*Mk* 14:33-34; *Heb* 5:7-8), 'he accepted it in an act of complete and free submission to his Father's will. The obedience of Jesus has transformed the curse of death into a blessing' (CCC, 1009).

Death is the passage to the fullness of true life. The Church, subverting the logic of this world, calls the Christian's day of death his *dies natalis*, the day of his heavenly birth, where 'there will be no more death, and no more mourning or sadness [for] the world of the past has gone' (*Apoc* 21:4). Death is the prolongation, in a new way, of life as the liturgy says: 'For your faithful, O Lord, life has changed not ended; while our earthly dwelling is destroyed, a new and eternal dwelling is prepared for us in Heaven' (*Missal*, Preface).

The death of a Christian is an event of grace, having, as it does, a positive value and significance in Christ and through Christ. Scripture teaches that: 'Life to me, of course, life is Christ, but then death would bring me something more' (*Phil* 1:21); 'here is a saying you can rely on: if we have died with him, then we shall live with him' (*2 Tm* 2:11).

According to the faith of the Church, 'to die in Christ' begins at Baptism. In Baptism, the Lord's disciples sacramentally die in Christ so as to live a new life. If the disciples die in the grace Christ, physical death seals that 'dying with Christ', and consummates it by incorporating them fully and definitively into Christ the Redeemer.

The Church's prayer of suffrage for the souls of the faithful departed implores eternal life not only for the disciples of Christ who have died in his peace, but for the dead whose faith is known to God (see Eucharistic Prayer IV).

The just encounter God in death. He calls them to himself so as to share eternal life with them. No one, however, can be received into God's friendship and intimacy without having been purified of the consequences of personal sin. 'The Church gives the name Purgatory to this final purification of the elect, which is entirely different from the punishment of the damned. The Church formulated her doctrine of faith on Purgatory especially at the Councils of Florence and Trent' (CCC, 1031).

Hence derives the pious custom of suffrage for the souls of the faithful departed, which is an urgent supplication of God to have mercy on the souls of the dead, to purify them by the fire of His charity, and to bring them to His kingdom of light and life. This suffrage is a cultic expression of faith in the communion of saints. Indeed, the Church in its pilgrim members, from the earliest days of the Christian religion, has honoured with great respect the memory of the dead; and 'because it is a holy and a wholesome thought to pray for the dead that they may be loosed from their sins' (*2 Mac* 12:46) she offers her suffrages for them. These consist, primarily, in the celebration of the holy sacrifice of the Eucharist, and in other pious exercises, such as prayers for the dead, alms deeds, works of mercy, and the application of indulgences to the souls of the faithful departed.

Directory on Popular Piety and the Liturgy, 249–52

Norms for Indulgences at the Commemoration of All Souls

1. From twelve o'clock noon on 1 November until midnight on 2 November, all who have confessed, received Holy Communion and prayed for the pope's intentions (one Our Father and Hail Mary, or any other prayer of one's choice) can gain one plenary indulgence by visiting a church or oratory, and there reciting one Our Father and the Apostle's Creed.

This indulgence is applicable only to the souls of the departed.
Confession may be made at any time within the week preceding or the week following 1 November.
Holy Communion may be received on any day from 1 November to 8 November.

2. The faithful who visit a cemetery and pray for the dead may gain a plenary indulgence applicable only to the Holy Souls on the usual conditions once per day from 1 to 8 November. The conditions mentioned above apply also for this.

What are Indulgences?

Indulgences are the remission before God of the temporal punishment due to sins whose guilt has already been forgiven. The faithful Christian who is duly disposed gains the indulgence under prescribed conditions for either himself or the departed. Indulgences are granted through the ministry of the Church which, as the dispenser of the grace of redemption, distributes the treasury of the merits of Christ and the Saints.

Compendium of the Catechism of the Catholic Church, 312
(published by Veritas, 2006). See CCC, 1471–9, 1498.

Lord God,
whose days are without end
and whose mercies beyond counting,
keep us mindful
that life is short and the hour of death unknown.
Let your Spirit guide our days on earth
in the ways of holiness and justice,
that we may serve you
in union with the whole Church,
sure in faith, strong in hope, perfect in love.
And when our earthly journey is ended,
lead us rejoicing into your kingdom,
where you live for ever and ever. Amen.

Order of Christian Funerals, 332

NOVEMBER 2023

1 Wednesday ALL SAINTS   Solemnity
White ✠   HOURS Proper. Te Deum. Complementary Psalms at Day Hour
                     MASS Proper Gloria. Creed. Preface: Proper
READINGS   **Apoc 7:2-4, 9-14. Ps 23:1-6, R/ cf. v 6. 1 Jn 3:1-3.
                     Mt 5:1-12.** *Lect* I:999 or II:1244

All Saints. 'The ultimate object of veneration of the Saints is the glory of God and the sanctification of man by conforming one's life fully to the divine will and by imitating the virtue of those who were pre-eminent disciples of the Lord. Catechesis and other forms of doctrinal instruction should therefore make known to the faithful that our relationship with the Saints must be seen in the light of the faith and should not obscure the "*cultus latriae*, due to God the Father through Christ in the Holy Spirit, but intensify it"' (*Directory on Popular Piety and the Liturgy*, 212).
                     EVENING PRAYER of All Saints
                     Night Prayer 2 of Sunday
No other celebrations, not even funeral Masses, are permitted today (see Lit. Note 8)
Achonry   Dedication of the Cathedral (see *Lit. Note 12*)

---

2 Thursday   **THE COMMEMORATION OF ALL THE FAITHFUL DEPARTED**
                                          (All Souls Day)

Violet/Black   HOURS from the Office for the Dead

                                          MASS Proper for the Dead. Preface: Proper

READINGS   **Is 25:6-9. Ps 26:1, 4, 7-9, 13-14, R/ v 1, Alt R/ v 13. Rm 5:5-11. Lk 7:11-17.** *Lect* I:1002 *or* Readings are chosen from Masses for the Dead. *Lect* III:849–90

All Souls. 'Indeed, the Church in its pilgrim members, from the very earliest days of the Christian religion, has honoured with great respect the memory of the dead; and "because it is a holy and a wholesome thought to pray for the dead that they may be loosed from their sins" (2 Mac 12, 46) she offers her suffrages for them. These consist, primarily, in the celebration of the holy sacrifice of the Eucharist, and in other pious exercises, such as prayers for the dead, alms deeds, works of mercy, and the application of indulgences to the souls of the faithful departed' (*Directory on Popular Piety and the Liturgy*, 251).

All priests may celebrate three Masses today, for only one of which may a stipend be taken. The other Masses have the intention for all the faithful departed and for the intentions of the Pope.

No other celebrations are permitted today. See pp. 167–168 on **Indulgences**.

---

3 Friday   **30th Week in Ordinary Time**

                                  St Malachy, bishop   Memorial

White   HOURS of the memorial. Psalter Week 3

                                  MASS of the memorial

Armagh   **St Malachy, bishop**   Feast
Down and
Connor   **St Malachy, bishop**   Feast

READINGS   **Rm 9:1-5. Ps 147:12-15, 19-20, R/ v 12. Lk 14:1-6.** *Lect* II:396

His love for the Jewish people is such that Paul is prepared to give his life for them. Jesus comes up against the Pharisees and teir literal interpretation of the Law.

St Malachy see *The Irish Calendar*, p. 191.

---

4 Saturday   **30th Week in Ordinary Time**

                                  St Charles Borromeo, bishop   Memorial

White   HOURS of the memorial. Psalter Week 3

                                  MASS of the memorial

READINGS   **Rm 11:1-2, 11-12, 25-29. Ps 93:12-15, 17-18, R/ v 14. Lk 14:1, 7-11.** *Lect* II:397

In early times the Jews were the only chosen people. But now in the time of 'election,' the time of the gospel, the Gentiles as well as the Jews are called. The Jews have rejected Christ while the Gentiles are converted. Paul's belief is that this alienation of the Jews is only temporary.

St Charles Borromeo, 1538–84, ordained priest and bishop in 1563 and resident Archbishop of Milan in 1563. He drafted The Catechism of the Council of Trent, having been prominent in the final sessions of that Council. Patron saint of catechists and seminarians.

NOVEMBER 2023

5 Sunday   THIRTY-FIRST SUNDAY IN ORDINARY TIME
Prisoners' Sunday

Green ✠   HOURS Proper. Te Deum. Psalter Week 3
          MASS Proper. Gloria. Creed. Preface: Sundays I–VIII

READINGS   **Mal 1:14-2:2, 8-10. Ps 130. I Th 2:7-9, 13. Mt 23:1-12.** *Lect* I:719.

Scripture speaks strongly against those who do not observe the law but still don't hesitate to impose the obligation on others. The failure is leading a double life and in having an inflated sense of their own importance.

No Masses for the dead, except funeral Masses, are permitted today (see Lit. Note 8)

St Martin de Porres, religious is not celebrated this year.

---

6 Monday   ALL THE SAINTS OF IRELAND   Feast
White   HOURS Proper (Divine Office, p. 460*)
          Te Deum. Psalter Week 3 at Day Hour
          MASS Proper. Gloria. Preface: Proper

READINGS   **Heb 11:2, 12:1-4, 15, 13:1 or Eccles (Sir) 44:1-15. Ps 125, R/ v 5. Lk 6:20-26.** *National Proper*

No Masses for the dead, except funeral Masses, are permitted today (see Lit. Note 8)

All the Saints of Ireland see *The Irish Calendar*, p. 192.

---

7 Tuesday   31st Week in Ordinary Time
Green   HOURS Psalter Week 3. MASS of choice
White   Optional memorial of **St Willibrord, bishop and missionary**

READINGS   **Rm 12:5-16. Ps 130. Lk 14:15-24.** *Lect* II:402

Mutual love binds all Christians together as one body. Each member works for the good of all

St Willibrord see *The Irish Calendar*, p. 192.

---

8 Wednesday   31st Week in Ordinary Time
Green   HOURS Psalter Week 3. MASS of choice

READINGS   **Rm 13:8-10. Ps 111:1-2, 4-5, 9, R/ v 5. Lk 14:25-33.** *Lect* II:404

The supreme law of love covers all our relationships with other people.

---

9 Thursday THE DEDICATION OF THE LATERAN BASILICA   Feast
White   HOURS Proper. Te Deum. Psalter Week 3 at Day Hour
              MASS Proper. Gloria. Preface: Proper
READINGS   **Ez 47:1-2, 8-9, 12 or 1 Cor 3:9-11, 16-17. Ps 45:2-3, 5-6, 8-9, R/ v 5. Jn 2:13-22.** Lect I:1006 or II:1250

The Church of St John on the Lateran in Rome is 'Mother and Head of all the churches of the City and the World'. It is the cathedral church of the Bishop of Rome, and was called 'St John' after the two monasteries once attached, dedicated to St John the Divine and St John the Baptist. It is however dedicated to the Most Holy Saviour.

No Masses for the dead, except funeral Masses, are permitted today (see Lit. Note 8)

---

10 Friday **31st Week in Ordinary Time**
               St Leo the Great, pope and doctor of the Church
                                                         Memorial
White   HOURS of the memorial. Psalter Week 3
               MASS of the memorial. Preface: Common or of the Saint
READINGS   **Rm 15:14-21. Ps 97:1-4, R/ cf. v 2. Lk 16:1-8.** Lect II:408

Paul speaks of his vocation as apostle to the Gentiles. His first words were always to the Jews, but he was rejected by them. Luke's Gospel addresses the pressing problem of how a Christian is to deal with money.

St Leo the Great, died 461, taught the two natures, human and divine, of Christ at the Council of Chalcedon, 451, and the primacy of the See of Peter.

---

11 Saturday **31st Week in Ordinary Time**
                 St Martin of Tours, bishop   Memorial
White   HOURS Proper of the memorial. Psalter Week 3 at Day Hour
                 MASS of the memorial. Preface: Common or of the Saint
READINGS   **Rm 16:3-9, 16, 22-27. Ps 144:2-5, 10-11, R/ v 1. Lk 16:9-15.** Lect II: 410

'Every practice that reduces persons to nothing more than a means of profit ... leads to idolising money and contributes to the spread of atheism. "You cannot serve God and mammon"' (CCC, 2424).

St Martin of Tours, 316–97, Bishop of Tours, apostle of rural Gaul, founder of monasteries. Patron of France, soldiers, beggars and innkeepers.

NOVEMBER 2023

12 Sunday   THIRTY-SECOND SUNDAY IN ORDINARY TIME
Green ✠   HOURS Proper. Te Deum. Psalter Week 4
              MASS Proper. Gloria. Creed. Preface: Sundays I–VIII
READINGS   **Wis 6:12-16. Ps 62:2-8, R/ v 2. I Th 4:13-18** (shorter form 4:13-14)**. Mt 25:1-13.** Lect I: 722

The door is closed against the bridesmaids who did not keep vigil nor trim their lamps. The concern of the Christian should be readiness for the call of the Lord, to seek the light of Christ in daily living, and to keep burning brightly the light received at baptism. It is true wisdom to be always eagerly longing for the Lord.
No Masses for the dead, except funeral Masses, are permitted today (see Lit. Note 8)
St Josaphat, bishop and martyr is not celebrated this year.

---

13 Monday   32nd Week in Ordinary Time
Green   HOURS Psalter Week 4. MASS of choice
READINGS   **Wis 1:1-7. Ps 138:1-10, R/ v 24. Lk 17:1-6.** Lect II:412

The Book of Wisdom was written in the second century BC for the large Jewish community in Alexandria. It encourages fidelity to traditional teachings, but is influenced by some Greek thought. It begins by teaching that religious faith and virtuous living are the basis of true wisdom and lead to immortal life.

---

14 Tuesday   32nd Week in Ordinary Time
Green   HOURS Psalter Week 4. MASS of choice
White   Optional memorial of **St Laurence O'Toole, bishop**
Dublin   **St Laurence O'Toole, bishop**   Feast
READINGS   **Wis 2:23-3:9. Ps 33:2-3, 16-19, R/ v 2. Lk 17:7-10.** Lect II:414

'God did not bring death, and he does not delight in the death of the living … It was through the devil's envy that death entered the world' (CCC, 413).
St Laurence O'Toole see *The Irish Calendar*, p. 192.
Dublin   **Dedication of the Cathedral** (see *Lit. Note 12*)

---

15 Wednesday 32nd Week in Ordinary Time
Green   HOURS Psalter Week 4. MASS of choice
White   Optional memorial of **St Albert the Great, bishop and doctor of the Church**
READINGS   **Wis 6:1-11. Ps 81:3-4, 6-7, R/ v 8. Lk 17:11-19.** Lect II:416

Rulers who acquire true wisdom will show concern for the poor and weak, the oppressed and alienated.
St Albert the Great, c. 1206–80, the Dominican theologian, who taught in Cologne, was called the 'Universal Doctor' for the vast range of his interests. Patron of scientists.

---

16 Thursday | **32nd Week in Ordinary Time**
Green | HOURS Psalter Week 4. MASS of choice
White | Optional memorial of **St Margaret of Scotland**
White | Optional memorial of **St Gertrude, virgin**
READINGS | **Wis 7:22-8:1. Ps 118:89-91, 130, 135, 175 R/ v 89. Lk 17:20-25.** Lect II:418

In praise of Wisdom, its nature and origin. This Wisdom, close to God, with his power and creating with him, anticipates the theology of the Spirit of New Testament times. A perfect number of twenty-one attributes are given to describe Wisdom.

St Margaret, 1045–93, wife of Malcolm III, King of Scotland, helped by her example and influence the work of reform in the Church.

St Gertrude, 1256–1302, a Benedictine nun, from the age of five she cultivated devotion to the Sacred Heart and advocated frequent Communion.

---

17 Friday | **32nd Week in Ordinary Time**
 | **St Elizabeth of Hungary, religious** | Memorial
White | HOURS of the memorial. Psalter Week 4
 | MASS of the memorial. Preface: Common or of the Saint
READINGS | **Wis 13:1-9. Ps 18:2-5, R/ v 2. Lk 17:26-37.** Lect II:420

Idolatry in whatever form is to be condemned. The study of nature should lead us to acknowledge the transcendent God, universal Creator. The beauty of the world is a work of art reflecting the beauty of its creator.

St Elizabeth of Hungary, 1207–31, queen at fourteen, widowed and exiled at twenty, Franciscan tertiary until her death at twenty-four. A woman of prayer and service of the poor.

---

18 Saturday | **32nd Week in Ordinary Time**
Green | HOURS Psalter Week 4. MASS of choice
White | Optional memorial of **The Dedication of the Basilicas of Ss Peter and Paul**
White/Green | Saturday Mass of the **Blessed Virgin Mary**
READINGS | **Wis 18:14-16, 19:6-9. Ps 104:2-3, 36-37, 42-43, R/ v 5. Lk 18:1-8.** Lect II:422

On the night of the Exodus the word of God is seen as the agent of God's power in the deaths of the first-born and the journey across the Red Sea. At his Second Coming the Word will again stand in judgement.

Dedication of the Basilicas of Ss Peter and Paul: Acts 28:11-16, 30-31. Ps 97:1-6, R/ v 2 . Mt 14:22-33. Lect II:1269

The dedication of the churches of St Peter and St Paul was observed on this date since 12th century. The present basilica of St Peter's was consecrated in 1626 and St Paul's Outside-the-Walls in 1854.

Killaloe | **Dedication of the Cathedral** (see Lit. Note 12)

NOVEMBER 2023

19 Sunday   **THIRTY-THIRD SUNDAY IN ORDINARY TIME**
World Day of the Poor

Green ✠   HOURS Proper. Te Deum. Psalter Week 1
MASS Proper. Gloria. Creed. Preface: Sundays I–VIII

READINGS   **Prov 31:10-13, 19-20, 30-31. Ps 127:1-5, R/ v 1. I Th 5:1-6. Mt 25:14-30** (shorter form 25:14-15, 19-20)**.** *Lect* I:725

The readings today emphasise fidelity and dedication to duty and work. It is more blessed to give: talents and gifts are given for the service of the community. The Christian is to be fully dedicated to working in service of others while watching and waiting for the life to come. There is always so much good to be done for others and so little time in which to do it!

Today is *World Day of the Poor*. Pope Francis in his apostolic letter *Misericordia et Misera*, marking the end of the Jubilee Year of Mercy, establishing this Day, said that it would serve as 'the worthiest way to prepare for the celebration of the Solemnity of Our Lord Jesus Christ, King of the Universe, who identified with the little ones and the poor and who will judge us on our works of mercy'.

---

20 Monday   **33rd Week in Ordinary Time**
Green   HOURS Psalter Week 1. MASS of choice

READINGS   **1 Mac 1:10-15, 41-43, 54-57, 62-64. Ps 118:53, 61, 134, 150, 155, 158, R/ cf. v 88. Lk 18:35-43.** *Lect* II:425

Antiochus Epiphanes began a forcible repression of Judaism. He imposed gentile practices on the Jews who before this had the Mosaic Law as their civil law. This had the result of producing resistance from those who remained faithful to the Law.

---

21 Tuesday   **33rd Week in Ordinary Time**
The Presentation of the Blessed Virgin Mary Memorial

White   HOURS of the memorial. Psalter Week 1
MASS of the memorial. Preface: Blessed Virgin Mary

READINGS   **Zec 2:14-17. Ps Lk 1:46-55, R/ v 49. Mt 12:46-50.** *Lect* II:1271

The feast of the **Presentation of the Blessed Virgin Mary** celebrates Mary in her grace-filled life, wholly given over to the Holy Spirit.

---

22 Wednesday 33rd Week in Ordinary Time
Green   HOURS Psalter Week 1. MASS of choice
Red   Optional memorial of **St Cecilia, virgin and martyr**

READINGS   **2 Mac 7:1, 20-31. Ps 16:1, 5-6, 8, 1, R/ v 15. Lk 19:11-28.** *Lect* II:430

A mother and her seven sons are ordered by the king to disobey the law.

St Cecilia, the patroness of music and musicians, was a third-century Roman Christian martyr. According to tradition, she refused to worship the Roman gods and was beheaded.

---

23 Thursday   **33rd Week in Ordinary Time**
St Columban, abbot and missionary   Memorial
White   HOURS of the memorial. Psalter Week 1
   MASS of the memorial. Preface: Common or of the Saint
READINGS   **1 Mac 2:15-29. Ps 49:1-2, 5-6, 14-15, R/ v 23. Lk 19:41-44.** Lect II:433

Mattathias is fired with zeal for fidelity to God's Law. All who are concerned for virtue and justice followed him. Jesus weeps over the unfaithful city that does not recognise the message of peace.
St Columban see The Irish Calendar, p. 192.

---

24 Friday   **33rd Week in Ordinary Time**
Ss Andrew Dŭng-Lạc, priest, and Companions, martyrs   Memorial
Red   HOURS of the memorial. Psalter Week 1
   MASS of the memorial
READINGS   **1 Mac 4:36-37, 52-59. Ps 1 Chr 29:10-12, R/ v 13. Lk 19:45-48.** Lect II:435

Judas proposed to cleanse and dedicate the Temple sanctuary. The annual Jewish festival of lights called Hanukkah is the commemoration of this rededication and is celebrated in late November-December, this year beginning on the evening of 7 December.
St Andrew Dŭng-Lạc and Companions. In the seventeenth, eighteenth and nineteenth centuries in Vietnam, many Christians suffered martyrdom. On 19 June 1988, Pope St John Paul II canonised 117 of these – ninety-six native Vietnamese men and women, eleven Dominican missionaries from Spain and ten French missionaries.

---

25 Saturday   **33rd Week in Ordinary Time**
Green   HOURS Psalter Week 1. MASS of choice
Red   Optional memorial of **St Catherine of Alexandria, virgin and martyr**
Red   Optional memorial of **St Clement I, pope and martyr** (see Collect, p. 181)
White   Optional memorial of **St Colman, bishop**
White/Green   Saturday Mass of the **Blessed Virgin Mary**
READINGS   **1 Mac 6:1-13. Ps 9:2-4, 6, 16, 19, R/ cf. v 16. Lk 20:27-40.** Lect II:437

The death of Antiochus Epiphanes is seen as a punishment for his pillaging of the Temple of God in Jerusalem.
St Catherine was martyred about 310 at Alexandria. Her body is venerated at the monastery on Mount Sinai.
St Clement, third successor of St Peter as bishop of Rome (88-97). His letter to the Corinthians called for peace and harmony in the life of that community. Exiled, he was martyred by drowning in Crimea. Later, his relics were brought to the church of San Clemente in Rome.
St Colman see The Irish Calendar, p. 192.
White   FIRST EVENING PRAYER of **Christ the King**

NOVEMBER 2023

26 Sunday **OUR LORD JESUS CHRIST, KING OF THE UNIVERSE**
Solemnity

White ✠ HOURS Proper. Te Deum. Psalter 1 at Day Hour
MASS Proper (RM p. 371). Gloria. Creed. Preface: Proper
READINGS **Ez 34:11-12, 15-17. Ps 22:1-3, 5-6, R/ v 1. 1 Cor 15:20-26, 28. Mt 25:31-46.** Lect I:729

Christ the King. At the end of our earthly life we will be judged on how we have lived and acted. At the end of time the kingdom of God will be established through the saving work of Christ. Then the Shepherd King will come to judge how we have loved. Our lives are to be characterised by a love that welcomes Christ in those most in need, and by joyful expectation of his glorious coming.

No other celebrations, not even funeral Masses, are permitted today (see Lit. Note 8)

---

27 Monday **34th Week in Ordinary Time**
Green HOURS Psalter Week 2. MASS of choice
White Optional Memorial of **St Fergal, bishop and missionary**
READINGS **Dn 1:1-6, 8-20. Ps Dn 3:52-56, R/ v 52. Lk 21:1-4.** Lect II:439

In these days leading into Advent, the theme of the end times predominates in the liturgy. The Book of Daniel encourages faithfulness to the practice of the faith, despite the material allurements of the world and different forms of persecution.

St Fergal, see *The Irish Calendar*, p. 192.

---

28 Tuesday **34th Week in Ordinary Time**
Green HOURS Psalter Week 2. MASS of choice
READINGS **Dn 2:31-45. Ps Dn 3:57-61, R/ v 59. Lk 21:5-11.** Lect II:442

'The Last Judgement will come when Christ returns in glory. Only the Father knows the day and the hour, only he determines the moment of its coming. Then through his Son Jesus Christ he will pronounce the final word on all history. We shall know the ultimate meaning of the whole work of creation and of the entire economy of salvation, and understand the marvellous ways by which his Providence led everything towards its final end. The Last Judgement will reveal that God's justice triumphs over all the injustices committed by his creatures and that God's love is stronger than death' (CCC, 1040).

---

29 Wednesday 34th Week in Ordinary Time

Green   HOURS Psalter Week 2. MASS of choice

READINGS   **Dn 5:1-6, 13-14, 16-17, 23-28. Ps Dn 3:62-67, R/ v 59. Lk 21:12-19.** Lect II:444

Belshazzar's Feast. 'You have been weighed in the balance and found wanting.' God punishes those who, instead of glorifying him in whose hands lies their fate, worship other gods and celebrate sacrilegious feasts.

Kildare and Leighlin Dedication of the Cathedral (see Lit. Note 12)

---

30 Thursday

Red   ST ANDREW, APOSTLE   Feast

HOURS Proper. Te Deum. Psalter Week 2 at Day Hour

MASS Proper. Gloria. Preface: Apostles I-II

READINGS   **Rm 10:9-18. Ps 18:2-5, R/ v 5. Mt 4:18-22.** Lect II:1279

St Andrew from Bethsaida was a disciple of John the Baptist when he was called by Jesus. He in turn brought his brother Peter to Jesus. He is said to have suffered martyrdom by crucifixion on this date, but the tradition of an X-shaped cross is much later. Patron of Scotland, Russia and fishermen.

No Masses for the dead, except funeral Masses, are permitted today (Lit. Note 8)

DECEMBER 2023

1 Friday 34th Week in Ordinary Time

Green   HOURS Psalter Week 2. MASS of choice

READINGS   **Dn 7:2-14. Ps Dn 3:75-8, R/ v 59. Lk 21:29-33.** Lect II:449

Again the four kingdoms of Babylon, Persia, Greece and Rome are represented by four beasts. After them will come the messianic King whose kingdom will be everlasting.

---

2 Saturday 34th Week in Ordinary Time

Green   HOURS Psalter Week 2. MASS of choice

White/Green   Saturday Mass of the **Blessed Virgin Mary**

READINGS   **Dn 7:15-27. Ps Dn 3:82-87, R/ v 59. Lk 21:34-36.** Lect II:452

God will permit a period of distress for a limited time, but after that will come a time of relief for his faithful people. Jesus warns us to hold fast during the days of trial and to be ready for his coming to receive his sovereignty.

Violet   FIRST EVENING PRAYER of **Advent**

LITURGICAL CALENDAR 2023–2024

Easter
Easter Sunday of the Resurrection of the Lord is 31 March 2024.

Ordinary Time
Ordinary Time in 2024 consists of thirty-four weeks. There are six weeks from 8 January (Monday after the Feast of the Baptism of the Lord) until 13 February (Tuesday before Ash Wednesday).
After Pentecost, Ordinary Time resumes from the seventh week on 20 May (Monday after Pentecost Sunday).

Lectionary
Sunday – Cycle B
Weekdays – Cycle 2

DECEMBER 2023

3 Sunday ✠	**FIRST SUNDAY OF ADVENT**	
	READINGS: Is 63:16-17, 64:1, 3-8. Ps 79:2-3, 15-16, 18-19, R/ v 4. 1 Cor 1:3-9. Mk 13:33-37. *Lect* I:5	
4 Monday	1st Week of Advent	
	St John Damascene, priest and doctor of the Church	
		Opt. Mem.
5 Tuesday	1st Week of Advent	
6 Wednesday	1st Week of Advent	
	St Nicholas, bishop	Opt. Mem.
	Galway: St Nicholas, bishop	Feast
7 Thursday	1st Week of Advent	
	St Ambrose, bishop and doctor of the Church	
		Memorial
8 Friday ✠	**THE IMMACULATE CONCEPTION OF THE BLESSED VIRGIN MARY**	Solemnity
	READINGS: Gn 3:9-15, 20. Ps 97:1-4, R/ v 1. Eph 1:3-6, 11-12. Lk 1:26-38. *Lect* I:1009 or II:1289	
9 Saturday	1st Week of Advent	
	St Juan Diego Cuahtlatoatzin	Opt. Mem
10 Sunday ✠	**SECOND SUNDAY OF ADVENT**	
	READINGS: Is 40:1-5, 9-11. Ps 84:9-14, R/ v 8. 2 Pt 3:8-14. Mk 1:1-8. *Lect* I:27	
11 Monday	2nd Week of Advent	
	St Damasus I, pope	Opt. Mem.
12 Tuesday	2nd Week of Advent	
	Our Lady of Guadalupe	Opt. Mem.
	St Finnian, bishop	Opt. Mem.
	Meath: St Finnian, bishop	Feast
13 Wednesday	2nd Week of Advent	
	St Lucy, virgin and martyr	Memorial
14 Thursday	2nd Week of Advent	
	St John of the Cross, priest and doctor of the Church	Memorial
15 Friday	2nd Week of Advent	
16 Saturday	2nd Week of Advent	

17 Sunday ✠ **THIRD SUNDAY OF ADVENT**
READINGS: Is 61:1-2, 10-11. Ps Lk 1:46-50, 53-54, R/ Is 61:10. 1 Th 5:16-24. Jn 1:6-8, 19-28. *Lect* I:48

18 Monday **3rd Week of Advent**
Memorial may be made of **St Flannan, bishop** (see *Lit. Note 8*) Opt. Mem.
Killaloe: St Flannan, bishop Feast

19 Tuesday **3rd Week of Advent**

20 Wednesday **3rd Week of Advent**
Memorial may be made of **St Fachanan, bishop** (see *Lit Note 8*) Opt. Mem.
Kilfenora: St Fachanan, bishop Feast

21 Thursday **3rd Week of Advent**
Memorial may be made of **St Peter Canisius, priest and doctor of the Church** (see *Lit. Note 8*) Opt. Mem.

22 Friday **3rd Week of Advent**

23 Saturday **3rd Week of Advent**
Memorial may be made of **St John of Kanty, priest** (see *Lit. Note 8*) Opt. Mem.

24 Sunday ✠ **FOURTH SUNDAY OF ADVENT**
READINGS: 2 Sm 7:1-5, 8-12, 14, 16. Ps 88:2-5, 27, 29, R/ cf. v 2. Rm 16:25-27. Lk 1:26-38. *Lect* I:70

25 Monday ✠ **THE NATIVITY OF THE LORD (CHRISTMAS)** Solemnity
READINGS: Vigil: Is 62:1-5. Ps 88:4-5, 16-17, 27, 29, R/ cf. v 2. Acts 13:16-17, 22-25. Mt 1:1-25 (shorter form 1:18-25). *Lect* I:99
Midnight Mass: Is 9:1-7. Ps 95:1-3, 11-13, R/ Lk 2:11. Ti 2:11-14. Lk 2:1-14. *Lect* I:104
Dawn Mass: Is 62:11-12. Ps 96:1, 6, 11-12. Ti 3:4-7. Lk 2:15-20. *Lect* I:104
Mass during the Day: Is 52:7-10. Ps 97:1-6, R/ v 3. Heb 1:1-6. Jn 1:1-18 (shorter form 1:1-5, 9-14). *Lect* I:109

26 Tuesday **St Stehpen, first martyr** Feast
27 Wednesday **St John, apostle and evangelist** Feast
28 Thursday **The Holy Innocents, martyrs** Feast
29 Friday **5th Day in the Octave of Christmas**
Memorial may be made of **St Thomas Becket, bishop and martyr** (see *Lit. Note 8*) Opt. Mem.
30 Saturday **6th Day in the Octave of Christmas**

31 Sunday ✠ **THE HOLY FAMILY OF JESUS, MARY AND JOSEPH**
Feast
READINGS: Year B: Gn 15:1-6, 21:1-3. Ps 104:1-6, 8-9, R/ vv 7, 8. Heb 11:8, 11-12, 17-19. Lk 2:22-40 (shorter form 2:22, 39-40) . *Lect* I:119 or Eccles (Sir) 3:2-6, 12-14. Ps 127:1-5, R/ cf. v 1. Col 3:12-21 (shorter form 3:12-17) Lk 2:22-40 (shorter form 2:22, 39-40). *Lect* I:114

ADDITIONS SINCE PUBLICATION OF *ROMAN MISSAL*
See Liturgical Note 24

Four optional memorials of the General Calendar displaced by higher ranking observances of the National Calendar as approved in 1998 have been assigned new dates.

St Ephrem, deacon and doctor of the Church
Optional Memorial 10 June

Pour into our hearts O Lord, we pray, the Holy Spirit,
at whose prompting the Deacon Saint Ephrem
exulted in singing of your mysteries
and from whom he received the strength
to serve you alone.
Through our Lord Jesus Christ, your Son,
who lives and reigns with you in the unity of the Holy Spirit,
God, for ever and ever.
Amen.

St Peter Claver, priest
Optional Memorial 10 September

O God, who made Saint Peter Claver a slave of slaves
and strengthened him with wonderful charity and patience
as he came to their help,
grant, through his intercession,
that, seeking the things of Jesus Christ,
we may love our neighbour in deeds and in truth.
Through our Lord Jesus Christ, your Son,
who lives and reigns with you in the unity of the Holy Spirit,
God, for ever and ever.
Amen.

St Martin de Porres, religious
Optional Memorial 5 November

O God, who led St Martin de Porres
by the path of humility to heavenly glory,
grant that we may so follow his radiant example in this life
as to merit to be exalted with him in heaven.
Through our Lord Jesus Christ, your Son,
who lives and reigns with you in the unity of the Holy Spirit,
God, for ever and ever.
Amen.

St Clement I, pope and martyr
Optional Memorial 25 November

Almighty ever-living God,
who are wonderful in the virtue of all your Saints,
grant us joy in the yearly commemoration of Saint Clement,
who, as a Martyr and High Priest of your Son,
bore out by his witness what he celebrated in mystery
and confirmed by example what he preached with his lips.
Through our Lord Jesus Christ, your Son,
who lives and reigns with you in the unity of the Holy Spirit,
God, for ever and ever.
Amen.

* * *

The optional memorial of Blessed Virgin Mary, Mother of the Church: the collect is
from the votive Mass, Our Lady, Mother of the Church (*RM*, p. 1252). The collect
for the memorial of Our Lady of Loreto is from the Common of the Blessed Virgin
Mary, Advent (*RM*, p. 963).

Blessed Virgin Mary, Mother of the Church
Optional Memorial Monday after Pentecost

O God, Father of mercies,
whose Only Begotten Son, as he hung upon the Cross,
chose the Blessed Virgin Mary, his Mother,
to be our Mother also,
grant, we pray, that with her loving help
your Church may be more fruitful day by day
and, exulting in the holiness of her children,
may draw to he embrace all the families of the peoples.
Through our Lord Jesus Christ, your Son,
who lives and reigns with you in the unity of the Holy Spirit,
God, for ever and ever.
Amen.

Our Lady of Loreto
Optional Memorial 10 December

O God, who, fulfilling the promise made to our Fathers,
chose the Blessed Virgin Mary
to become the Mother of the Saviour,
grant that we may follow her example,
for her humility was pleasing to you
and her obedience profitable to us.
Through our Lord Jesus Christ, your Son,
who lives and reigns with you in the unity of the Holy Spirit,
God, for ever and ever.
Amen.

* * *

ROMAN MISSAL ADDITIONS

The optional memorial of St Paul VI is celebrated on the anniversary of his ordination as priest. The collect here is from the Common of Pastors: Pope (*RM*, p. 984). The optional memorial of St John XXIII is celebrated on the anniversary of the opening of the Second Vatican Council. The optional memorial of St John Paul II is celebrated on the anniversary of the inauguration of his ministry as universal Pastor of the Church.

St Paul VI, pope
Optional Memorial 29 May

Almighty ever-living God,
who chose Pope Saint Paul the Sixth to preside over your whole people
and benefit them by word and example,
keep safe, we pray, by his intercession,
the shepherds of your Church
along with the flocks entrusted to their care,
and direct them in the way of eternal salvation.
Through our Lord Jesus Christ, your Son,
who lives and reigns with you in the unity of the Holy Spirit,
God, for ever and ever.
Amen.

St John XXIII, pope
Optional Memorial 11 October

Almighty ever-lasting God,
who in Pope Saint John the Twenty-Third,
have given a living example of Christ, the Good Shepherd,
to shine throughout the world,
grant us, we pray,
that, through his intercession,
we may joyfully pour out
an abundance of Christian charity.
Through our Lord Jesus Christ, your Son,
who lives and reigns with you in the unity of the Holy Spirit,
God, for ever and ever.
Amen.

St John Paul II, pope
Optional Memorial 22 October

O God, rich in mercy,
who willed that Pope Saint John Paul the Second
should preside over your universal Church,
grant, we pray, that instructed by his teaching,
we may confidently open our hearts to the saving grace of Christ,
the sole Redeemer of the human race,
who lives and reigns with you in the unity of the Holy Spirit,
God, for ever and ever.
Amen.

* * *

In some places the optional memorial of Bl. John Sullivan is observed on 8 May.

Bl. John Sullivan, priest
Optional Memorial 8 May

God, Father of mercies,
who taught your Priest, Blessed John Sullivan,
to contemplate Christ crucified and imitate his compassion,
grant that we may follow his example
and grow every day in loving you above all things.
Through our Lord Jesus Christ, your Son,
who lives and reigns with you in the unity of the Holy Spirit,
God, for ever and ever.
Amen.

* * *

The memorial of Ss Martha, Mary and Lazarus replaces the memorial of St Martha (29 July) (decree 2 February 2021). To the memorial of St Martha is added her sister Mary and brother Lazarus. The following is an interim collect

Ss Martha, Mary and Lazarus
Memorial 29 July

Grant, we pray, almighty God,
that the example of your Saints may spur us on to a better life,
so that we, who celebrate the memory of Saints Martha, Mary and Lazarus,
may also imitate without ceasing their deeds.
Through our Lord Jesus Christ, your Son,
who lives and reigns with you in the unity of the Holy Spirit,
God, for ever and ever.
Amen.

* * *

The proper collect for the optional memorial of St Faustina is not available as the Liturgical Calendar goes to print. The collect here is from the Common of Virgins (RM, p. 1003).

St Faustina Kowalska, virgin
Optional Memorial 5 October

Hear us, God our Saviour,
that, as we rejoice in commemorating the Virgin blessed Faustina,
we may be instructed by her loving devotion.
Through our Lord Jesus Christ, your Son,
who lives and reigns with you in the unity of the Holy Spirit,
God, for ever and ever.
Amen.

THE IRISH CALENDAR

The Church has also included in the annual cycle days devoted to the memory of the martyrs and the other saints. Raised up to perfection by the manifold grace of God, and already in possession of eternal salvation, they sing God's perfect praise in heaven and offer prayers for us. By celebrating the passage of these saints from earth to heaven, the Church proclaims the paschal mystery achieved in the saints who have suffered and been glorified with Christ; she proposes them to the faithful as examples drawing all to the Father through Christ, and through their merits she pleads for God's favours.

Sacrosanctum Concilium, Constitution on the Sacred Liturgy, 104

JANUARY

3rd: St Munchin (Mainchin) is the patron saint of the diocese of Limerick. His traditional birthplace is Dal Cais, where a parish and old graveyard Cell Mainchin (Kilmanaheen) existed. In the seventh century he was granted Inis Sibtonn (Ibton) in the tidal waters of Limerick in the region of which he founded a church and had a thriving religious community.

5th: (Dublin): St Charles of St Andrew. John Andrew Houben was born in Holland in 1821. He took vows as a Passionist in 1846 and came to Mount Argus in 1857. It was there he spent most of his priestly life. His ministry in the confessional was renowned and the poor of Dublin found in him a strong support. He died on 5 January 1893. St Charles was canonised on 3 June 2007.

15th: St Ita was born in Co. Waterford of noble and Christian parents. Early on she set her mind on serving Christ in religious life. She founded a monastery in Killeedy, Co. Limerick, which attracted a great variety of young people. She was given the title 'foster-mother of the saints of Ireland'. She died in 570.

16th: St Fursa was born in Ireland and became one of the great monastic missionaries abroad. He went first with his brothers Foillan and Ultan to live the monastic life in East Anglia. But as great numbers continued to visit him there he left Foillan as abbot and sought refuge in France around 644. A patron gave him a hermitage at Lagny on the Marne. He died about 650 at Mézerolles and was buried in Péronne, which became a great centre of devotion to him.

30th: St Aidan or Maedoc (Mogue) was born around 550, probably in Co. Cavan. Aidan studied under David in Wales, and on his return he founded a monastery at Ferns. He became bishop there and was renowned for his generosity and kindness. He died in 626 and his Lives testify to his popularity both in Cavan and in Ferns.

30th (Dublin, Meath): Bl. Margaret Ball was imprisoned for teaching Catholicism, harbouring priests and having Mass celebrated in her home. The harsh conditions of Dublin Castle wore down this old lady of gentle birth, and she died there in 1584. **Bl. Francis Taylor** was born in Swords, Co. Dublin and was elected Mayor of Dublin in 1595. For his Catholic faith he was put in prison for seven years and died of the hardships suffered there on 30 January 1621 at the age of seventy.

FEBRUARY

1st: St Brigid is renowned for her hospitality, almsgiving and care of the sick. She was born c. 454. When she was young her father wished to make a very suitable marriage for her but she insisted in consecrating her virginity to God. She received the veil and spiritual formation probably from St Mel and stayed for a period under his direction in Ardagh. Others followed her example and this led her to found a double monastery in Kildare with the assistance of Bishop Conleth. She died in 524 and her cult is widespread not only throughout Ireland but in several European lands. The St Brigid's Cross, in legend used by Brigid to explain the Christian faith, remains a popular sign of God's protection.

7th: St Mel died in 488. He is said to have been a Briton who came to Ireland with Patrick, with whom he worked until he was ordained in Ardagh. He is one of the earliest Irish saints and gave the religious veil to Brigid.

11th: St Gobnait is one of the best loved saints in west Cork but only traditions concerning her life survive. The main part of her life was spent in Ballyvourney, Co. Cork, where there has always been a deep devotion to her, and which is a place of pilgrimage on this day and on Pentecost. Her gifts of caring for and curing the sick have been a significant part of her cult through the centuries. Happily her memorial coincides with the World Day for the Sick.

17th: St Fintan was born in Leinster. He received his religious formation in Terryglass, Co. Tipperary, under the abbot Colum, and was deeply influenced by his penitential practices and the severity of the Rule. Fintan made his own foundation in Clonenagh, Co. Laois. He died in 603.

MARCH

1st: St David is the patron saint of Wales, where he was an abbot and bishop in the sixth century. Several Irish saints were his pupils and he influenced monastic development in Ireland. He died around 601.

5th: St Kieran. Kieran of Saigir was born in Cape Clear, Co. Cork. He is numbered among the pre-Patrician saints of Ireland. He went to the Continent, where he was baptised and later ordained priest and bishop. He returned to his father's territory, Ossory, where he lived as a hermit. Disciples soon joined him and Saigir became a well-known monastery.

8th: St Senan was born near Kilrush, Co. Clare. His family were prosperous farmers. His vocation seems to have resulted from an experience of danger from the sea. His early studies were mainly made at the monastery of Kilnamanagh. His principal monastic foundation was on Scattery Island, near Kilrush, in the Shannon Estuary. He was anamchara to Ciaran of Clonmacnois and Brendan, and died in 544.

11th: St Aengus (Oengus) was a monk in Clonenagh, Co. Laois, who came to the monastery at Tallaght at the end of the eighth century during the abbacy of Maelruain to spend a period under his direction. He was renowned for his devotion to both foreign and native saints and composed two martyrologies. He returned to Clonenagh, where he became abbot and bishop. He died around 824.

17th: St Patrick was born very probably in the early years of the fifth century in the Roman colony of Britain. He was taken captive at the age of sixteen and brought to Ireland where he was sold as a slave. He tended herds on Slemish mountain for six years. His captivity had a very positive effect on his spiritual life. He prayed many times each day, his faith growing stronger and his love and reverence for God increasing. He escaped back home at the age of twenty-two. It was obvious to him that God was calling him to return to convert the Irish. The voice of the Irish was calling him to come and walk among them once more. He studied probably in France, returned to Ireland as a bishop c. 457–61 or as early as 432 according to another tradition. His mission was not immediately greatly successful but eventually he would make a tremendous number of converts. Two writings survive: the *Letter to Coroticus*, a protest to the soldiers of a British prince who had killed some converts and sold others as slaves, and his *Confession*, written near the end of his life, showing him as one living by the faith he preached and allowing Christ to direct his whole life. He died in 491, though again other dates have been suggested, 480 or as early as 461.

21st: St Enda is considered to be one of the three great late vocations (athlaech) of Ireland. His sister, Faenche, a nun, set his thoughts on a religious vocation. He made a small foundation in Cell Aine, Co. Louth, and, after studies in Scotland under Ninian, made several foundations in the Boyne valley. On Faenche's urging he went to Aran. He died probably in 520 and is considered as one of the early models of ascetic monasticism in Ireland.

24th: St Macartan belongs to a very early generation of saints in Ireland and is recognised as the first Bishop of Clogher. He is known as Patrick's 'Strong Man' for his dedication and faithfulness.

APRIL

1st: St Ceallach (Celsus) was born in 1080. He became Abbot of Armagh in 1105 and was ordained priest. He was influenced by the reform then in progress in Munster. He presided at the Synod of Rathbreasail in 1111. In 1129, on a visitation of Munster, he died and is buried in Lismore in accordance with his own request.

18th: St Laserian (Molaise) worked in both Ireland and Scotland in the seventh century and later entered the monastery at Leighlin, where he became abbot. His monastery thrived and later gave its name to the diocese established in 1110. He adapted Church discipline in accordance with the practices of Rome and introduced the Roman method of dating the celebration of Easter. Laserian died in 639.

27th: St Asicus was St Patrick's expert craftsman in metal work and accompanied him on his journeys. He was left in charge of the church in Elphin which Patrick is said to have founded.

MAY

4th: St Conleth is believed to have come from the Wicklow area. While living as a hermit he was persuaded by Brigid to act as priest for her community in Kildare. He was venerated as a great saint and Cogitosus, in his Life of Brigid, calls him bishop and abbot of the monks of Kildare. He was buried beside Brigid in the great church there.

5th: Bl. Edmund Rice (1762–1844) came from Callan, Co. Kilkenny. After his young wife's early death, he sold his possessions and dedicated his life to the education of the poor. To advance the work, he gathered other like-minded men who took religious vows together to work for the Catholic education of boys. He is a model of patient and cheerful acceptance of the sufferings God sends, a true lay apostle and a deeply committed religious.

8th: Bl. John Sullivan was born in Eccles Street, Dublin, on 8 May 1861 and baptised in St George's Church of Ireland, Temple Street and was brought up in the Christian tradition of his father. He went to Portora Royal School in Enniskillen and then studied classics and law at Trinity College, Dublin, and at Lincoln's Inn, London. At the age of thirty-five he was received into the Roman Catholic Church and returned to Dublin, living a very simple life style. He entered the Society of Jesus in 1900, ordained priest in 1907 and then spent the greater part of his life at Clongowes Wood College, Co. Kildare. His reputation for holiness and as a person of prayer spread rapidly and he was always available to the sick, the poor and anyone in need. He died 19 February 1933. His declaration as blessed on 13 May 2017 at St Francis Xavier Church, Gardiner Street, Dublin, was the first ever beatification celebrated in Ireland.

10th: St Comgall was born around 516 in Co. Antrim. His father was a soldier and wished his son to follow in his steps but Comgall wished to become a soldier of Christ. He studied under Finnian of Moville and deepened his life of prayer to counteract his temptations to boredom and homesickness. He was persuaded to become a priest and then established a monastery at Bangor around 555–8, which attracted people like Columbanus. He also founded a monastery at Tiree in Scotland. He died after a long illness at Pentecost 602 or 605.

15th: St Carthage (or Mochuta) hailed from a rich family in Kerry. As he loved the chanting of the psalms, the local king arranged for him to become a priest. Having spent a year possibly at Bangor he founded his own monastery at Rahan in 595. It grew rapidly. However, opposition made him move southwards around 637. Along with hundreds of monks and their patients from the leper colony, he finally arrived at Lismore, where he made a foundation. He died in 638.

16th: St Brendan was a Kerryman who was born in 486. He studied at Clonard under Finnian. His name is connected with many places in Kerry such as Ardfert and Mount Brandon. He visited Scotland and reached the Hebrides and possibly areas beyond. He founded a monastery in Clonfert in 568 and died there in 578.

JUNE

3rd: St Kevin was a native of Leinster and grew up in Kilnamanagh, where he received his early religious formation. Wishing to be a hermit, he crossed the mountains to Glendalough and settled in Disert Caoimhghin at the foot of the upper lake. But disciples began to gather round him. Gradually the great monastic settlement grew and spread through the glen after his death in 618.

6th: St Jarlath is said to have been a disciple of St Enda, and was also taught by St Benignus. He became abbot bishop of the monastery he founded at Tuam in the sixth century.

7th: St Colman (Mocholmoc) of Dromore, Co. Down, spent most of his life in that area. Possibly he studied under Caetan of Nendrom, Co. Down, and was persuaded by St Mac Nissi to settle at Dromore c. 514.

9th: St Columba, also known as Colum Cille, was born in Gartan, Co. Donegal, in 521 and was of royal lineage. He studied under St Finnian of Moville and St Finnian of Clonard. He founded monasteries in Derry, Durrow, Iona and possibly Kells. He left Ireland, either for penance or to be a pilgrim for Christ, but Iona became his principal foundation. From it missionaries undertook the conversion of Northumbria. Columba is noted for his great love for people and for all living creatures. He died 9 June 597.

14th: St Davnet lived and died at Tydavnet at Sliabh Beagh, Co. Monaghan. Tradition speaks of St Davnet as a virgin and founder of a church or monastery. A bachall (staff) said to have been hers has been preserved and in the past it was used as a test of truth.

19th: (Cashel and Emly) Bl. Dermot O'Hurley and Companions. Archbishop Dermot O'Hurley of Cashel was martyred in 1584. His companions, honoured on this day, are Bishop Terence Albert O'Brien, OP, John Kearney, OFM and William Tirry, OSA.

20th: The Irish Martyrs. Seventeen Irish martyrs, men and women, cleric and lay, put to death for the Catholic faith between 1579 and 1654 were beatified by Pope John Paul II in 1992: Dermot Hurley, Archbishop of Cashel, hanged 20 June 1584 at Hoggen Green. Conor O'Devany, Bishop of Down and Connor, hanged, drawn and quartered. Patrick O'Loughran, chaplain to the O'Neill family, and Maurice McKenraghty, chaplain to the Earl of Desmond, both hanged. Also hanged were Dominicans Terence O'Brien and Peter Higgins, Franciscans John Kearney, Patrick O'Healy and Conrad O'Rourke, Augustinian William Tirry, and a Jesuit lay brother, Dominic Collins. Lay people Francis Taylor, Mayor of Dublin, and Margaret Ball died of ill treatment: the Wexford martyrs, a baker, Matthew Lambert and a group of sailors, Robert Meyler (Tyler), Edward Cheevers and Patrick Cavanagh were hanged, drawn and quartered on 5 July 1581. Six Catholics of Irish birth or connection executed for the faith in England had already been beatified in 1929 and 1987: John Roche (alias Neale), John (Terence) Carey, Patrick Salmon, John Cornelius (alias John Conor O'Mahoney), Charles Meehan, Ralph Corby (Corbington).

JULY

1st: St Oliver Plunkett from Irish nobility whose family supported King Charles I. Ordained in Rome in 1654, he became a professor of theology from 1654 until appointed Archbishop of Armagh in 1669. He ministered in Armagh, though forced to work in a covert way during the suppression of priests. He was arrested and tried at Dundalk in 1679 for conspiring against the state. It was seen that Oliver would never be convicted in Ireland, and he was moved to Newgate Prison, London. He was found guilty of high treason 'for promoting the Catholic faith', and was condemned to a gruesome death. He was hanged, drawn and quartered on 1 July 1681 at Tyburn, in London. He was the last Catholic to die for his faith at Tyburn, and the first of the Irish martyrs to be beatified in 1920. He was canonised by Pope Paul VI on 12 October 1975. He is buried at Downside Abbey, England; his head is venerated in St Peter's Church, Drogheda.

6th: St Moninne of Killeavy was one of Ireland's early women saints. After instruction on the religious life, she founded a community which initially consisted of eight virgins and a widow with a baby at Sliabh Gullion, Co. Armagh. They lived an eremitical life, based on that of Elijah and St John the Baptist. Moninne died in 517 or 518.

7th: St Maelruain (Maolruain), bishop and abbot, founded the monastery of Tallaght, Co. Dublin, in 774 which introduced a reform. Important liturgical and spiritual writings emerged from this movement known as the Célí Dé reform. He died in 792.

8th: St Kilian was born in the parish of Mullagh in the diocese of Kilmore. With eleven companions he left Ireland and became known as the apostle of Thuringia and eastern Franconia. With Kolonat and Totnan he was put to death in 689. There is a very strong devotion to him in Würzburg, where his remains lie, and also throughout the Bavarian countryside.

24th: St Declan is considered to be one of the pre-Patrician saints. He was of noble blood. Colman, a local priest, baptised him. Later he went to Europe to continue his studies where he was ordained priest and possibly bishop. He settled in Ardmore and evangelised the Decies country.

AUGUST

9th: St Nathy is said to have been born in the barony of Leyny, Co. Sligo. He made a foundation in Achonry, where many students gathered to learn from him. He is buried in Achadh Cain.

9th: St Felim was born in the sixth century in Breifne. He was a hermit near Kilmore, Co. Cavan, where he later founded a monastery. He is patron of Kilmore diocese.

12th: St Muredach is regarded as the founder of the church at Killala. He may also be the founder and patron of the monastery of Inishmurray off the Sligo coast.

12th: St Attracta lived in the sixth or seventh century. Local tradition remembers her great healing powers. Her convents were famous for hospitality and charity to the poor.

12th: St Lelia (Liadain) had a church at Kileely, near Thomond Bridge. She is said to have been baptised by St Patrick.

13th: St Fachtna (also called Fachanan) founder of the monastery of Ross Carbery (Ross Ailithir). He died around 600. His monastery became the principal monastery of west Cork and later had a famous scripture school.

17th: Our Lady of Knock. The story of Knock began on the 21 August 1879 when Our Lady, St Joseph and St John the Evangelist appeared at the south gable of Knock Parish Church. This miraculous apparition was witnessed by fifteen people, young and old. Knock is an internationally recognised Marian Shrine. Saint John Paul II visited Knock as part of his 1979 papal pilgrimage to Ireland. Pope Francis went to Knock and prayed at the Shrine before the final Mass of the World Meeting of Families at the Phoenix Park, Dublin, on Sunday, 26 August 2018. The date of the memorial is within the annual novena conducted at the Shrine. Pope Francis, on the Feast of St Joseph, 19 March 2021, declared Knock to be an International Shrine of Eucharistic and Marian Devotion.

23rd: St Eugene (Eoghan) lived in the sixth century and was said to have been taken by pirates to Britain. On obtaining his freedom he went to study at Candida Casa. Returning to Ireland he made a foundation at Kilnamanagh in the Wicklow hills, but his principal foundation was at Ardstraw (Ard Sratha), Co. Tyrone.

30th: St Fiacre was an Irishman who went abroad to seek a hermitage. He passed through Normandy and eventually met Faro, who was a great patron of Irish pilgrims at Meaux. Fiachre was given a hermitage near Breuil and there he stayed until his death around 670.

31st: St Aidan of Lindisfarne was of Irish descent and was a monk of Iona. When Oswald, the exiled King of Northumbria who had fled for refuge to Iona, returned to his throne in 634, he invited Aidan to come to reconvert his people. Aidan made his headquarters at Lindisfarne. With the aid of the king as interpreter he was very successful in his mission. He died in 651.

SEPTEMBER

4th: St Mac Nissi. Oengus Mac Nissi took his name from his mother Cnes or Ness. It is claimed that Patrick baptised him and taught him the psalms. He chose the district of Connor for his hermitage, but later became bishop of his clan. He died early in the sixth century.

9th: St Ciaran was born in Roscommon around 512. He came to Clonmacnois in January 545 where he founded a monastery which was to become one of the most renowned in Europe. He died at the age of thirty-three while the monastery was still being built.

12th: St Ailbe is sometimes claimed as one of the pre-Patrician saints, but the annals note his death in 528. A tradition held that he went to Rome and was ordained bishop by the pope. He founded the monastery of Emly which became very important in Munster. A ninth-century Rule bears his name.

23rd: St Eunan (Adomnán) was born in Donegal around 624 and died in 704. He became a monk in Iona and was chosen abbot there in 679. One of his writings is the Life of Colum Cille.

25th: St Finbarr came to Loch Irce (Gougane Barra) and lived there as a hermit. When disciples gathered round him he moved to Cork at the mouth of the Lee where he founded a monastery which became a famous centre of learning.

OCTOBER

3rd: Bl. Columba Marmion. Joseph, his baptismal name, was born in Dublin in 1858 and ordained priest in Rome in 1881. He served as curate in Dundrum Parish and then as professor in Holy Cross College, Clonliffe, before entering the Abbey of Maredsous, Belgium, in 1886. Elected as abbot, he received his abbatial blessing on 3 October 1909. He died on 30 January 1923. His trilogy, *Christ, the Life of the Soul, Christ in His Mysteries* and *Christ, the Ideal of the Monk,* has been some of the most influential spiritual writings of the twentieth century, nourishing the lives of generations of seminarians, priests, religious sisters and monks. His writings, letters and retreats fulfilled his aim in life: to bring people to God and to bring God to people. He was beatified in Rome on 3 September 2000.

9th: St John Henry Newman was beatified by Pope Benedict XVI at Cofton Park, Birmingham, on 19 September 2010 and canonised 13 October 2019. The memorial of the new saint is 9 October, the anniversary of his reception into the Catholic Church on 9 October 1845. The Church in Ireland is deeply aware of St John Henry's gentle scholarship, deep human wisdom and profound love for the Lord. It also recalls his connections with Ireland. Though his project on the establishment of the Catholic University of Ireland was not a great success, his reflection on education was written in part when he lived in Dublin and has remained a vital contribution to an understanding of Christian education. Invited to Ireland in 1850, he became Rector of the Catholic University of Ireland in 1854 until his resignation in 1858.

11th: St Canice was born in Co. Derry around 527 and died in 603. Though his people were poor, he studied at Clonard under Finnian and at Glasnevin under Mobhi. A deep friendship developed between himself and Columba, with whom he worked for a time in Scotland, where he set up a number of churches. In Ireland his principal foundation was in Aghaboe in Ossory, but this was replaced centuries later by his church in Kilkenny.

16th: St Gall was a monk of Bangor and set out with Columbanus for the Continent. When Columbanus was exiled from France, Gall accompanied him to Bregenz on Lake Constance. When Columbanus crossed into Italy, Gall remained in Switzerland. He lived in a hermitage, which later became the monastery of St Gallen. He died around 630.

25th (Cloyne, Cork and Ross): Bl. Thaddeus MacCarthy was born in 1455. His appointment as Bishop of Ross was opposed and Innocent VIII then appointed him Bishop of Cork and Cloyne. He set out as a humble pilgrim to Rome where he was confirmed as Bishop of Cork and Cloyne. On his return journey in 1492 he died at Ivrea in Italy.

27th: St Otteran, a descendant of Conall Gulban, is usually identified with Odhran who preceded Columba in Iona. His death is recorded in 548 and his grave was greatly revered in Iona. He was chosen by the Vikings as patron of the city of Waterford in 1096 and later patron of the diocese.

29th: St Colman hailed from Kilmacduagh, Co. Galway, in the seventh century. After studying in Aran, where he founded two churches on Inis Mór, he returned to make a foundation at Kilmacduagh.

31st (Cloyne): Bl. Dominic Collins was born around 1566 in the city of Youghal, Co. Cork. In 1598, after a military career, he entered the Society of Jesus as a Brother. He returned to Ireland in 1601, but on 17 June 1602 he was captured by the English who tried in vain to make him abjure his faith. Condemned to death, he was hanged in his native city on 31 October 1602.

NOVEMBER

3rd: St Malachy was born near Armagh in 1094. He became Vicar of Ceallach, the reforming Bishop of Armagh, and he continued this work of reform as Bishop of Connor and, later, Bishop of Armagh. Earlier he had restored the monastery of Bangor and in 1142 founded the monastery of Mellifont, the first Cistercian house in Ireland. He had visited St Bernard at Clairvaux on a journey to and from Rome in 1139. He also introduced the Canons Regular into Ireland. In 1148 Malachy set out from Ireland to meet the Pope but died on his way at Clairvaux, where he caught fever and died in the arms of Bernard and is buried in the abbey church.

6th: All the Saints of Ireland. 'In the communion of saints, many and varied spiritualities have been developed throughout the history of the Churches … The different schools of Christian spirituality share in the living tradition of prayer and are essential guides for the faithful. In their rich diversity they are refractions of the one pure light of the Holy Spirit.' (CCC, 2684)

7th: St Willibrord was born in Northumbria in 658. He entered the Benedictine order and was sent to study, including spending twelve years, 678–690, at the monastery of Rath Melsigi, near Milford, Co. Carlow before going, with eleven companions, to evangelise Frisia. He established a mission at Utrecht and in 695 was ordained Archbishop of Utrecht by Pope Sergius I. He founded a monastery at Echternach in Luxembourg in 700, where he died in 739.

14th: St Laurence O'Toole was born in Castledermot, Co. Kildare, in 1128. He studied at Glendalough, becoming a monk there and later its abbot in 1148. In 1162 he was chosen as the first native Archbishop of Dublin. He followed the reforming methods of Ceallach and Malachy, introducing the Canons Regular to minister in the Cathedral, upholding the rights of the Church, caring for the people. He attended the Third Lateran Council in 1179 and, returning as Papal Legate, he held synods to extend reform. He worked for peace and reconciliation and died on a mission of mediation with King Henry II and the Irish rulers at Eu in Normandy in 1180.

23rd: St Columban (also known as Columbanus) was born around 543. He became a monk of Bangor and later principal teacher there. In 591, desiring to 'go on pilgrimage for Christ', he set out with twelve companions and came to Burgundy. He established monasteries at Annegray, Luxeuil and Fontaine according to the severe Irish rule. Later he founded Bregenz in Austria and his greatest foundation at Bobbio, near Genoa, where he died in 615. He is remembered as one of the greatest of the Irish missionary monks.

25th: St Colman was born around 530, probably in west Cork. A bard by profession, he is reputed to have been influenced by St Brendan to become a priest. His apostolate was to east Cork and his main foundation was at Cloyne.

27th: St Fergal (Virgil) lived first in France and then in Bavaria, where he founded the monastery of Chiemsee. He was appointed Bishop of Salzburg around 754 and died in 784, leaving a reputation for learning and holiness.

DECEMBER

12th: St Finnian studied in Idrone (Co. Carlow) and later in Wales and on his return he settled in Clonard, Co. Meath, around 520, where he established a famous school. His pupils, among whom were Canice, Colum Cille and Brendan, were the initiators of the great monastic expansion in Ireland. He died in 549 and is remembered as the tutor of the saints of Ireland.

18th: St Flannan lived in the seventh century and was the son of a king of Thomond. He entered Molua's monastery at Killaloe and became abbot there. He is remembered as a great preacher.

20th: St Fachanan. Although little is known with certainty about Fachanan, a strong tradition from early times links him with Kilfenora and records that he founded a church or monastery there in the sixth century. He is venerated as the patron of the diocese of Kilfenora, now part of Galway.

Obituary List

July 2021

5   Carroll, Gerard (Ardagh & Clonmacnois), An Tinteán, Templemichael Glebe, Longford Town, Longford

5   McNamara, Donatus (OFMCap), Glin, Co. Limerick and Capuchin Friary, Camarino, Lusaka, Zambia

7   O'Brien, Donal (Cloyne, PP), Ballyvourney, Co. Cork

10   Cronin, Peter (SSC), St Columban's Missionary Society

10   McGillicuddy, Cornelius (Dublin), former CC Dollymount

10   Tuohy, Thomas (SM), Cherryfield Nursing Home, Milltown, Dublin 14

11   Brady, Edward (White Fathers), Missionaries of Africa, Cypress Grove, Dublin

11   Denny, Martin (CP), St Paul's Retreat, Mount Argus, Dublin 6W

12   Keating, Denis (OP), St Mary's, Pope's Quay, Cork

14   McLaughlin, Pat (CSsR), St Gerard's, 722 Antrim Road, Newtownabbey, Co. Antrim

14   O'Donnell, Terry (IC), Drumcondra & Cork

18   Ruddy, Joseph (MSC), Missionaries of the Sacred Heart, Croí Nua, Rosary Lane, Taylor's Lane, Galway

18   Ward, Conor (Dublin, Mgr), former PP Clonskeagh and Professor of Social Science UCD

23   O'Rourke, John J. (Cashel & Emly, AP), Gortnahoe, Thurles, Co. Tipperary

28   Carr, Frank (SSC), St Columban's Missionary Society

29   Culloty, Tom (Galway), Scarteen Lower, Newmarket, Co. Cork

30   McCaughey, Vincent (CP), St Paul's Retreat, Mount Argus, Dublin 6W

August 2021

3   Cronin, Con (SPS, Cork & Ross), The Presbytery, Passage West, Co. Cork

6   Carlin, Neal (Derry), St Anthony's Retreat Centre, Dundrean, Burnfoot, Co. Donegal

11   Nyland, Patrick (PJ) (SDB), Salesian House, 45 St Teresa's Road, Crumlin, Dublin 12

12   Burke, Edward (OFM), Dún Mhuire, Seafield Road, Killiney, Co. Dublin

14   O'Brien, Christopher (Armagh), Haroldstown, Tobinstown, Tullow, Co. Carlow

14 O'Laoghaire, Seán (Kildare & Leighlin, PE),
   Gowran Abbey Nursing Home, Gowran, Co. Kilkenny
15 O'Connor, Dermie (CSsR), St Patrick's, Esker, Athenry,
   Co. Galway
19 Kane, Michael (SPS), St Patrick's, Kiltegan
20 Corkery, Jackie (Cloyne, Canon), 26 Cairn Woods, Ballyviniter,
   Mallow, Co. Cork
20 McQuillan, Ignatius (Derry), 51 Seacoast Road,
   Limavady, Co. Derry
24 Wadding, George (CSsR), 461/463 Griffith Avenue, Dublin 9
26 Foley, Gerard (CSSp), Holy Spirit Missionary College,
   Kimmage Manor, Dublin 12
30 Olden, Michael (Waterford & Lismore, Mgr), Woodleigh,
   Summerville Avenue, Waterford

September 2021

2 Mullan, Patrick J. (Derry), 53B Brisland Road, Eglinton, Derry
4 Crotty, Oliver (Dublin), co-PP Glendalough/Rathdrum/
   Roundwood
4 Fitzgerald, Gerald (CSSp), Provincial House,
   34 Collinsgrove Road, Scarborough, Ontario, MIE 3S4, Canada
7 Byrne, James Alphonsus (SPS), St Patrick's, Kiltegan
9 Mullan, Aidan (Derry), 6 Victoria Place, Derry
10 McGauran, Francis (Elphin), Cuilmore, Strokestown,
   Co. Roscommon
23 O'Sullivan, Brendan (OMI), Oblate Fathers, House of Retreat,
   Tyrconnell Road, Inchicore
24 Bellew, Gerry (SSC), St Columban's Missionary Society
24 Lalor, John (SPS), St Patrick's, Kiltegan

October 2021

1 Butler (Duggan), John (SDB), Salesian House, Don Bosco Road,
   Pallaskenry, Co. Kildare
2 Powell, Oliver (Opus Dei), Knapton House, Monkstown,
   Co. Dublin
5 Ó Dálaigh, Michéal (Cork & Ross, PE, Dean),
   Bushmount Care Home, Drimoleague,
   former PP Curraheen Road, Cork

7   O'Driscoll, Liam (Cork & Ross, Archdeacon), Hollymount, Lee Road, Cork, former PP Clogheen/Kerry Pike

8   Brazil, Sean (SSC), St Columban's Missionary Society

13   Galvin, Gerard (Cork & Ross, PE), Ardmore, Timoleague, Co. Cork, former PP Muintir Bháire

14   Browne, Thomas (SPS), St Patrick's, Kiltegan

21   Egan, Seamus (SSC), St Columban's Missionary Society

22   O'Neill, Daniel (MSC), Carraig na bhFear, Co. Cork

27   McCaughey, George (SDB), Salesian House, Celbridge, Co. Kildare

27   Ó Dálaigh, Tadhg (MSC), Woodview House, Mount Merrion Avenue, Blackrock, Co. Dublin

November 2021

1   O'Shea, Fintan (OFM), 4 Merchant's Quay, Dublin 8

2   Cooney, Kevin (SM), Cerdon, St Mary's Road, Dundalk, Co. Louth

3   Sheedy, Michael (Killaloe), Kilrush, Co. Clare

7   O'Carroll, Caimin (Killaloe), Doora-Barefield, Co. Clare

15   O'Rourke, Denis M. (SPS), St Patrick's, Kiltegan

20   Flynn, James (IC), Clonturk House, Drumcondra

22   Burke, Cormac (Opus Dei, Mgr), Strathmore, Kenya

25   O'Brien, Patrick (Tuam, PP), Parochial House, Caherlistrane, Co. Galway

26   Swan, Colum (Kildare & Leighlin, PE), Bon Secours Care Village, Mount Desert, Cork

December 2021

10   Freeney, Paul (Dublin), former PP Beechwood Avenue

11   O'Donoghue, Hughie (CSsR), Redemptorists, Cebu City, Philippines

11   Treacy, Thomas (SMA), African Missions, Blackrock Road, Cork

12   Ryder, John (Derry), 16 Whitehouse Park, Derry

18   Foley, Edward (OP), St Saviour's, Dublin

19   McCrory, Gerard (Dromore, Canon), Ballynahinch, Co. Down

20   Kearns, John (SPS, Clogher, CC), Loughside Road, Garrison, Enniskillen, Co. Fermanagh

21   McNamara, Kevin (Kerry), St Agatha's Parish Centre, Headford, Killarney, Co. Kerry

22   Murphy, Canice (OP), St Saviour's, Waterford
31   Boyle, Hugh (SDB), Salesian House, 45 St Teresa's Road,
      Crumlin, Dublin 12

January 2022

1   Forbes, Ciarán (OSB), Glenstal Abbey, Murroe, Co. Limerick
1   Lavery, Pat (CSsR), Fortaleza, Brazil
6   McCormick, Paul (Down & Connor, Deacon),
      54 St Patrick's Avenue, Downpatrick
7   Flynn, Leo (SPS), St Patrick's, Kiltegan
12   Bingham, Michael (SJ), Iona, 211 Churchill Park, Portadown,
      Northern Ireland
15   Travers, Charles (Elphin, Mgr), 1 Convent Court, Roscommon
16   O'Doherty, Micheál (Kerry), St Joseph's Nursery Home,
      Killorglin, Co. Kerry
20   Bracken, PJ (Clonfert), Portumna Retirement Village,
      Portumna, Co. Galway
22   Maloney, Peter Cecile (SVD), Castlerea, Co. Roscommon
23   Byrne, Patrick (SPS), St Patrick's, Kiltegan
31   Dennehy, Philip (Dublin), former PP Athy

February 2022

9   Corcoran, Philip (Dublin), former PP Confey
9   Larkin, Patrick (Armagh), Carlingford Nursing Home,
      Old Dundalk Road, Carlingford, Co. Louth
11   McGinley, Séamus (Armagh), Parochial House, 2 Tullynure Road,
      Cookstown, Co. Tyrone
11   Reynolds, Michael (CSSp), Holy Spirit Missionary College,
      Kimmage Manor, Dublin 12
14   O'Doherty, Donal (Dublin, Mgr), former PP Dundrum
18   Carroll, Patrick F. (Dublin, Canon), former moderator Cabra/
      Cabra West/Phibsborough
18   Lee, Angelus (OFM), 4 Merchant's Quay, Dublin 8
27   Gavigan, James (Opus Dei), Knapton House, Monkstown,
      Co. Dublin
27   McGrane, Camillus (John) (OSM, Dublin),
      former CC Marley Grange, Servite Community,
      25 Hermitage Grove, Rathfarnham, Dublin 16
28   O'Connell, John (Dublin), former PP Bray: Holy Redeemer

March 2022

1   Lawlor, John (Kerry), Fatima Nursing Home, Tralee
3   Raftery, Gregory (Galway, Kilmacduagh & Kilfenora), Laatzen, Germany
6   Kavanagh, Robert (SPS), St Patrick's, Kiltegan
14   Fox, Christopher Peter (MHM), Mill Hill Missionaries, St Joseph's House, 50 Orwell Park, Rathgar, Dublin 6
19   Casey, James (CSsR), St Patrick's, Esker, Athenry, Co. Galway
21   Poland, James (Dromore), Saval, Newry, Co. Down
25   Dooher, Patrick (SSC), St Columban's Missionary Society
25   McCormack, James (CM), Vincentian Community Residence, St Paul's, Sybil Hill, Raheny, Dublin
26   Moriarty, James (Kildare & Leighlin, Dublin), bishop emeritus of Kildare & Leighlin and former auxiliary bishop of Dublin
26   O'Sullivan, Richard (SSC), St Columban's Missionary Society
28   McGrath, Sean (SPS), St Patrick's, Kiltegan
28   O'Kane, Patrick (Derry), 1 Aileach Road, Ballymagroarty, Derry
31   Kennedy, Colm (SDB), Salesian House, 45 St Teresa's Road, Crumlin, Dublin 12

April 2022

2   O'Halpin, Aodh (SSC), St Columban's Missionary Society
3   Breslin, Eamonn (CSsR), Mount St Alphonsus, Limerick City
3   O'Gorman, Dan (SSC), St Columban's Missionary Society
5   Kelly, Patrick James (CSSp), Holy Spirit Missionary College, Kimmage Manor, Dublin 12
7   Corrigan, Kevin (CSSp), Holy Spirit Missionary College, Kimmage Manor, Dublin 12
10   Doyle, Owen (SSC), St Columban's Missionary Society
10   McGreevy, Mark (OP), St Catherine's, Newry
12   Mowles, Alan (SDB), Salesian House, 45 St Teresa's Road, Crumlin, Dublin 12
14   Cargan, John (Derry), 4 Garvagh Road, Kilrea, Co. Derry
15   Doyle, Noel (SSC), St Columban's Missionary Society
16   Daly, Kevin (OCSO), Mount Saint Joseph Abbey, Roscrea
17   Reihill, Seamus (SPS), St Patrick's, Kiltegan
19   McCarthy, John (Tuam, PE), Knock, Co. Mayo
26   Clarke, Paddy (SSC), St Columban's Missionary Society, former CC Willington

26 Donovan, Jeremiah (OMI), Oblate Fathers, House of Retreat, Tyrconnell Road, Inchicore
27 McHugh, Patrick (Clogher, Canon), 5 Killynoogan Road, Kesh, Co. Fermanagh
27 O'Brien, Michael Peter (MHM), Mill Hill Missionaries, St Joseph's House, 50 Orwell Park, Rathgar, Dublin 6

May 2022

2 McKenna, Owen (SMA), African Missions, Blackrock Road, Cork
3 Fullerton, Robert (Down & Connor, Canon), 501 Ormeau Road, Belfast
4 Regan, James (SPS), St Patrick's, Kiltegan
5 Hoey, Eamon (CSsR), St Joseph's Monastery, Dundalk, Co. Louth
7 Doran, Joseph (Dublin), adm. Kilbride and Barndarrig
14 Houston, Joe (SSC), St Columban's Missionary Society
16 Murphy, Brian (OSB), Glenstal Abbey, Murroe, Co. Limerick
21 Carrigan, Bill (SSC), St Columban's Missionary Society
21 Hannon, Martin (Opus Dei), Knapton House, Monkstown, Co. Dublin
23 Gray, Francis (Ardagh & Clonmacnois), Mohill, Co. Leitrim
29 Carolan, Edward (OMI), Oblate Fathers, House of Retreat, Tyrconnell Road, Inchicore

June 2022

1 McDonagh, Donald J. (SPS), St Patrick's, Kiltegan
7 Lawlor, Brendan (Killaloe), Tulla, Co. Clare
8 Corr, Sean (SSC), St Columban's Missionary Society
8 Fagan, Hugh (CSSp), Holy Spirit Missionary College, Kimmage Manor, Dublin 12
11 Brennan, Loughlin (Cashel & Emly, PP), Murroe, Co. Limerick
13 Madden, James (Down & Connor), 1A Glenview Street, Belfast
13 McCaffrey, Ultan (OFM), Franciscan Friary, Liberty Street, Cork
13 McCreave, Eamon (Paul) (OSM), Servite Community, 10 Main Street, Benburb, Co. Tyrone, Northern Ireland
22 Flynn, John (SMA), African Missions, Blackrock Road, Cork
26 Quinn, Brian (Raphoe, PP), Provincial House, Gortlee, Letterkenny, Co. Donegal
26 Woods, Thomas (Meath, Mgr), Mullingar, Co. Westmeath

July 2022

- 3 Cronin, Isidore (OFM), Franciscan Friary, Liberty Street, Cork
- 4 Murphy, Brendan (SVD), Bay Street, Louis/Mississippi, USA
- 5 Kilkelly, Christopher (Tuam, PE), Trinity Care Nursing Home, Dublin
- 8 Moran, Bill (SSC), St Columban's Missionary Society
- 14 Russell, Thomas (OFM), Franciscan Friary, Clonmel, Co. Tipperary
- 19 Gillooly, Thomas (SPS), St Patrick's, Kiltegan
- 19 Murphy, Pat (Kerry), Fatima Nursing Home, Tralee
- 26 Bermingham, James (SPS), St Patrick's Missionary Society

Addendum

November 2020

- 20 Connolly, Diarmuid (Dublin, Canon), former PP Castleknock
- 22 Kearney, Thomas (SMA), SMA House, Wilton, Cork

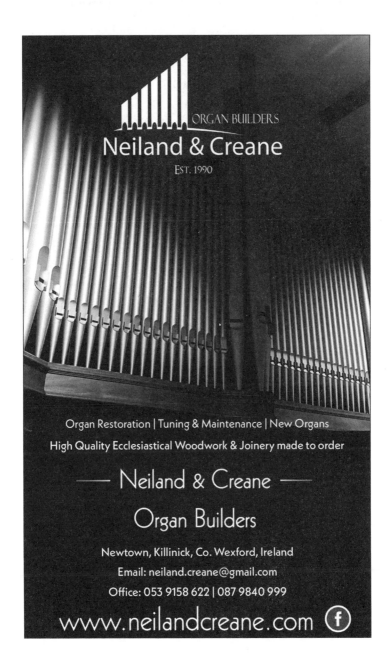

FOUNDED 1782

SAINT KIERAN'S COLLEGE KILKENNY

www.stkieranscollege.ie

ST KIERAN'S IS A CATHOLIC DIOCESAN COLLEGE UNDER THE PATRONAGE OF THE BISHOP OF OSSORY

Its objectives are the advancement of Catholic religion and education by providing a well-rounded academic education for second level students and supporting faith formation in the Diocese of Ossory as a pastoral centre and home for many diocesan initiatives.

- **SECONDARY SCHOOL** which promotes real excellence in education and formation to 800 pupils, with a wide range of sporting, co-curricular and extra-curricular activities.

- **ASPAL** the home for Ireland's leading digital learning platform for all involved in ministry and the faith life of our parishes and dioceses. A collaboration of Ossory Adult Faith Development, St Patrick's Pontifical University, supported by The Benefact Trust.

- **MYFAITH** the home for this innovative online parish based programme of preparation for the Sacraments of First Holy Communion and Confirmation. Supporting children and their families on this important journey.

- **CENTRE FOR RETREAT AND THEOLOGICAL REFLECTION** which offers parish evenings and weekend retreats and on-going formation courses for clergy and laity.

- **PASTORAL AND FAITH DEVELOPMENT** which supports parishes, various groups and people of our Diocese to deepen their understanding of faith, through reflection, lectures and various other initiatives.

- **THE HOME FOR LIGHTHOUSE STUDIOS, THE KILKENNY RESEARCH & INNOVATION CENTRE** and so much more.

Further information:
The President, St Kieran's College, Kilkenny.
Tel: +353 (0)56 7721086 Email: president@stkieranscollege.ie

DIVINE MASTER CENTRE

Dedicated as a place of hospitality and welcome
Retreat spaces to rest and encounter the Eucharistic Jesus in the spirit of Bethany

LITURGICAL CENTRE

For liturgical and religious items for homes, churches, chapels, and prayer spaces.
Gifts and handmade cards for religious and other special occasions.
Online catalogue: www.liturgical.centre.ie

Ministry of prayer, support and service to priests and those called to serve others in the Church.

ATHLONE
8 Castle Street, Athlone
Co. Westmeath
T: 09064 92278

DUBLIN
Newtownpark Avenue
White's Cross, Blackrock
Co. Dublin A94 V670
T: 01 2886414 • E: dublin@pddm.org
www.pddm.ie

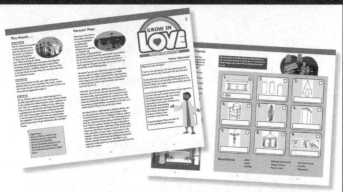

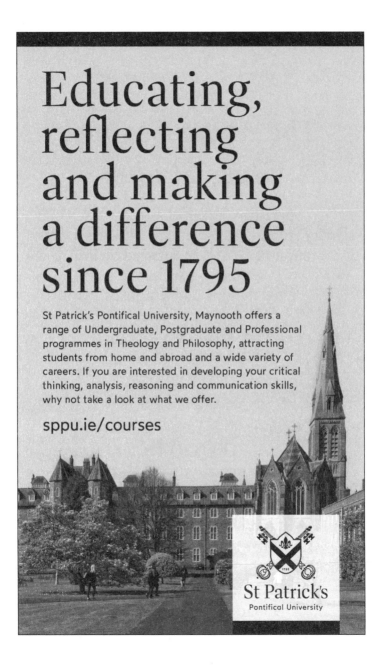

Ar fáil anois, trí Ghaeilge!

PARISH SACRAMENTAL PROGRAMME OF PREPARATION
Reconciliation First Holy Communion Confirmation

MyF@ith.ie

- Join with ICH THUS and teacher-led **online interactive classes** for both children and parents.
- Build module-by-module on the journey to being fully prepared **in the company of your family.**
- **Come together in your parish** to continue the learning.

- Age appropriate online interactive games/ challenges/quizzes/moments of prayer for each module to **reinforce learning.**
- **Log out/Log in** and pick up from where you left off.
- Supports for Group Leaders and **encourage weekly children's Mass attendance.**

Encourage weekly attendance and active participation at Mass with resources for every Sunday

Supporting Leaders for group meetings with notes, questions and tasks for each module

Explore the Church Seasons. Reinforce the learning with Advent and Lenten Workbooks

Register your Parish online at MyFaith.ie or tel. 056 7753628

213

Index of Advertisers